MARCEL BREUER

MARCEL BREUER DESIGN AND ARCHITECTURE

Vitra Design Museum

CATALOGUE

Edited by: Alexander von Vegesack, Mathias Remmele
Concept, editorial work: Mathias Remmele, Alexandra Pioch
Image rights: Kerstin Meyer-Ebrecht, Alexandra Pioch
Graphic design: Thorsten Romanus
Editorial assistance: Jane Havell
Translations: Jeffrey Lieber, Ian Pepper, Julia Thorson
Typesetting: Print Media Works, Schopfheim
Lithography and printing: GZD, Ditzingen
Production coordinator: Elke Henecka

EXHIBITION

Conception: Mathias Remmele
Assistant: Alexandra Pioch
Organisation: Alexandra Pioch, Mathias Remmele
Exhibition design: Dieter Thiel
Graphic design: Thorsten Romanus
Model construction: Ursula Burla, Daniel Christen, Dirk von Kölln,
Oswald Dillier, Marc Gehde, Valerie Hess, Raphael Höglhammer,
Markus Kummer, Horst Steiner
Technical execution: Thierry Hodel, Stefani Fricker
Media and publicity: Gabriella Gianoli

Die Deutsche Bibliothek lists these publications in the
Deutsche Nationalbibliografie; detailed bibliographic data may be
obtained online at http://dnb.ddb.de.

ISBN 3-931936-42-2
Printed in Germany

©© 2003 Vitra Design Stiftung gGmbH
and the authors, Charles-Eames-Str. 1,
D-79576 Weil am Rhein
1st edition, 2003

"Marcel Breuer – Design and Architecture" is a project of the
Vitra Design Museum.

EXHIBITION VENUES

Vitra Design Museum Weil am Rhein
Vitra Design Museum Berlin
Further venues to follow

CONTENTS

8 FOREWORD 1

AN INTRODUCTION > M. REMMEI

TUBULAR STEEL FURNITURE" > (

148 THE FURNITURE OF MARCE

> D. CACCIOLA 166 THE ARCHI

174 BAMBOS – THE YOUNG MA

188 ON HOUSES AND PALAC

HOUSES > J. DRILLER 258 EI

DISCOURSES OF THE VERNACU

308 WORKING WITH MARCEL BR

COMPLEX > G. D. GRAWE

> I. HYMAN

432 BIOGRAPHY 446 FURTHE

MARCEL BREUER, DESIGN AND ARCHITECTURE –

E

50 MARCEL BREUER – "INVENTOR OF BENT

MÁČEL   116 MARCEL BREUER FURNITURE

BREUER IN PRODUCTION BY GAVINA UND KNOLL

ECT I. M. PEI ABOUT HIS FRIEND MARCEL BREUER

TER HOUSES BY MARCEL BREUER > L. SCHÖBE

S: REMARKS ON MARCEL BREUER'S RESIDENTIAL

COUNTERING AMERICA: MARCEL BREUER AND THE

AR FROM BUDAPEST TO BOSTON > B. BERGDOLL

EUER > R. F. GATJE   332 THE PARIS UNESCO

60 THE LATER MODERNISM OF MARCEL BREUER

402 CHURCHES AND MONASTERIES

R READING, PHOTO CREDITS, AUTHORS

With this retrospective on the work of Marcel Breuer, the Vitra Design Museum continues its series of monograph exhibitions dedicated to central figures of twentieth-century architectural and design history. Following presentations of Charles and Ray Eames, Frank Lloyd Wright, Ludwig Mies van der Rohe, Verner Panton and Luis Barragán, the focus now on Breuer's oeuvre represents a logical choice. For in the history of industrial furniture design (a core competence of the Vitra Design Museum), it was not merely as the "inventor" of tubular steel furniture that Breuer played a decisive role. The thoroughness with which he explored the creative possibilities of a certain material, taking into account the technical aspects of production methods, is evidence of his "industrial thinking" and a key reason for the enduring popularity of many of his furniture designs.

Breuer's significance for the development of twentieth-century design is reflected in the collection of the Vitra Design Museum, which has one of the most comprehensive and complete bodies of Breuer's works. And with the archive of Anton Lorenz, a long-time business partner of Breuer, the museum holds one of the outstanding collections of source material on the history of tubular steel furniture, containing important documents particularly in regard to the development of Breuer's furniture design. The collection and archive thus provided a solid basis for putting together a retrospective on the work of this innovative designer.

The professed goal of the exhibition and catalogue, however, is not solely to pay tribute to Breuer's contributions to twentieth-century design and domestic culture, but also to showcase examples from his extensive architectural oeuvre. The Vitra Design Museum thus hopes to bring renewed public attention to Breuer's work as an architect, an area that has somewhat been neglected, and to encourage a long overdue and fundamental reassessment of his achievements in architectural design. The success of an exhibition and catalogue project of this scope depends on the contributions of numerous individuals both within the museum and at outside institutions, to whom we would like to take this opportunity to express our gratitude.

First and foremost, we extend our thanks to Alexandra Pioch. Without her dedication, competence and judiciousness, the entire Breuer project would never have come together.

Kerstin Meyer-Ebrecht and Rebekka Tanner actively supported exhibition preparations during their two-month internships at the Vitra Design Museum. Especially fruitful and helpful in developing the exhibition concept were discussions with Joachim Driller, Isabelle Hyman and Hans Hagemeister. On repeated occasions, the project team was able to count on the selfless assistance of Breuer's former partner Bob Gatje. The other partners Herb Beckhard, Tician Papachristou and Hamilton Smith were also a source of valuable advice and suggestions. Going above and beyond their catalogue essays, Gabriele Grawe, Donatella Cacciola and Lutz Schöbe are greatly appreciated for the commitment and support they lent to the Breuer project. Uli Fiedler not only offered his expert knowledge but also helped

with the organisation of loaned pieces for the exhibition.

Under the direction of professors Natalina Di Iorio, Frédéric Dedelley and Mathias Remmele at the School of Art and Design in Basel, fourth semester students in the interior design department developed design proposals for the Breuer exhibition. Dieter Thiel guided the semester project as an outside expert. Several of the ideas developed in the course were incorporated into the conception and design of the exhibition. Above all, we would like to thank the students Silvia Fiammengo, Esther Schlup and Daniel Christen for their contributions as well as for their special efforts Valerie Hess, Raphael Höglhammer and Markus Kummer.

Special thanks also go to numerous public and private archives and collections, without whose help the exhibition would not have been possible. This applies in particular to the two institutions housing a large part of the Breuer estate: the Smithsonian Archives of American Art in Washington, D.C., and the Department of Special Collections at the Syracuse University Library. The respective keepers of the Breuer holdings, Jean Fitzgerald and Kathleen Manwaring, readily provided the project with all manner of assistance. Our thanks also go to Wendy Hurley in Washington and Peter Verheyen in Syracuse as well as to the other staff members at both institutions. With her unceasing helpfulness, Sabine Hartmann at the Bauhaus Archive Berlin greatly contributed to the preparation of the catalogue and exhibition. Valuable support was further provided by:

Dr Klaus-Jürgen Winkler of Bauhaus University in Weimar; Jerry Anderson of the University of St Mary in Bismarck; Sister Audrey of the Annunciation Priory of St Mary in Bismarck; Piriya Vongkasemsiri of the Chicago Historical Society; T.O. Immisch of the Moritzburg State Gallery in Halle; Larissa Gentile of the Whitney Museum of American Art in New York; Brother Allen Reed at St John's Abbey in Collegeville; Rev. Thomas G. Simons, Pastor of St Francis de Sales in Muskegon; Sister Imelda at the Baldegg Convent; Dr Matthias Schirren at the Archives of the Academy of Arts in Berlin; Dr Eva-Maria Barkhofen and Ms Linnemann of the Berlinische Galerie; Lucien and Judith Hervé in Paris; Manfred Ludewig in Berlin; Peter Lepel of the company Embru in Rüti; the photographers Lee D. Ewing in Washington, D.C., and Ralph Liebermann in Williamstown; Linda A. Reynolds of Williams College in Williamstown; the architects Beat Jordi in Berne and Franz Staffelbach in Zurich.

Within the Vitra Design Museum, the project team is particularly indebted to support in word and deed rendered by Stefani Fricker, Kathrin Kessler, Sixta Quassdorf, Alexa Tepen, Grażyna Ubik, Jochen Eisenbrand, Thierry Hodel, Serge Mauduit, Andreas Nutz, Roman Passarge, Michael Simolka and Frank Ubik. Finally we would like to thank Thorsten Romanus for his dedication in developing the catalogue layout and Dieter Thiel for his fruitful and enjoyable collaboration in the creative implementation of the exhibition concept.

Alexander von Vegesack
11   *Mathias Remmele*

MARCEL BREUER DESIGN AND ARCHITECTURE – AN INTRODUCTION

MARCEL BREUER DESIGN AND ARCHITECTURE – AN INTRODUCTION

MATHIAS REMMELE

It is astonishing how differently the creative legacy of Marcel Breuer is perceived and regarded around the world today, more than twenty years after his death.

In Europe Breuer is known foremost as a designer, as the creator of the "Wassily" chair and the cane-backed "Cesca" chairs, and as a famous Bauhaus student and "Young Master". Few here seem to know about the importance of his second career as an architect, which after a slow beginning in Europe in the early 1930s was fully launched with his emigration to America in 1937. And yet, from the beginning of the 1950s until his retirement in 1976, Breuer belonged to the first truly global generation of modern architects, with offices in New York and Paris and clients throughout the entire western world.

The case could not be more different in the United States, where Breuer is, unsurprisingly, best known as an architect; and, informally speaking, as one of many other important figures of the modern movement who came from Europe, where before his emigration he had also designed some furniture. Breuer's contribution to architectural history in the United States rests first on his reputation as an admired teacher at Harvard, and then as a sought-after and successful architect, more than on his furniture designs. How high his role is regarded can be seen in a recent overview of American art, in which the chapter on post-war architecture is entitled "Breuer, Mies, and the International Style."[1]

On the other side of these more general perspectives was the professional estimation of Breuer's work, which was the same on both sides of the Atlantic. This was summed up in 1981, the year of Breuer's death and the high point of post-modernism, by J. Stewart Johnson, Design Curator at The Museum of Modern Art, who predicted: "Breuer will be

1 In additon to the publicatons by Driller, Hyman and Gatje, the numerous small events celebrating Breuer's 100th anniversary in the USA last year are a clear indication of this.

14

◂ Marcel Breuer, c. 1952
Photo: Hans Namuth

better remembered for his furniture designs than for his architecture."[2] Seen from today's vantage point, this is certainly a judgement rooted in its time. And yet, allowing for changes in taste, it makes sense when viewed in the context of Breuer's biography, considering the circumstances and opportunities that chance afforded him.

In the field of design Breuer had an uncommonly auspicious beginning. He was, quite plainly, in the right place at the right time. Endowed with great talent and favoured by Gropius, he found at the Bauhaus – from every point of view – ideal conditions for the development and realisation of his revolutionary projects. The time was ripe for new ideas and experiments; the avant-garde was clamouring for designs that would express the spirit of the age, and Breuer strove unleashed from tradition and impinging Beaux-Arts standards. Would it otherwise have been possible for a 23-year-old to produce such an absolutely perfect work as the "Wassily" chair?

In the field of architecture Breuer was, perhaps, born too late. By 1932, when he built the Harnischmacher House in Wiesbaden, fulfilling a long-desired dream, the icons of classic modernism – Le Corbusier's Villa Savoye, Gropius's *Meisterhäuser* in Dessau, and Mies van der Rohe's Barcelona Pavilion, to name only a few – had already been built and their creators, all of them one generation older than Breuer, had already established themselves as the masters of the modern movement.

In spite of all his later successes, Breuer never succeeded in overcoming this disadvantage. No single building of his design is seen as having the epochal significance of the "Wassily" chair. In architecture, he does not belong to the heroes of the first generation of modernists, but rather to the less regarded masters of post-war modernism,

2 Cited after Isabelle Hyman: Marcel Breuer, Arcitect. The career and the buildings, New York 2001, p. 7.

whose achievements were considered ambiguous in the last quarter of the twentieth century.

It is for these reasons that the Vitra Design Museum has decided to present both parts of Marcel Breuer's oeuvre in a balanced manner. We hope that through this long-planned travelling retrospective his architectural works will be rediscovered, re-evaluated and advanced alongside the furniture designs, whose importance for the history of twentieth-century design remains undisputed.

This aim is also reflected in the essays in the exhibition catalogue, in which the architecture is given prominence. To a large extent, Breuer's furniture designs have already been the subject of assiduous research by Christopher Wilk, Magdalena Droste, Manfred Ludewig, Otakar Máčel, Friederike Mehlau-Wiebking, Arthur Rüegg and Ruggero Tropeano. In this field there is little new knowledge waiting to be discovered. Only in the case of the plywood furniture is there a need for further research; the influence of Breuer's interiors on the lifestyle culture of the mid-twentieth century has also not been researched as intensely and brought to light as fully as could be wished. The catalogue raisonné of Breuer's furniture and interior designs planned by the Vitra Design Museum seeks to fill these gaps.

Every retrospective of Breuer's work has had to confront the problem that his career is seemingly divided into two parts: in his early work furniture and interiors are dominant, whereas later on architecture clearly plays the major role. Although this rigid distinction is blurred when his oeuvre is seen in its entirety, it is nevertheless difficult to view the different fields of his activity in an integral way and to package them in an exhibition, as perhaps can

◂ Marcel Breuer and A. Elzas, De Bijenkorf Department Store, Rotterdam, The Netherlands, 1955–57, site office.

be done in the case of Mies van der Rohe, Alvar Aalto or Arne Jacobsen, whose furniture and interiors were often specifically created for buildings of their own design. But from very early on, at least since the middle of the 1920s, Breuer thought of himself as an architect, though he continued to create furniture and interiors until the end of his career.

There are, in fact, certain threads that bind together the various fields of his activity, foremost among them his interest in problems of construction and his desire to stage them in an expressive way. "You exploit a structural system with passion as well as logic. A spirit of construction is there and an instinct for achievement. (...) There is enjoyment and a sence of creation in making the most out of a structural system. Not acrobatics, but a search for possibilities." [3] What Breuer says in this remark regarding his architecture is also applicable to his furniture designs. His passion for construction and his extraordinarily developed instinct for innovation unite his furniture designs and his buildings. Throughout his career Breuer made repeated use of certain formal elements, which became leitmotifs in his work; these are also linking threads thematised in the exhibition.

3 Cited after Marcel Breuer. 1921–1962, Introduction and captions by Cranston Jones, Stuttgart 1962, p. 19.

▾ Armchair from the Sommerfeld House, Berlin, 1921.
▸ Haus am Horn, Weimar, 1923, dressing table, lady's bedroom.

MATERIAL

As a designer Marcel Breuer worked with four distinct materials one after another: wood, tubular steel, aluminium and plywood. We can divide his furniture designs into four categories, four chronological periods corresponding to the change in materials.

His basic interest in construction is evident even in his earliest works. In the lounge chairs and tables he created for the Sommerfeld House as a 20-year-old Bauhaus student there is, apart from their strong cubic form, a clear division between the wooden construction and the leather-covered cushions. The thrill Breuer clearly felt in experimenting with structure is even more evident in the dressing table he created a year later, exhibited in the first Bauhaus exhibition at Haus am Horn. This object is less a piece of furniture then a small constructivist architectural project. The same can be said for the very well known "Lattenstuhl", whose complex structure cannot be explained by function alone.

With the tubular steel furniture, Breuer's style became more sober, but these pieces are also defined by their construction. The "Wassily" chair, for example, can be read as a classic club chair that has been stripped to expose skin and bones, clearly exhibiting its constructive lines. In his tubular steel furniture designs, Breuer investigated in a systematic way the constructive possibilities of the material and, in some designs, such as the "Wassily" (B5, B11), we can follow through many different versions his struggle to combine construction and comfort, handling and production in the finest possible manner.

The epochal significance of Breuer's idea to use tubular steel for the production of furniture can hardly be overestimated. Commercially his invention might not have been successful at the start, but it appealed to the European avant-garde, who gave it an

◄ Ise and Walter Gropius in their living room, Dessau, c. 1927.

▼ Apartment of Hans Scharoun, Berlin, c. 1929.

overwhelmingly positive reception. Tubular steel essentially became the material of modern furniture design. It corresponded perfectly with the vision then being advanced of a living machine aesthetic. It stood for technology, industry, serial production, standard, functionality and hygiene – concepts and values central to the international modern movement. Following Breuer's lead, Mies van der Rohe, Le Corbusier and many other propagators of the modernist aesthetic used this material for their own furniture designs.

In the second half of the 1920s furnishing with tubular steel was an avowal of solidarity for modernism – and not only in the neighbourhood of the Bauhaus, where Gropius, Kandinsky and Moholy-Nagy were furnishing their own homes with Breuer's pieces. In Berlin one could find Breuer's creations in Hans Scharoun's apartment, in Paris in the apartment of Mallet-Stevens, and in Helsinki at Aino and Alvar Aalto's. By 1928, after their full swing to modernism, they brought Breuer's tubular steel furniture into their offices and private apartments in a very noticeable way.

His aluminium furniture was also inspired by a constructive idea – the distinctive quality of these designs lies in the transfer of the cantilever principle from tubular steel to aluminium.

Breuer's work with plywood also began with an astonishing act of translation: the well-known Isokon lounge chair is formally and constructively based on the aluminium lounge chair he had created in 1933–34 in collaboration with the Swiss company Embru. The line of plywood furniture is additional proof of his joy in experimenting and of his ability to recognise the innate constructive possibilities of a certain material. That his proposals in the field of plywood furniture were not always perfect is perhaps not an indication of a weaker

▾ Apartment of Aino and Alvar Aalto, Turku, Finland,
    1927–28, living room.
▾▾ Apartment of Aino and Alvar Aalto, living room.
▸ Office of Aino and Alvar Aalto, Turku, Finland,
    c. 1927–28.

interest in furniture design, but the result of a lack of collaboration with a technically competent producer, such as Aalto profited from in his plywood furniture designs created at this time.

In addition to their constructive aspects, it is interesting to see in Breuer's plywood furniture his flirtation with organic forms, for with these designs he had moved away from the design ideals of his earlier Bauhaus period.

HOUSES

Breuer's single family houses, largely thanks to Joachim Driller's notable book on the subject, are today regarded as his most important contribution to the field of architecture. To be sure, Breuer devoted himself more intensively to the design of single family houses than any other building type, so that few of his contemporaries have as similar and as broad an oeuvre in this field. Even at the Bauhaus, his architectural projects were concerned with the topic of houses, and his first realised buildings belong to this category. The Doldertal Houses in Zurich, the three houses he built for himself in the United States, the MoMA "House in the Garden" and the late villas all received international recognition in their own time.

Out of the abundance of single family houses – so numerous that a complete overview is impossible – we can isolate four basic types, based on Driller's research. Most of Breuer's works in this field can be classified more or less clearly into these basic categories. For the purposes of the exhibition, we have chosen one typical example of each of the four types.

Breuer's house in Lincoln, Massachusetts, the first house he built for himself in the United States, is best representative of his multi-level houses, in which a huge two-storey living room lies in the centre of the floor plan. The Robinson House is the best and most interesting example of his binuclear houses, in which semi-public spaces (kitchen, dining room and living room) are clearly separated from the private living spaces of the house (bedrooms and bathrooms). Breuer's first house in New Canaan, Connecticut, the second he built for himself in the US, embodies the long-house type with its striking linear ground plan. Finally, the Staehelin House in Feldmeilen, near Zurich, belongs to the type of the large villas and is impressive for the solution he found for a complex and diverse system of rooms.

Apart from the innovative solutions he devised for floor plans, which subsequently influenced many other architects, Breuer's single family houses are remarkable for his choice of materials and for his thoughts concerning the relationship between interior and exterior space. In this, he was in clear contrast with other masters of the modern movement, in that he advocated a distinct separation between the built and the natural worlds.

By all accounts, the informal character of Breuer's houses corresponded to his own lifestyle. They seem intimate even when grand, are unpretentious, and he did not put the will of the architect above the desires of the inhabitants. Surely, these are the reasons for their popularity and long-lasting influence.

Besides steel and glass, concrete is the crucial material for architecture in the twentieth century. In the 1950s, while Mies van der Rohe became the grand master of steel and glass architecture in the US, Breuer concerned himself with reinforced concrete, and with this material he created his own distinctive design vocabulary. He was impressed by the natural qualities and constructive possibilities of concrete, by its austere beauty, and the impression of heaviness, massiveness and solidity that it could give. The often cited model of Le Corbusier was of less decisive significance for the development of Breuer's concrete architecture than his introduction to the Italian engineer Pier Luigi Nervi, with whom he had a fruitful and inspiring collaboration on the UNESCO headquarters in Paris. Nervi's polished, daring and elegant concrete constructions can be counted among the masterpieces of twentieth-century architectural engineering.

From Nervi, Breuer took the idea of construction defining the space of a room, and he achieved this more purely and with less compromise than anywhere else in his four churches, which are presented in the exhibition under the banner "Spaces". Breuer saw rooms as sacred in which construction and dimension were more than simply functional. But, as in every case, his fascination for certain ways of constructing stood at the beginning of his design process.

For St John's, the first church he built, he used specially constructed folded concrete walls to cover an immense space without columns. The interior of the church is defined by sharp-edged and uncovered concrete folds, which give the space, as paradoxical as it may sound, an expressive but simultaneously calm and contemplative character.

24

For both St Mary's and St Francis de Sales he used the complex space configuration of the hyperbolic paraboloid. In the case of St Mary's, he used a thin, but very strong shell construction to create a softly undulating roof. In the case of St Francis de Sales, he chose a very unusual solution, constructing the two side walls of the church out of non-weight-bearing hyperbolic paraboloids. In this way, he generated a very dramatic and dynamic space, one that can surely be counted among the more unusual architectural creations of the century. Compared with these spaces, the monastery church at Baldegg, with its strong concrete beams, seems fairly conventional. That Breuer renounced a more mannered style of construction makes this late work, all in all, the most dignified church he built during his long career.

VOLUME

Among the most impressive of Breuer's architectural achievements are those buildings that project a monumental presence through their volume alone. These solitary, sharp-edged and unified volumes are convincing because of their proportions and their sculptural qualities. Their forms seem to be generated through the principle of subtraction, as if a building could be hewn out of a bigger, even more massive volume: opening up, hollowing out and cutting in, but also a remarkable sensation of emergence – these are the characteristics of those buildings that occupy an exceptional position in Breuer's oeuvre. That he used homogeneous materials for the sweeping façades of these buildings – sometimes reinforced concrete, at other times natural stone – amplifies the monolithic impression they project. The position and dimension of the small number of windows on the façades were always carefully chosen. The

◀ Marcel Breuer and Hamilton Smith, Begrisch Hall,
University Heights, New York 1959–61.
◀▾ Marcel Breuer and A. Elzas, De Bijenkorf
Department Store, Rotterdam, The Netherlands,
1955–57, east façade.
▾ Marcel Breuer and Hamilton Smith, Atlanta
Central Public Library, Atlanta, Georgia, 1977–80,
south-west façade.

windows impart a sense of tension and minimise the impression of an overwhelming monumentality, which is usually the result of expansive, cohesive volumes.

A significant volume is a characteristic of many of Breuer's buildings – particularly the churches and the Y-shaped administration buildings (UNESCO in Paris, and IBM in the south of France and in Florida). In the churches, Breuer was less concerned with volume as it appeared from the exterior than he was with defining the interior space through a certain means of construction. In the case of the administration buildings, the physicality of the robust, highly structured façades, with their many windows, diminishes the monolithic impression and allows volume to recede.

The buildings presented in the exhibition that belong to this special category – Begrisch Hall (a lecture hall in the Bronx which originally belonged to New York University), the De Bijenkorf Department Store in Rotterdam, the Whitney Museum in New York, and the Central Library in Atlanta – are each remarkable for the pregnancy and the unity of their volumes. They prove in an impressive way Breuer's often-doubted ability to work with massive building volumes. Seen from today's perspective, they remain fresh and timeless as do only few other buildings of the time.

CANTILEVER

Ever since Lissitzksy's utopian "Sky Hook" design, the cantilever has been counted among the iconic motifs of modernism. This constructivist architectural fantasy stands as an example of the belief in progress and the enthusiasm for technology at the time Breuer's career began. Breuer himself repeatedly used this motif in his designs and his architecture, always reinterpreting it anew over the course of many decades. This is certainly evident in his cantilever tubular steel chairs, in which the delight in the constructive possibilities of the material is staged in such a way as to highlight the design's functional advantages.

The cantilever motif can be found in Breuer's architecture quite early on. The stair-like plan he proposed in 1928–29 for a hospital in Elberfeld had no chance of being built, but was reformulated in his offset two-storey houses, and even the Whitney Museum can be read as a late reference to the earlier design. Among the most impressive buildings in which Breuer used the cantilever motif are Begrisch Hall and the Grand Hôtel Le Flaine, which dramatically and precariously extends out over a rocky cliff in the vacation village of the same name. A love of aesthetics overtakes structural stability in the daring cantilever balcony he designed for his own house in New Caanan, Connecticut; years after its construction, even when a wall had to be built under the balcony for extra support, Breuer continued to publish it in its original form.

LYING RECTANGLE

A distinct creative element of Breuer's interiors – and later also of many of his buildings – is the motif of the lying rectangle, which is sometimes enlarged to a horizontal strip. The first unmistakable formulation of this motif is in the Berlin apartment of the theatre director Erwin Piscator, which Breuer designed and furnished in 1927. For the dining room he created a hanging sideboard spread along the side wall of the room at a height of around one metre. From then on, this kind of sideboard belonged to the standard repertoire of Breuer's interiors – though the materials and size would vary – and not only during his time in Berlin. In England, and later on in America, he designed for himself and his clients many of these box-like furniture pieces. In his single family houses he often used built-in cabinets instead of hanging volumes on the wall, but for the cabinets' sliding doors he always chose this motif of the lying rectangle.

We can also find this creative element in his public spaces: it may be in the form of a blackboard in a lecture hall, or carved into the altar wall in a church. The remarkable fact is that Breuer developed this creative element in his design and also used it in his architecture. The visual rendering of the hanging sideboard on the wall of the Piscator dining room can be found again – to use only this very impressive example – twenty-three years later on the façade of the Thompkins House on Long Island, where Breuer turned the design upside down. He uses it sometimes as a strip of windows, and sometimes as a negative space in a façade, as in the Beijenkorf Department Store in Rotterdam, and sometimes in the very volume of a building itself, as in the Wolfson Trailer House in Salt Point, New York. The lying rectangle is, in its different formulations, one of the central elements in Breuer's creative vocabulary and a strong connection between his design and his architecture.

◄◄ From top to bottom:
· Harnischmacher House, Wiesbaden, 1932.
· Marcel Breuer and Hamilton Smith, St John's Abbey
  and University Complex, Science Building,
  Collegeville, Minnesota, 1964–66, lecture hall.
· Marcel Breuer and Herbert Beckhard, Torin
  Corporation, Penrith, Australia, 1976, entrance area.
◄ From top to bottom:
· Geller House I, Lawrence, Long Island, New York,
  1945, dining room with built-in cabinet.
· Marcel Breuer, Robert Gatje, Mario Jossa, Baldegg
  Cloister, Sonnhalde Nursing School, Baldegg,
  Switzerland, 1968–72, chapel.
· Marcel Breuer and Hamilton Smith, Grand Coulee
  Power Plant and Dam, Washington, 1972–75,
  visitors' balcony.
▼ Wolfson Trailer House, Pleasant Valley, New York,
  1950, south view.
▶ Marcel Breuer and Herbert Beckhard, Geller House II,
  Lawrence, Long Island, New York, 1968–69, dining
  area.

TEXTURES

Something similar can be said about the textures Breuer used to structure and enliven large surfaces. He often preferred simple geometrically defined patterns – simple stripes arranged to create overlapping patterns, series of rows, or graphic repetitions conveying variation, run like a red ribbon through his oeuvre. Striped patterns can already be found as early as 1923 in the dressing table exhibited in the first Bauhaus exhibition at Haus am Horn, and in the writing table of the same year. Since the end of the 1920s, at the latest, Breuer used these patterns for the design of surfaces in space. This can be seen in his own apartment in Berlin, as well as in the entry of the Heinersdorf House, which is covered with glass mosaic stones. In the house Breuer built for himself in Lincoln, Massachusetts, striped patterns abound – in the furniture, in the wall coverings, in the venetian blinds, and in the textiles he used to create optical divisions in rooms.

The house in Lincoln is also one of the early examples of his use of a striped pattern in the design of the outside surface of a house. In the case of wooden constructions, the striped pattern is a natural result of the wooden slats used for the covering – whether vertical, horizontal or diagonal, the use of varying placements shows that he was very aware of the patterns he created and of the constructive function of the slats, the Cesar Cottage being a striking example of this. Something similar can be said about the striped patterns seen on the concrete buildings, which are of course the imprint of the wooden-slat moulds used to shape the concrete.

In addition to striped patterns, Breuer often combined different geometric shapes – rectangles and squares in the case of the gymnasium of the elementary school in Bantam,

34

◄ From top to bottom:
· Breuer House I, Lincoln, Massachusetts, 1939, living
 room with view of built-in shelving, stairs, dining
 and sleeping areas.
· Eastern Airlines Ticket Office, Boston,
 Massachusetts, 1945, waiting area.
· Caesar Cottage, Lakeville, Connecticut, 1952,
 side view.

▸ Marcel Breuer and O'Connor & Kilham, Bantam
Elementary School, Bantam, Connecticut, 1954–56,
gymnasium.
▾ United States Embassy, The Hague, The Netherlands,
1956–59.

Connecticut; trapezoidal forms on the façade of the US embassy at The Hague, and a honeycomb pattern on the main façade of the Beijenkorf Department Store in Rotterdam, which is also a play on the name of the store, which means "beehive". The sun-protecting and visibility screens made out of red brick-stone are a special category – when seen from a distance they look like fine-netted fabric. In the case of Hunter College in New York these screens appear like a second, semi-permeable skin in front of the building, and produce a poetic play of light and shadow on the façade.

All these textures once again attest to Breuer's strong interest in materials, in the optical and physical qualities of their surfaces, and on the emotional effects they could induce. They prove his mastery in skilfully combining materials to create contrasts between colours and tones, bright and dark, rough and smooth, hard and soft, natural and artificial. Instead of artificially produced and applied ornament he worked with the textures inherent in the natural materials themselves, and the textures he could create, for example with a material such as concrete, in the process of construction.

◄ From top to bottom:
· Hooper House I, Baltimore, Maryland, 1948–50.
· Thompson House, Ligonier, Pennsylvania, 1947–49,
garden façade with roof of the pergola and exterior
staircase.
· Marcel Breuer and Herbert Beckhard, Koerfer House,
Moscia, Switzerland, 1963–66, detail photograph of
exterior staircase.
▶ Marcel Breuer and Herbert Beckhard, Gagarin
House I, Litchfield, Connecticut, 1956–57,
east façade.

CRYSTALLINE FORMS

The crystalline forms Breuer began to develop in the 1950s for his concrete buildings are characteristic of his late period. They are without precedent in his design vocabulary, and are distinct from the other central motifs he used, though he began to use them in his interiors, particularly in the sharp-edged concrete chimney sculptures, and in the furniture for the church spaces. These forms begin to appear in the UNESCO project. In the St John's Abbey church they are for the first time fully developed. From then on, Breuer regularly used crystalline forms to articulate the important parts of the buildings. Often remarked on are the concrete columns and the prefabricated concrete façade elements of the IBM buildings in the south of France and Florida. This kind of façade element, from which Breuer's office created again and again new, geometrically complex variations, had to serve different functions: first, it carries air-conditioning ducts and electric wiring; second, it provides protection from the sun, a theme Breuer was preoccupied with throughout his entire career; third, it gives the façades a tremendous physicality and depth. The end result is that our impression of the building constantly changes depending on the weather, the day, the season, and on our particular viewpoint.

The façade elements fabricated in series are in accordance with a central aim of Breuer: "Architecture has to create forms which stand repetition."[4]

4 Marcel Breuer, "Individual Expression Versus Order", quoted in Cranston Jones, ed. Marcel Breuer: Buildings and Projects 1921–1961. New York, 1962, p. 10.

◀ Marcel Breuer and Hamilton Smith, St John's Abbey, Collegeville, Minnesota, 1954–68, west side of the cloister church.

▼ St John's Abbey, crypt, Chapel of the Brothers.

▼▼ Marcel Breuer and Hamilton Smith, Grand Coulee Power Plant and Dam, Washington, 1972–75, exterior view of the turbine hall.

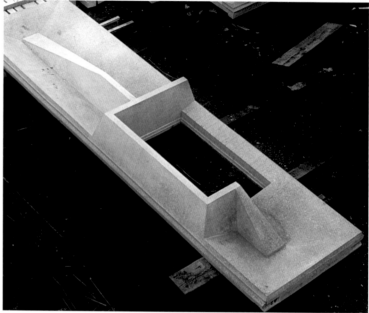

◄ Marcel Breuer and Hamilton Smith, Torin
   Corporation, Nivelles, Belgium, 1963–64,
   reinforcement for a façade element.
◄▼ Torin Corporation, view of façade with entrance.
▼ Torin Corporation, entrance façade.
▼▼ Torin Corporation, façade detail.

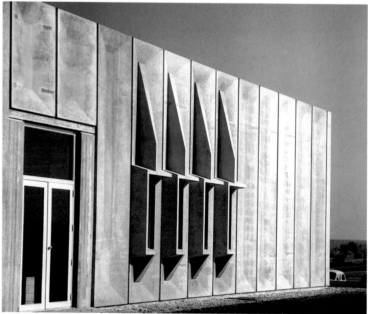

◀ Marcel Breuer and Herbert Beckhard, University
of Massachusetts, Murray Lincoln Campus Center,
Amherst, Massachusetts, 1967–70, façade detail.
▼ Marcel Breuer and Hamilton Smith, student
residence of St John's University, Collegeville,
Minnesota, 1965–67, façade detail.

Economically, it made sense to use standardised elements, especially for large projects. Accordingly, Breuer used them for the façades of administration buildings, factories, scientific and university buildings, dormitories, apartment houses and hotels. The expressive, unique character of these buildings is a result of these crystalline forms. However, in some cases, the repetition of the same element borders on a mechanical rigidity and spiritlessness, which was often a complaint against late modern architecture in general, for even the best formal element cannot withstand endless repetition.

The very uniqueness of the crystalline forms inspires a search for their origin. Some, like I. M. Pei, see the roots of these forms in cubism. While there are certain formal analogies with cubism, this hypothesis has never been thoroughly researched. Isn't the visual language of Paul Klee – there is, after all, a biographical connection between them – more likely to be one of Breuer's important sources of inspiration?

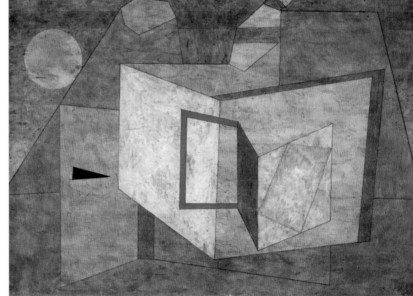

MARCEL BREUER – "INVENTOR OF BENT TUBULAR STEEL FURNITURE"

MARCEL BREUER – "INVENTOR OF BENT TUBULAR STEEL FURNITURE"

OTAKAR MÁČEL

Introduction

"The tubular steel chair is as truly a part of the heroic period of the new architecture as are the transparent sheets of glass that replace bearing-walls. The tubular chair also draws upon the new potentialities evident in our period – media that were accessible to all eyes, but that remained useless as long as their implications were not grasped."[1] Such was the verdict of Sigfried Giedion, advocate and chronicler of modernist architecture, who in this quotation also pinpoints the position of the bent tubular steel chair in the history of architecture. The man who was the first to comprehend the possibilities lying there "accessible to all eyes" was Marcel Breuer.

Breuer contributed to modern design in two areas. In the decades following World War II, he was regarded as an internationally successful architect, one rarely associated with furniture design. As a young man at the Bauhaus, however, he appeared to stand on the threshold of a brilliant career as a designer of furniture and interiors. This state of affairs changed with his emigration to the UK, and later to the USA. Today, his training – fragmentary studies at the Vienna Art Academy and a certificate of apprenticeship from the Bauhaus – would hardly constitute the official qualifications required to take up an architectural practice. This problem, admittedly, was one he would have shared with Peter Behrens and Mies van der Rohe.

In order to grasp and to exploit the possibilities that lay "accessible to all eyes" in those days, Breuer needed no official certificate. What was required instead was the capacity to draw inspiration from the beauty of the machine and from industrial production. Alongside the machine aesthetic (a typical source of inspiration for the contemporary avant-garde), Breuer's central European origins were probably of significance for the invention

1 Sigfried Giedion, Mechanization takes command (Oxford, 1948), p. 488.

of tubular steel furniture. The bentwood furniture so prevalent in the lands of the old Hapsburg monarchy betray certain affinities with tubular steel furniture: the rounded cross-section of the "building material" employed, its flexibility and transparency, and the linearism that so decisively shapes the items of furniture fashioned from it. Even the idea itself of fashioning a chair from a continuous tube had been anticipated in bentwood work: the so-called "demonstration armchair" exhibited by August Thonet at the Paris World's Fair of 1876 consisted entirely of a pair of long, multipally bent wooden bars. Even the runners, which count as the most important formal element of many tubular steel designs, were already familiar from bentwood rocking chairs, or from the chairs of Josef Hoffmann, for instance, especially his "Sitzmaschine" (machine for sitting), designed in 1905.

Marcel Breuer was at once the first and the most significant designer of tubular steel furniture, and a series of monographs about his work exists. None the less, the historiography of design betrays several blind spots concerning this topic. We know, for example, little about his initial attempts at designing furniture made of aluminium. Up to the present day, his early designs for chairs without rear legs cannot be dated via reference to published drawings, definitely documented public presentations or other evidence, although this is perfectly possible in the case of furniture designed by Mies van der Rohe and Mart Stam. Even regarding the invention of the principle of the chair without rear legs, dissension has long prevailed in the literature; as a consequence, the attribution of authorship assigned to various models is subject to change.[2] To compound the confusion, a trial over the artistic copyright of the cantilevered chair, initiated in Germany in 1933, led to altered attributions of several designs in the Thonet catalogue. Contributing to the complicated historical issue is the fact

2 For a critical survey of the literature on the history of the chair without back legs, see Otakar Máčel, Der Freischwinger. Vom Avantgardeentwurf zur Ware (Delft, 1992), pp. 21–38.

that not only is archival material relevant to the history of tubular steel furniture divided between Europe and the United States, it is also distributed among various locations within Europe. Much material, moreover, has gone missing, for instance the Thonet Archive during World War II. The Anton Lorenz Archive – crucially important for the history of tubular steel furniture – contains hardly any documents from the years 1928–29.

A wealth of general information, on the other hand, is available about Breuer's tubular steel furniture. Much is to be found in monographs on his architecture, and in any publication dealing with modern furniture design. Literary references ar not, however, uniformly accurate or reliable. With regard to Breuer's furniture, two monographs are especially noteworthy. The first is by Christopher Wilk, and appeared in English under the title *Marcel Breuer: Furniture and Interiors,* as the catalogue accompanying the Breuer exhibition at the Museum of Modern Art in New York in 1981. The other was written by Manfred Ludewig and Magdalena Droste; their trilingual monograph (in German, English and French), *Marcel Breuer: Design,* appeared in 1992 on the occasion of an exhibition in Berlin's Bauhaus Archive, and has been reprinted several times. Wilk, who worked in the USA, relied principally on materials preserved in American archives, and was supported in his researches by Breuer himself. Based upon the expertise of the collector Ludewig, the volume by the German authors is lavishly supplied with colour illustrations and draws on materials held by the Bauhaus Archive in Berlin, where Droste then worked as a curator.

▸ Gerrit T. Rietveld, "Roodblauwe stoel", 1918,
  Collection of the Vitra Design Museum.
▸▸ Slat chair ti 1a, 1924, Collection of the
  Vitra Design Museum.

"Wassily" – the Beginnings

The origin of the first tubular steel chair – known today as the "Wassily" chair – has become a legend of design history. According to statements by Breuer, it was the curved tubular steel handlebars of his Adler bicycle that caused him to hit upon the idea of constructing a chair from this material. He wrote to the bicycle manufacturer with a request that the necessary tubular steel be made available to him, but the firm found the idea crazy and refused to make a shipment. The firm of Mannesmann, widely known as a producer of tubular steel, was more commercially oriented, and sent the desired material to Dessau. Assisted by a metalsmith, Breuer built his first tubular steel chair from this supply. Since then, the myth of Mannesmann's "precision tubing" has been closely bound up with the beginnings of tubular steel design.

The entire story played itself out in 1925, when the Bauhaus was relocated from Weimar to Dessau. The new building, designed by Gropius, was not yet ready, and the workshops found temporary accommodations in the town's art gallery. Marcel Breuer was twenty-three years old and had already produced various furniture designs in wood. His works between 1922 and 1925 betray the distinct influence of the aesthetic of the Dutch De Stijl group. It is hardly surprising, then, that his first tubular steel chair – the club armchair – bears visible traces of the De Stijl aesthetic. Disregarding the outer differences in materials, it might well be compared to Gerrit Rietveld's "Red-Blue Chair", since both are reduced to elementary components, which are then exposed undisguised. The parts are set one against the next and connect, rather than interpenetrate.[3] Both chairs consist of transparent arrangements of surfaces and lines, the bent tubing of the club armchair already betraying a tendency towards the new, functional design.

3 Reyner Banham had already referred to this relationship in his Theory and Design in the First Machine Age (London, 1975; 1st edn 1960), p. 198. Incidentally, because of the numerous welds, this similarity is least evident in the case of the first prototype of the club armchair.

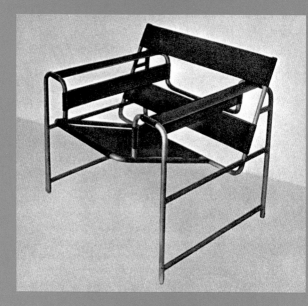

◄◄ Original model for the steel club armchair, 1925.
◄ Steel club armchair, small series, Dessau, 1926.
◄▼ Steel club armchair B3, Standard Möbel/Thonet, 1927–28, Alexander von Vegesack Collection.
▸ Steel club armchair B3, Standard Möbel, 1927, Collection of the Vitra Design Museum.
▼ Steel club armchair B3, Thonet, 1930–31, Alexander von Vegesack Collection.

THONET

THONET

THONET

MOBILI DI ACCIAIO

Thonet

1931

SISTEMA ARCHITETTO MARCEL BREUER

RIO 14
NO
ittoria 16

▸ French patent specification, application of
9 September 1927, issued 21 July 1928.

In 1927, Breuer commented on his first tubular steel chair: "Two years ago, when I saw my first finished steel club armchair, I thought that among all of my pieces to date, it would earn me the most criticism. In both external appearance and in material expression, it is the most extreme; it is the least artistic, the most logical, the least 'cosy', the most machine-style. What actually happened was the opposite of what I had expected."[4] To be sure, the club armchair was highly unusual in appearance. Although it had no moveable parts, it none the less appeared far more "machine-like" than Rietveld's chair. The open construction contributed to this impression, as did the nickel-plated tubing, which seemed more industrial than domestic. In Breuer's formulation ("the least artistic, the most logical"), the functionalist aesthetic is distinctly audible. Because the armchair was reduced to the necessary constructive elements as well as featuring other rational characteristics (it was easily disassembled, lightweight and hygienic), it was not viewed as "artistic". Art, at least as defined up to that time, was conceived as a kind of supplement to the basic essence of a given object.

Breuer's initial concerns about potential criticisms were not unfounded. The first prototype of the club armchair, presumably completed in the second half of 1925, and documented only by a photograph from January 1926,[5] was not yet a fully realised piece of furniture. Although the runners are already included in this design, the chair still stood on four little feet, and moreover showed numerous welds. Three additional phases of reworking would prove necessary for Breuer to arrive at its definitive structure in 1927–28. In the course of this development, welds came to be avoided, so that the tubing only had to be screwed together after being bent into shape. The originally open upper part of the backrest was also

4 Marcel Breuer (1927), "Metallmöbel", in Werner Gräff, ed., Innenräume. Räume und Inneneinrichtungsgegenstände aus der Werkbundausstellung "Die Wohnung", insbesondere aus den Bauten der städtischen Weissenhofsiedlung in Stuttgart (Stuttgart, 1928), p. 133.

5 For Lucia Moholy-Nagy's photograph of the club armchair at the Breuer exhibition in Dessau's Kunsthalle, see Robin Krause, "Die frühen Stahlrohrmöbel von Marcel Breuer", in Margret Kent-gens-Craig, ed., Das Bauhausgebäude in Dessau 1926–1999 (Basel, 1998), p. 36.

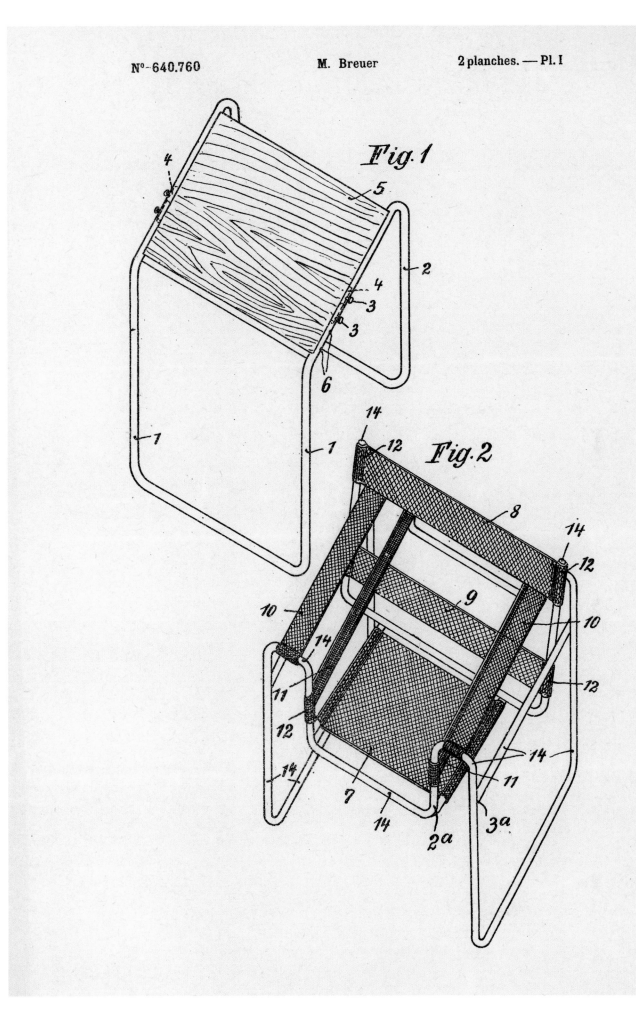

Fig.1

Fig.2

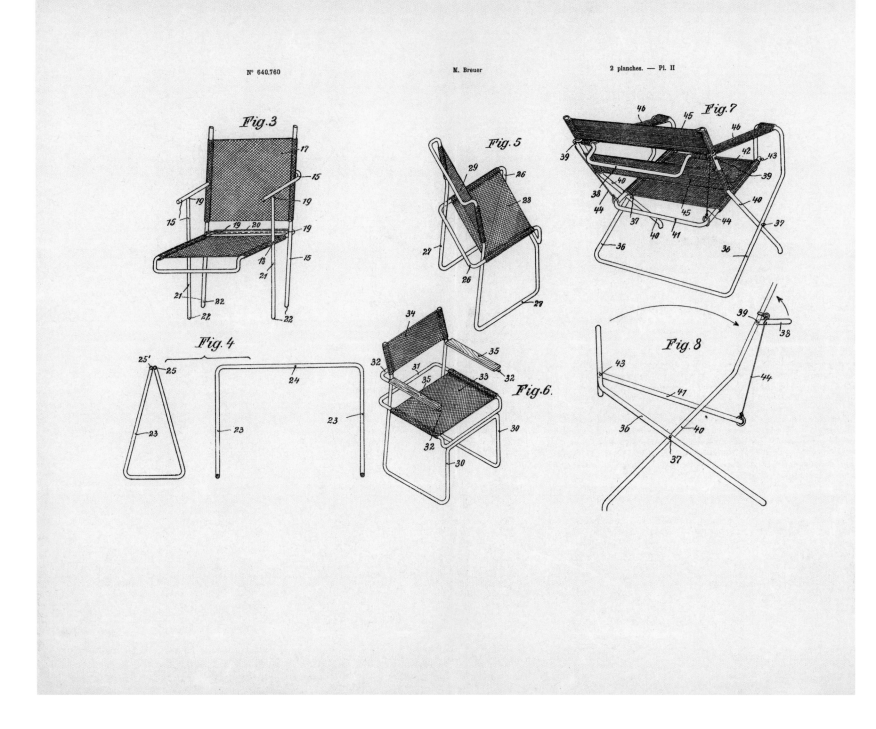

Fig. 3

Fig. 4

Fig. 5

Fig. 6.

Fig. 7

Fig. 8

◀ French patent specification, application of
9 September 1927, issued 21 July 1928.

later closed. A version deviating in constructive terms, and manufactured by Thonet, is known from the period 1930–32.[6] The re-edition of the armchair, manufactured from the 1960s, goes back to the "final version" of the design, as produced in 1927 by Standard Möbel.

The Continuous Line

Alongside improvements in the club armchair, Breuer also worked on new models in tubular steel. These included a folding chair for the auditorium of the Bauhaus and a stool for its cafeteria, as well as a studio table, two chairs and an armchair. The chair without armrests was a prototype of the later B5 and B6 models. The chair with armrests was never produced in this form. The armchair was a foldable version of the club armchair. These models are known through various photographs of the rooms of the Bauhaus and from drawings in Breuer's French patent specification. This patent document may also serve as a source for dating the design *ante quem*. The patent was issued only in July of 1928, but it refers to "brevets déposées en Allemagne" between September 1926 and March 1927. The application for Breuer's registered design for "metal furniture" in the German patent newsletter contains no illustrations and no detailed explanations of the models.[7] For this reason, the drawings in the French patent specification are especially interesting. There are two sheets, one showing the stool and the club armchair, the other containing the remaining furniture. The illustrations on the first sheet are on a smaller scale and are inferior in graphic quality to those on the second sheet. On the basis of these differences, it can be assumed that the illustrations

6 The club armchair was still listed in the Thonet catalogue "Stahlmöbel-Preisliste Nr.3/-1932" (valid beginning July 1932), but was absent beginning with the catalogue "Thonet 3209". The best reproductions of the various versions of the club armchair appear in Manfred Ludewig and Magdalena Droste, Marcel Breuer. Design (Cologne, 1992), pp. 62 ff.

7 DRGM No. 964 585 from 13 September 1926 (see the Berlin patent sheet of 14 October 1926, p. 1255). French patent: Brevet d'Invention, Groupe 9, Classe 4, No. 640.769, enquiry of 12 September 1927, issued on 21 September 1928. The second application in Germany is supposed to have taken place on 25 March 1927.

on the first sheet are older, and that, accordingly, the stool was the second oldest or even the first model.[8]

The new designs show that Breuer had freed himself from the De Stijl aesthetic and now strove for a solution that did more justice to the materials. The models are no longer produced by adding various elements, but are instead shaped by a continuous line of bent steel tubing. This is especially true of the supports of the studio table; for the chair without armrests constructed from two closed lines; and for the stool. The last is the only model that uncompromisingly embodies the new form and the new spirit. Instead of rendering the constructive arrangement visible, Breuer has allowed himself to be guided by a characteristic of tubular steel, namely its flexibility. The tubing was bent in such a way as to produce a continuous line, lending the compact and transparent stool its special character. When compared with the first prototype of the club armchair, the runners here are already lucidly developed. The quality of the stool lies in its simplicity. Sigfried Giedion commented: "The tubing flows in an endless line, as in the Irish interlacement work. And instead of the two-dimensional structure, we have a spatial one, stressing transparency, expressing the new spatial conception of our time."[9] Christopher Wilk too paid tribute to this simple piece of furniture: "the stool ... had a refined and elegant design – it was also Breuer's favourite. It was marked by a distinct originality of conception that demonstrated Breuer's move away from the complexity of constructivism and toward a mode of design that was more personal."[10] The stool, also referred to as a side or tea table, was later manufactured as a set of four in four different sizes. It came to be a very popular and frequently copied item.

8 For more detail, see Krause 1998, pp. 28–41.

9 Giedion 1948, p. 491.

10 Christopher Wilk, Marcel Breuer: Furniture and Interiors (Museum of Modern Art, New York, 1981), p. 43.

11 Arthur Ruegg, "Die schweizerische Entwicklung 1925–1935", in Friederike Mehlau-Wiebking, Arthur Ruegg, Ruggero Tropeano, Sigfried Giedion, Schweizer Typenmöbel 1925–1935. Sigfried Gideon und die Wohnbedarf AG (Zurich, 1989), p. 13.

◄ Stacking tables B9, Polish Thonet Catalogue, 1930.

 **MEBLE STALOWE**

B 9—9 c

Stolik poczwórny do herbaty

z rury stalowej z drewnianemi płytami politurowanemi		wysokość	szerokość	głębokość
	B 9	45 cm	45 cm	39 cm
	B 9 a	50 cm	52 cm	39 cm
	B 9 b	55 cm	59 cm	39 cm
	B 9 c	60 cm	66 cm	39 cm

The Origin of the Bauhaus Furnishings

Where were the first items of tubular steel furniture produced? We know with certainty that production did not take place in the Bauhaus workshops, and that the company Standard Möbel, founded by Breuer and Lengyel, initiated production at the earliest at the end of 1926. The question remains, then, of where the tubular steel furniture with which the Bauhaus building was equipped from 1926 was actually made. Breuer had experience with furniture manufacture in wood, but not in metal. In order to produce the first prototypes of his club armchair, he needed advice and assistance. Breuer is supposed to have undertaken his first attempts at bending tubular steel in Weimar in 1923, aided by Karl Jucker, a silversmith.[11] In Dessau, he found a competent assistant in Karl Körner, a master fitter in the training workshop of the Junkers Company, which built aeroplanes. Still other sources claim that he worked with Georg Flechtner, an artistic metalworker.[12] What remains certain, in any event, is that the first tubular steel furniture had its origins outside the Bauhaus workshops. The connection with the Junkers plant appears plausible for a young "Bauhäusler" with an interest in industrial production. And there is a practical reason for such a collaboration: Junkers had experience with processing metal tubing and sheet metal, especially aluminium. This might explain Breuer's statements about his beginnings with duralumin, and about the "corpus furniture" (no longer extant) in the Weissenhofsiedlung, made of sheet steel.[13] A statement by an aircraft mechanic, Fritz Müller, confirms Breuer's connection to the Junkers plant. Müller, apprenticed in 1925 to the master fitter Körner, witnessed the first attempts with tubular steel furniture.[14] According to Müller, Breuer had weekly contacts with Körner between September 1925 and November 1926, and was still having wire models of his chairs made at Junkers up to July 1928. Müller also confirms Breuer's experiments with aluminium.

12 For Körner, see Helmut Erfurt, Der Stahlrohrstuhl – sein Entwicklungsweg durch das Industriedesign, Beiträge zur Stadtgeschichte 4 (Dessau, 1986), p. 36. For G. Flechtner, see Ludewig and Droste 1992, p. 3.

13 Breuer 1927, pp. 133 f. The "corpus furniture" is said to have stood in the Peter Behrens house, No. 31, but Karin Kirsch's Die Weiße-hofsiedlung. Werkbund-Ausstellung "Die Wohnung" – Stuttgart 1927 (Stuttgart, 1987), in which the interior furnishings are described rather precisely, makes no mention of it.

14 Tecta, ed., Marcel Breuer erfindet den Stahlrohrstuhl. Ein Gesprächsprotokoll von Helmuth Erfurth und Fritz Müller (Cologne, 2002).

In the evolution of the stool, attempts were made with steel as well as with aluminium tubing. The stool made of aluminium tubing, now in the collection of the Stuhlmuseum (Museum of the Chair) at Burg Beverungen, may have come about during this series of attempts. According to Müller's recollections, the design of the stool postdated the first prototypes of the club armchair, but it did have an influence on the articulation of the runners of the armchair.

Despite these contacts, there was no question of serial production of Breuer's early tubular steel furniture at the Junkers plant – only tryout models and individual pieces were produced there. Metal furniture for the Bauhaus building, and presumably also for the Master Houses, was supplied by at least seven different companies.[15] This finding is consistent with Müller's statement: "several small companies and plumbers in Dessau repeatedly manufactured various construction parts according to our specifications and assembled them."[16]

Robin Krause has impressively depicted the laborious production of the first tubular steel furniture.[17] Individual tasks, from bending to nickel-plating, screwing together, assembly, etc., were performed by different companies, a circumstance detrimental to precision of execution. This experience may have been an added incentive for Breuer to take the manufacture of his designs into his own hands. Moreover, the Bauhaus director Walter Gropius wanted to reserve the right to produce and market Breuer's tubular steel furniture to the Bauhaus as an institution, any income being always welcome there. In spring 1926, the Bauhaus was still corresponding with its patent attorney concerning possible legal protection of the club armchair, but by summer these communications had ceased. In the mean time,

15 Krause 1998, p. 38.

16 Tecta 2002, p. 35.

17 Krause 1998, p. 38.

Breuer's interests had taken him in a new direction. Presumably near the end of 1926 or the beginning of 1927, together with his compatriot Kálmán Lengyel, he founded the company Standard Möbel in Berlin to attend to the manufacture of all his tubular steel designs to date. He did this without Gropius's knowledge, and by April 1927 Breuer and his director were in dispute. Breuer argued that the tubular steel chairs were his private affair – not unlike the paintings marketed by the institute's artist-teachers for their own profit. In order to keep Breuer at the Bauhaus, Gropius finally yielded.[18] Incidentally, the status of this endeavour as a "private business" was no obstacle to Herbert Bayer designing the first Standard Möbel catalogue, nor to its being printed in the Bauhaus printing shop that year.

18 Christian Wolsdorff, "Stühle, Tische, Betten, Schränke. Das Bauhaus und die Möbel", in Bauhausmöbel. Eine Legende wird besichtigt! (catalogue of the Bauhaus Archive, Berlin, 2002), p. 44.

The "Standard Möbel" Era

In 1927, tubular steel furniture remained largely unknown to the public. The clientele was restricted to the circle around the Bauhaus itself, and no serious manufacturer was willing to contemplate such a hazardous undertaking. Standard Möbel was the first manufacturer to specialise in contemporary tubular steel furniture – although it was not a large factory, but instead a workshop that produced only a limited number of pieces. The name of the operation was programmatic, an expression of the functionalist aesthetic: from now on, not individualised pieces of furniture but standardised items, serially produced from steel tubing (the material of the future), would inhabit light-flooded apartments. Above and beyond "practical utility, construction and economy", the first catalogue also mentions the establishment of types: "One type has been elaborated for each necessary mode of application, and then improved to such a degree that no subsequent variation would have been possible."[19] This interpretation of the concept of standardisation goes back to Le Corbusier and Amedé Ozenfant, who had already defined the standard as the norm of the machine aesthetic in their 1921 essay "Le Purisme". Le Corbusier's book *Towards a New Architecture,* which dealt with similar questions, had just appeared in 1926.[20]

What kind of "standard furniture" was offered by the company that called itself by this name? The product range was modest: Bayer's catalogue featured only ten models, all the work of Breuer. Three new Breuer models were added to the second catalogue – entitled "The New Furniture", it appeared in 1928 and was designed by Lengyel – along with four items of tubular steel furniture designed by Lengyel. Among the most important models presented in 1928 was the "final version" of the club armchair. Accompanied by a version with armrests (B11), the B5 chair was now ready for serial production. Along with the stool, offered as a nest of four tea tables, two models are conspicuous for being based formally on continuous lines: the chair B6 and the table B10. Both possess a convincing simplicity and lucidity. In the B6 chair, the contour of the tubing resembles that of the stool, while the table features a novel and original solution – its feet are shaped into a bowed form that ensures the stability of the whole. Also remarkable is the chair with armrests (B11), which exemplifies the difficulties arising from the design principle of the continuous line when armrests are involved. The chair was composed of four, later of three, components. The composition of all models was simple: nickel-plated tubular steel (beginning in 1928, a chromed version was available for a surcharge of 10 per cent), fabric coverings and black lacquered wood. The catalogue offered no information about the colours of the fabric coverings.

19 Standard-Möbel-Katalog "Breuer Metallmöbel," 1927; ed. Tecta (Lauenförde, 1992).

20 Le Corbusier, Towards a New Architecture (John Rodker, London, 1926; reprinted as a Dover Edition, 1986), pp.139–148. See also Winfried Nerdinger, "Le Corbusier und Deutschland," in: Arch+, 1987, No. 90, p. 83 f..

RÜCKENLEHNSTUHL mit Stoffbespannung

Sitzhöhe 45 cm

B5

TEETISCHE

B9-9c

in 4 verschiedenen **Größen**

L15 **LIEGE-GESTELL** mit Stoffbespannung

B13 **BETT**

mit Sprungfedermatratze

WIR bringen das Möbel der neuesten Zeit, des modernen Menschen, der seine Umgebung nicht mit unzweckmäßigem Kram bengt und sich mit klarem Geiste in sonnigen Räumen unge- zwungen bewegt ● UNSER Konstruktionselement ist Stahlrohr ● WIR schaffen auf einfachste Art und mit einfachsten Mitteln Möbel, die sich allen Ansprüchen des modernen Kultur- menschen anpassen ● UNSERE Möbel befriedigen das Schönheitsgefühl des Menschen, der mit seinem ganzen Schaffen und Denken im Tempo des XX. Jahrhunderts wurzelt ● Wenden Sie sich an uns, verlangen Sie Vorschläge für Einrichtungen jeder Art ● WIR beraten Sie kostenlos ●

M. BREUER **B**

KLUBSESSEL mit Stoffbespannung

B3

Gewicht	. . . . ca. 6 kg
Gesamtbreite	. . . . ca. 77 cm
Gesamttiefe	. . . . . ca. 67 cm
Gesamthöhe	. . . . . ca. 74 cm

PREIS-LISTE
STAHLROHRMÖBEL D.R.G.M. ● D.R.P. ● AUSL.-PATENTE

Typ		RM
B. 1	**Theaterstuhl** m. Stoffbespannung und Klappsitz (bei mindest 50 Stück)	32.—
B. 3	**Klubsessel** m. Stoffbespann. Sitzhöhe ca.45 cm	66.—
B. 4	" " " zusammenklappb.	60.—
B. 5	**Rückenlehnstuhl** m. Stoffbespann. 85cm hoch, 45 cm breit, 50 cm tief	36.—
B. 6	**Rückenlehnstuhl** mit Holzsitz und -lehne, 88cm hoch, 42 cm breit, 40 cm tief	26.—
B. 7	**Drehstuhl** mit Holzsitz und Stoffrückenlehne	34.—
B. 8	**Hocker** m. Stoffsitz, 35 × 35 cm, Sitzhöhe 45 cm	26.—
B. 9	**Teetisch** od. **Hocker** m.Holzpl.35×35, Höhe 45cm	19.—
B.9a	" " " 42×35, " 50 "	22.—
B.9b	" " " 46×35, " 55 "	25.—
B.9c	" " " 56×35, " 60 "	29.—

Typ		RM
B.10	**Tisch**, quadratisch, mit Holzplatte 70×70 cm, Höhe 68 cm	66.—
B. 11	**Armlehnstuhl** mit Stoffbespannung, 88 cm hoch, 48 cm breit, 50 cm tief	48.—
B.12	**Ablegetisch** mit Doppelplatte, Größe wie B. 9c	42.—
B.13	**Bett** mit Sprungfedermatratze, 200 × 100 cm	80.—
L.14	**Tisch**, rund mit Holzplatte, 60 cm Durchmesser, Höhe 68 cm	50.—
L.15	**Liegegestell** mit Stoffbespannung, 180×75 cm,	80.—
L.16	**Schrank** mit Sperrholz für Wäsche, Kleider, Geschirr usw. a) 180×120 cm, 55 cm tief ●	160.—
	b) 135×160 " 55 " "	150.—
	c) 135× 80 " 55 " "	100.—
L.17	**Stehlampe**, verstellbar, Höhe 165 cm komplett	120.—

Ausführung der Typen zu obigen Preisen:
Metallteile aus Präzisions-Stahlrohr **vernickelt.**
Holzteile schwarz **gebeizt.**
Stoffbespannung: schwarz, rostfarb.od.grau, Eisengarnstoff.
Stahlrohr in **verchromter** Ausführung ca. 10% Aufschlag.
Holzplatten in **schleiflackiert,** Ausführung ca. 20% Aufschlg.
Kleine **Abweichungen** von den Katalogabbildungen vor-
behalten!

Preise verstehen sich ab Berlin ohne Verpackung u. Transport.
Verpackung wird zum Selbstkostenpreis berechnet und nicht
zurückgenommen.
Transport geschieht auf Gefahr des Bestellers.
Zahlung sofort nach Rechnungserhalt.
Reklamationen werden nur binnen 5 Tagen berücksichtigt.
Gerichtsstand: Berlin-Mitte.

KLUBSESSEL zusammenklappbar

Sessel zusammengeklappt nur 15 cm tief

B4

Gewicht	. . . . ca. 5 kg
Gesamtbreite	. . . . ca. 77 cm
Gesamttiefe	. . . . . ca. 61 cm
Gesamthöhe	. . . . . ca. 70 cm

STEHLAMPE verstellbar nach jeder Richtung

L17

ABLEGETISCH

B12

Größe wie B9 c

L16a mit Inneneinteilung für jeden Verwendungszweck

SCHRANK

TISCH

Sitzhöhe 45 cm

B11

B10

ARMLEHNSTUHL mit Stoffbespannung

▾ Walter Gropius, Weissenhofsiedlung, House 16,
Stuttgart, 1927, furnishings by Marcel Breuer.
▸ Walter Gropius, Weissenhofsiedlung, House 16,
with furnishings by Marcel Breuer.

Outside the Bauhaus, the contemporary, increasingly matter-of-fact and functional interior décor received notice only in June 1927, when the Werkbund exhibition "The Apartment" opened its doors at the Weissenhof in Stuttgart. Here, modern architecture and the new interior were presented to a wide public. In the model houses, people saw bright, airy rooms with spartan furnishing, devoid of ornamentation. The comparatively "empty" rooms with their built-in cabinets and clinical-seeming tubular steel furniture were really "the most machine-like and the least cosy". A series of architects displayed metal furniture designs. Alongside Breuer, these were Ernst Haefeli, Arthur Korn, Ludwig Mies van der Rohe, Jacobus Johannes Pieter Oud, the brothers Bodo and Heinz Rasch, Sybold van Ravesteyn and Mart Stam. Breuer supplied the furnishings for apartments Nos. 16 and 17 in the house designed by Gropius, and for No. 30 in the house by Stam.

Although contemporary steel furniture conveyed an impression of industrial serial production, most of the items exhibited in Stuttgart were, in truth, one-offs. Only those models designed by Breuer, Korn and Mies van der Rohe were actually offered for sale after the exhibition. An understanding of the potentialities of the new materials was not evident in all models. The chairs by Haefeli, Oud and Ravesteyn, for example, which stood on four feet, were dependent upon customary construction as normally executed in wood. Two of the tubular steel chairs in particular stood out by virtue of their unconventional forms: they lacked rear legs. The seats of these skeletal-appearing chairs, their forms (not unlike the now familiar Breuer models) shaped by lucid lines of tubing, floated in the air. The elasticity of the cold-pulled tubular steel, optimally exploited here, led to completely new forms. The designers of these chairs were Mart Stam and Ludwig Mies van der Rohe. The idea for a chair

▼ Mart Stam, tubular steel chair without back legs,
L. & C. Arnold, 1927, design of 1926, Collection of
the Vitra Design Museum.

▶ Ludwig Mies van der Rohe, tubular steel chair
without back legs, metal workshop of Joseph Müller,
1927, Collection of the Vitra Design Museum.

without back legs, and composed of tubing bent at right angles, had been elaborated and sketched out by Stam in Stuttgart in November 1926, during preparations for the exhibition. Mies van der Rohe had immediately taken up the idea, and worked it up further in altered, namely in rounded form.[21] Apart from formal contrasts, there were two technical differences between their designs. Stam's chair was painted and, because of a manufacturing problem, had no bounce. The bends were too strong, and the tubing – with a diameter of 20 mm and a thickness of 2 mm – was too weak to endow the chair with the required stability; the problem had been solved by stiffening the construction of the tubing by equipping it with iron inserts, as a consequence of which all springiness had been eliminated. Mies van der Rohe's chair was nickel-plated, and because of the use of stronger steel tubing, had plenty of bounce. For the history of design, it is instructive to realise that in August 1927 Mies van der Rohe had already submitted a patent application for his chair, which was accepted, after numerous delays, at some point during the same year. Stam had hoped to see serial production of his chairs begin as soon as possible, but the manufacturer of the prototypes, L. & C. Arnold of Schorndorf (a renowned maker of iron furniture) showed no interest. Thereafter, Stam concentrated principally on architecture.

Breuer's contribution to the interior decor of the Weissenhofsiedlung was relatively limited, since in furnishing the apartments he was dependent upon the views of Gropius and Stam. Things were very different with the commission to decorate the Berlin apartment of theatre director Erwin Piscator. "Nothing is to be used from the old apartment ... Do everything new, from the bottom up, according to the principle: from the door in the corridor all the way to the last little pantry door, everything in a unified style. Only the most

21 On Stam, see Werner Möller, Otakar Máčel: *Ein Stuhl macht Geschichte* (Munich, 1992), pp. 22–28. For Mies van der Rohe, see Otakar Máčel, "Vom Serienmöbel zum Designklassiker. Die Metallmöbel von Ludwig Mies van der Rohe," in Alexander von Vegesack, Mateo Kries, *Mies van der Rohe. Möbel und Bauten in Stuttgart, Barcelona und Brno* (Milan, 1998), pp. 20–28.

indispensable furniture, so that space remains."[22] Such was Hildegard Piscator's request. In the Piscator apartment, Breuer really did design everything in a unified style. As the "necessary apparatuses of contemporary life", his tubular steel furniture gave shape to the empty space, as he later formulated it in *Das Neue Frankfurt* (The New Frankfurt): "the furniture, even the walls of the room, are no longer massive, monumental ... they are much more airily open, sketched, so to speak, into space; they neither hinder movement, nor the freedom of the gaze to wander through space."[23] A characteristic element of the design is the narrow, elongated horizontal wall cupboard in the dining room, which would continue to find frequent application in Breuer's interiors. The Piscator bedroom, designed in part to accommodate gymnastics practice, anticipated the House for a Sportsman, shown in 1931 at the Berlin Building Exhibition. With this interior, Breuer discovered a formal language that would be virtually prototypical for his work in coming years. His strivings for a matter-of-fact aesthetic sobriety, thanks to which "the new space ... would represent no self-portrait of the architect" (as he had formulated it in *Das Neue Frankfurt*), placed him in a paradoxical situation: it was, in fact, precisely through their formal reductiveness and economy that his interiors betrayed their author's identity.

22 Prager Tagblatt, 25 October 1928; cited after Wolsdorff 2002, p. 31; Wilk 1981, pp. 61–64; Ludewig and Droste 1992, p.19, pp. 74–77.

23 Marcel Breuer, "metallmöbel und moderne räumlichkeit," in Das Neue Frankfurt (1928), No.1, p.11.

▾ Piscator apartment, workroom.
▾▾ Piscator apartment, living room.
▸ Piscator apartment, bedroom.

▸ De Francesco apartment, Berlin, 1929, bedroom.

The Decisive Years

In many respects, the years 1928 and 1929 were of signal importance for Breuer. Together with Gropius, he left the Bauhaus; he completed his corpus of tubular steel furniture with cantilevered chairs and new tables; he closed a contract with Thonet, which lent sales of his furniture considerable momentum. Finally, Anton Lorenz surfaced at this time as managing director of Standard Möbel; he would soon assert the firm's control over Breuer's designs.

In early 1928, when Walter Gropius took his leave as director of the Bauhaus, Bayer, Breuer and Moholy-Nagy followed. Breuer went to Berlin, where he settled as an independent architect, remaining active there until 1933. While he also completed designs for larger projects, he primarily executed renovations and interior décor commissions, perpetuating the style he had invented for the Piscator apartment. Among his best-known works from these years are, among others, the Da Francesco, Boroschek and Vogler apartments in Berlin, as well as the Harnischmacher apartment in Wiesbaden.

One might assume that in the aftermath of the Weissenhof exhibition, public awareness of tubular steel furniture would have had a beneficial impact on the receipts of Standard Möbel. But the reverse was the case. In fact, business was so bad that on 30 July 1928 Breuer transferred his rights to the company against reimbursements from sales. According to documents that came to light during later legal proceedings, Breuer is also supposed to have committed himself to surrendering all new designs to Standard-Möbel.[24] This contract was agreed under the supervision of Anton Lorenz, the company's new managing director. Lorenz, another Hungarian, was originally a teacher of geography and history. He had lived in Germany since 1919, and came to Standard Möbel in late 1927 through his acquaintance

24 Typewritten duplicate of verdict 216/33b.C.128.30 of the civil division 16b of the district court I. in Berlin from 21.X. 1932, p.7, "Prozess Lorenz kontra Thonet".

◄ Levi gymnastics studio, Berlin, 1930.
▼ Boroschek apartment, Berlin, 1930, living room.

with Lengyel. Beginning in 1928, he assumed responsibility for the manufacture of furniture in a workshop in Teltower Straße in Berlin.[25]

     Breuer also finalised a contract with Thonet in July 1928. The manufacturer of bentwood furniture had early recognised the potential of the new tubular steel designs, and had begun making preparations for its manufacture in 1928, in both Germany and Paris. This initiative was comparatively risky – as yet there existed no market for the product, and hence no guarantee of profit in the short term. The precise date that production commenced is unknown, but the earliest signs date from January 1929, when an advertisement appeared in the magazine *Innendekoration* (Interior Decoration) with an illustration of a tubular steel table by Breuer and a wooden chair by Adolf Schneck. Both designers were mentioned by name in the advertisement, then a novel practice for Thonet. The Breuer table (B18) did not come from the Standard Möbel selection. Like the table models B19, B21–23, B26 and B27, it had been newly designed especially for Thonet.[26] For Thonet, in addition, Breuer had also designed his first chair without back legs, then known in German as a "Kragstuhl", meaning "overhanging" or "cantilevered" chair.

25 Wilk 1981, p. 73.

26 Wilk 1981, p. 78–82.

The First Cantilevered Chair

Numerous myths have grown up around the chair without rear legs. Yet little is known with any certainty about this chapter of design history. It has been repeatedly asserted that Breuer designed the first such chair exclusively for Thonet, and hence independently of his connection to Standard Möbel and to Lorenz. But when its operations were taken over by Thonet, Standard Möbel held four prototypes for a chair without rear legs, which have become the objects of dispute. Breuer's contribution to their design remains unclear.

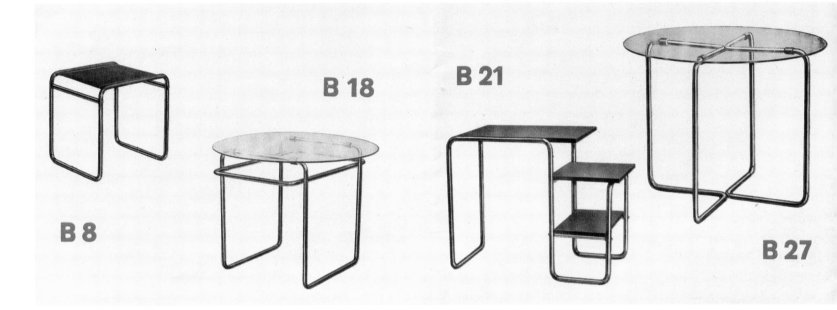

Many people have regarded Breuer as the inventor of the cantilevered chair, since Mart Stam withdrew to Switzerland in 1966, disappearing for ever from public view, while Breuer's designs had just begun second lives in new editions. In an interview with Christopher Wilk at the end of his life in 1979, Breuer himself asserted that Stam had stolen his idea for the cantilevered chair when he had informed Stam about the concept during the latter's visit to Dessau. Stam, in turn, who was also questioned by Wilk, replied that the story was based on fantasy, that he had never even met Breuer at the Bauhaus.[27] Today, so many years after the controversial events, these statements by old rivals can hardly be introduced for evidential purposes. If we take the literature on faith, then we must conclude that by 1928 Breuer had already designed almost all of the models of the chair without rear legs. Yet this claim, raised only after the war, probably on the basis of Breuer's own assertions, has never been supported by concrete or dateable documentary sources. That nearly all of the models were already available in 1928, at least as ideas, would be possible only if Breuer had designed them "for the drawer". The Thonet catalogues from 1929 to 1931 give an impression, conversely, of the gradual development of his tubular steel models without rear legs.

What appears certain is that the simple cantilevered chair and the version of it with armrests, later labelled B33 and B34, have their origins in the year 1928, as the first models. Comparable prototypes were in existence in early 1929 at Standard Möbel, and the oldest known Thonet catalogue too, composed of separate leaflets, shows only these two models without rear legs. With the chair B33, Breuer's point of departure was Stam's conception of a cubic form. However, he used thicker tubing and a wider bend radius, so that the chair requires no inner strengthening of the tubing and thus acquires its springiness. This model

27 See Máčel 1992, p. 61 f.

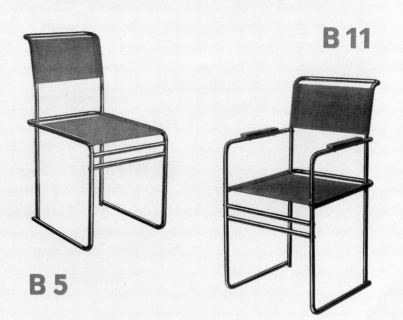

B 5

B 11

B 3

B 9-9c

B 12

B 10

B 22

B 19

B 2

B 34

B 33

B 26

B 26

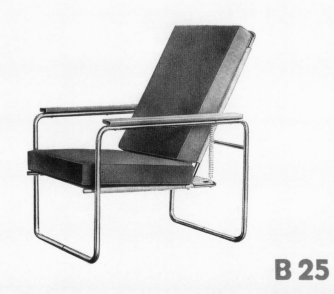

B 25

◄ Poster, Thonet Mundus, 1928.

▾ Side table B23, Polish Thonet Catalogue, 1930.
▸ Side table B23, c. 1930, Collection of the
   Vitra Design Museum.
▸▸ Thonet poster, 1934.

MEBLE STALOWE

B 23

Stolik z dwoma płytami ze szkła kryształowego
z rury stalowej

Cała wysokość	74 cm
Cała szerokość	53 cm
Cała głębokość	53 cm
Rozmiar płyt szkl. . . . . 66 x 48·5 cm
Wysokość do I-szej płyty . . .	37 cm
Wysokość do II-ej płyty . . .	67 cm

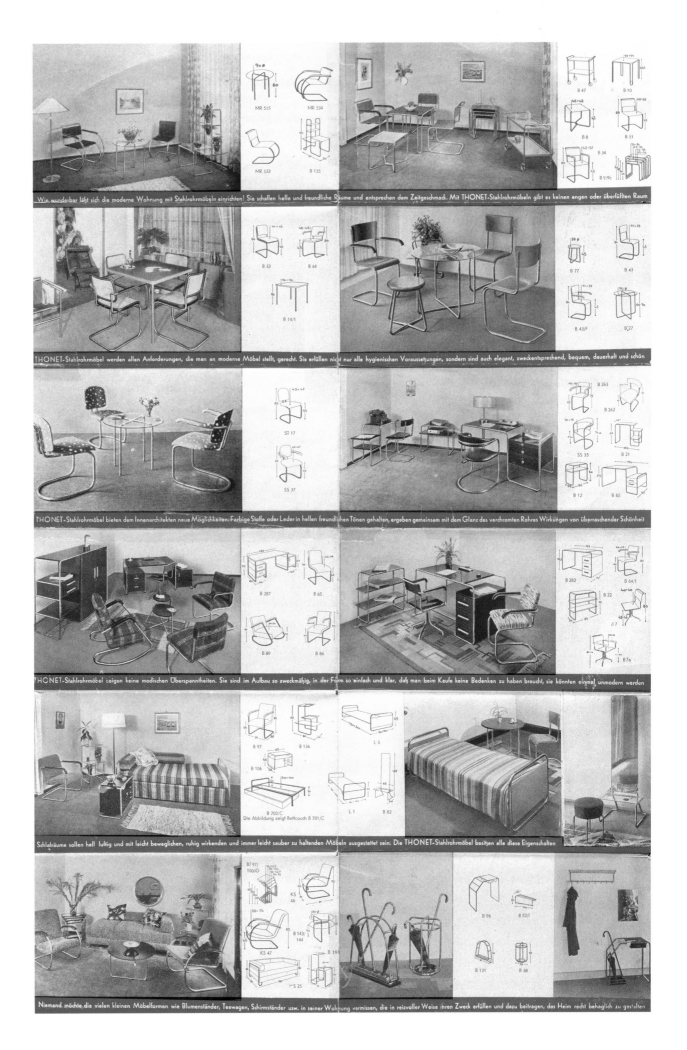

Wie wunderbar läßt sich die moderne Wohnung mit Stahlrohrmöbeln einrichten! Sie schaffen helle und freundliche Räume und entsprechen dem Zeitgeschmack. Mit THONET-Stahlrohrmöbeln gibt es keinen engen oder überfüllten Raum

THONET-Stahlrohrmöbel werden allen Anforderungen, die man an moderne Möbel stellt, gerecht. Sie erfüllen nicht nur alle hygienischen Voraussetzungen, sondern sind auch elegant, zweckentsprechend, bequem, dauerhaft und schön

THONET-Stahlrohrmöbel bieten dem Innenarchitekten neue Möglichkeiten. Farbige Stoffe oder Leder in hellen freundlichen Tönen gehalten, ergeben gemeinsam mit dem Glanz des verchromten Rohres Wirkungen von überraschender Schönheit

THONET-Stahlrohrmöbel zeigen keine modischen Überspanntheiten. Sie sind im Aufbau so zweckmäßig, in der Form so einfach und klar, daß man beim Kaufe keine Bedenken zu haben braucht, sie könnten einmal unmodern werden

Schlafräume sollen hell, luftig und mit leicht beweglichen, ruhig wirkenden und immer leicht sauber zu haltenden Möbeln ausgestattet sein. Die THONET-Stahlrohrmöbel besitzen alle diese Eigenschaften

Niemand möchte die vielen kleinen Möbelformen wie Blumenständer, Teewagen, Schirmständer usw. in seiner Wohnung vermissen, die in reizvoller Weise ihren Zweck erfüllen und dazu beitragen, das Heim recht behaglich zu gestalten

was not painted, but instead nickel- or chrome-plated. The most important difference between the two consisted of a formal detail: with Stam's chair, the steel tubing ran upwards from seat to backrest at a 90-degree angle. While this achieved a lucid and severe contouring, it made for uncomfortable sitting. Breuer, by contrast, bent the steel tubing beneath the backrest gently backwards. This improved comfort and gave the chair a more elegant appearance. It was only in Breuer's reworked shape that the chair without back legs was widely disseminated and copied by nearly every manufacturer of tubular steel furniture. The cantilever motif, incidentally, also occupied Breuer in his architectural work. In 1928, he designed a hospital in Wuppertal-Elberfeld with a terrace-style layout, its façade articulated into an arrangement of successively overhanging storeys.

The "gentle curve" is also emblematic of a divergent conception of the Neue Sachlichkeit (the New Objectivity, or Sobriety). Stam was an adherent of the fundamentalist wing of the modernist movement in architecture, with its orientation to social science, and he detested the curved line. Breuer, equally a modernist by conviction, was instead fascinated by the machine aesthetic. The aforementioned curve is recognisable in models B33, B32 and B64 in the illustrations of all Thonet catalogues. Whether it was correctly and consistently applied in the manufacturing process is not entirely certain. Deviations from the illustrated models were always possible. In the mid-1930s, Stam was contracted by Lorenz to draw corrections for, among others, the models B32, B33 and B64; his emendations eliminated the curve once again.[28] A chair (ST12) manufactured by DESTA, which resembled the B33, had no curve, since it had been derived directly from Stam's version of the chair without back legs.

28 Möller/Máčel 1992, pp. 88 ff.; Máčel 1992, pp. 99.

◄ Chair with armrests B64, 1928, Collection of the
Vitra Design Museum.
▼ Chair B32, 1928, Collection of the
Vitra Design Museum.

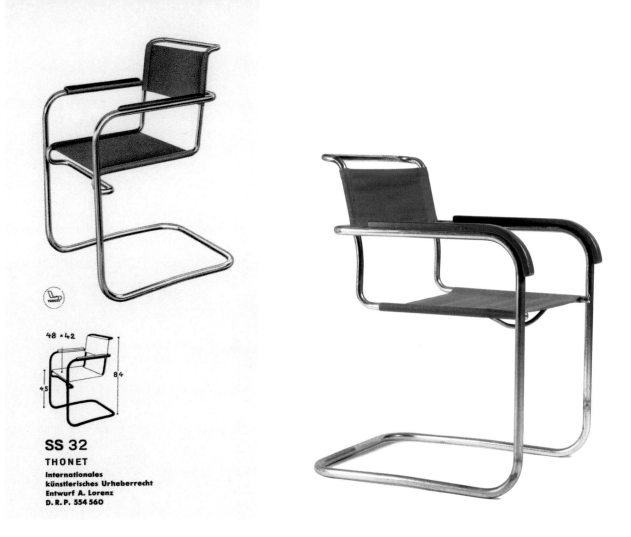

SS 32
THONET
Internationales
künstlerisches Urheberrecht
Entwurf A. Lorenz
D. R. P. 554 560

The chair with armrests (B34) is composed of two parts: the supporting structure, including armrests, is formed from a closed, continuous line of tubing, while the seat component is shaped from an open line of tubing, which is then suspended within the supporting structure. The tubing of the seat element terminates where it meets the legs on the inner sides of the supporting structure. Later, Breuer modified this design slightly to produce the model B30, in which the tubing of the seat terminates not at the sides but instead where it abuts the legs at right angles. With the first prototype of this model by Standard Möbel, which may be identical with an illustration in Wilk, the seat element had a different appearance.[29] It was composed of a closed line and not only had an upper offset, but an offset below as well, intended to make the chair more stable as a whole. This solution was unusual for Breuer in formal terms. In February 1929, Lorenz had already made patent claims[30] and later exploited the design in his DESTA operation alongside his own models. Apart from the case of the Breuer armchair B24, Breuer and Thonet never made use of this version of the seating element.[31]

The Conflict

On 11 April 1929, Standard Möbel closed its doors.[32] On the same day, Thonet took over the rights to all of its models, together with the entire inventory of materials, products and catalogues. In return, Thonet paid out 30,000 Reichsmarks to the creditors of Standard Möbel. Together with its "own" Breuer models, Thonet now had the disposal of the largest and most diverse selection of tubular steel furniture in the world. Yet in the process of surrendering the entire inventory of furniture, Lorenz had withheld four prototypes. One of

29 Wilk 1981, ill. 69, p. 73.

30 Registered design No. 1 069 697, inquiry of 12 February 1929. The accompanying drawings show, as is usual, various versions of the seat, but at the same time various versions of chairs without either back or front legs.

31 The B24 surfaces in Thonet's catalogues beginning in 1933, and then under the name of Lorenz; Thonet catalogue Meubles en tubes d'acier 3311, 1933, p. 12.

32 For a time, the name Standard Möbel remained associated with the co-founder Kálmán Lengyel.

◄◄ Chair with armrests B34, Thonet, 1928 (the same
model appears in the DESTA catalogue of 1929
under the designation SS32, designed by Anton
Lorenz).

◄ Chair with armrests B34, variant from the Thonet
detached card catalogue of 1930–31, Collection of
the Vitra Design Museum.

▸ Chair with armrests, model B30, Thonet detached
card catalogue of 1930–31.

these, bearing the designation L33, was similar to the Thonet model B33, and the others were combined with the new seat and backrest Lorenz had patented two months earlier (L34). His motives for this behaviour were mercantile in nature: Lorenz expected to achieve commercial success with the prototypes. After he had invited Mies van der Rohe, in vain, to collaborate with him, Lorenz closed a licence agreement on 18 April with Mart Stam for his chair without back legs. On the same day, Lorenz wrote to Thonet: "Unfortunately, your keen desire to have the models . . . L33 and L34 handed over to you cannot be fulfilled, since the legal patents and copyrights are the property of Mr. Lorenz, and he has no intention of transferring them to you."[33]

Lorenz must have realised that Thonet was preparing to commence manufacture of Breuer's cantilever designs, and wanted to stay a step ahead of the competition. Once Thonet actually began production, Lorenz initiated legal proceedings at Berlin district court between July and September 1929. Armed with the Stam licence and his patent application, he complained of an infringement of his copyrights. In September, he founded the company DESTA in Berlin – in the very same location where Standard Möbel had earlier resided – and began to produce tubular steel furniture. Thus it came to pass that the simple cantilevered prototype L33 came to be manufactured by Thonet as the B33, designed by Breuer; and by DESTA as the ST12 (without curve), designed by Stam; while the prototype L34 surfaced at Thonet as the B34, designed by Breuer; and at DESTA as the SS32, designed by Lorenz. At their fronts, both of the last-named chairs had differing termini of their seat elements: with the B34, the line of the tubing was open, while with the SS32 it was closed by an offset. This is how things remained until at least June 1932. It seems doubtful that Breuer was also the

33 Cited after the type-written duplicate of the default judgment I.244/1931 of the I. civil court of appeal of the supreme court from 27 February 1932, p. 15.

- Chair with armrests, model B25, Thonet detached card catalogue of 1930–31.
- Tubular steel chair B5, 1st version, 1927, Alexander von Vegesack Collection.
- Tubular steel chair for the Bauhaus Building (precursor to the B5), 1926, Bauhaus-Archiv, Berlin.
- Tubular steel chair B5, 2nd version, Polish Thonet catalogue, 1930.

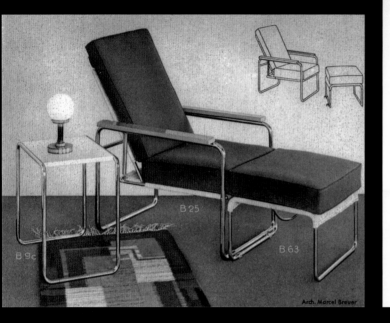

B 5

Krzesło z rury stalowej

siedzenie i oparcie wykonane z kolorowej specjalnej materji parcianej t. zw. „Eisengarnstoff"

Cała wysokość . . . . 86 cm
Cała szerokość . . . . 45 cm
Cała głębokość . . . . 59 cm
Głębokość siedzenia . . . . . . 45 cm
Szerokość siedzenia . . . . . . 42 cm
Wysokość siedzenia . . . . . . 47 cm

▸ Tubular steel chairs, models B11 and B5, 3rd version,
Thonet, 1933.
▾ Tubular steel chairs, models B11 and B5, 4th version,
Thonet, 1935.

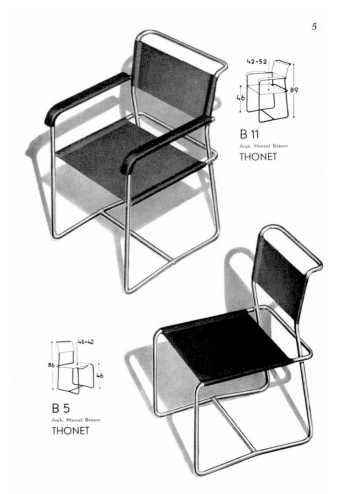

B 11
Arch. Marcel Breuer
THONET

B 5
Arch. Marcel Breuer
THONET

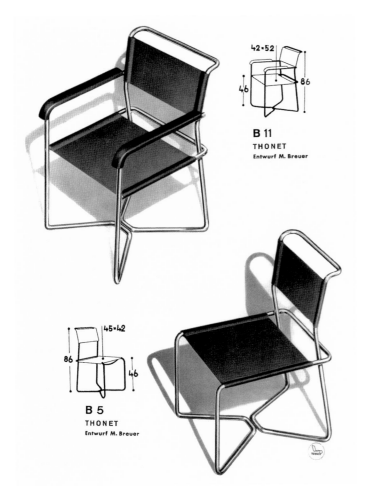

B 11
THONET
Entwurf M. Breuer

B 5
THONET
Entwurf M. Breuer

◀ Easy chair with armrests, model B35, Thonet, 1928–29, Collection of the Vitra Design Museum.

▶ Thonet detached card catalogue, 1930–31.

author of models ST12 and SS32, since both chairs lack characteristically Breueresque traits. During the period when Lorenz and Thonet were embroiled in this lawsuit, Breuer was active in Berlin as a freelance. During the trial, he appeared only as a witness. He designed additional chairs for Thonet, which completed the company's assortment in the area of tubular steel furniture. As already mentioned, the simple cantilevered chair (B33) and the version with armrests (B34) were the first designs Breuer had done especially for Thonet. In what is presumed to have been the first Thonet catalogue,[34] we find Breuer's furniture exclusively. Alongside the two cantilevered chairs, the upholstered easy chair B25 also appears, with a seat hanging from a pair of spiral springs at the rear. Breuer utilised this alternative to the system without back legs on only one occasion.[35]

Remarkable also are the chairs B5 and B11, which were shown here in their penultimate versions: the runners were additionally connected at the rear of the chair by a segment of tubing. The subsequent Thonet catalogue (c. 1930) also contained only Breuer designs, or else models that had been attributed to Breuer. New designs were the chairs B32 (later reissued as "Cesca"), B35 and B36.[36] The model B11 had already attained its ultimate form; the B5 remained unchanged to begin with. A notable novelty was represented by the armchair B35. It inspired conviction by virtue of its lucid, open contours and offered a more comfortable seat than the club armchair. Open lines were also characteristic for the model B32 (the variant with armrests was not illustrated). In the 1960s, this model, with which Breuer has connected the simple principle of the chair without back legs with the classical Thonet tradition, was reissued by Dino Gavina and named "Cesca" after Breuer's daughter Francesca. After the war, among all the items of early tubular steel furniture, this elegant chair

34 The sole edition of this catalogue I am aware of is now in the possession of the Vitra Design Museum. It comes from the Polish retail shop Thonet Meble Stalowe; the price list, however, is dated "wrzesień" (September) 1930.

35 The use of spiral or leaf springs for tubular steel furniture was exceptional. See Jan van Geest, Otakar Máčel, Stühle aus Stahl. Metallmöbel 1925–1940 (Cologne, 1980), pp. 100, 111, 144 f.

36 Stahlrohr-Möbel Thonet-Mundus, catalogue of the Vienna retail shop, c. 1930; a price list which would permit the more precise checking of the selection is missing. According to Wilk, the B36 was not designed by Breuer; Wilk 1981, p. 185.

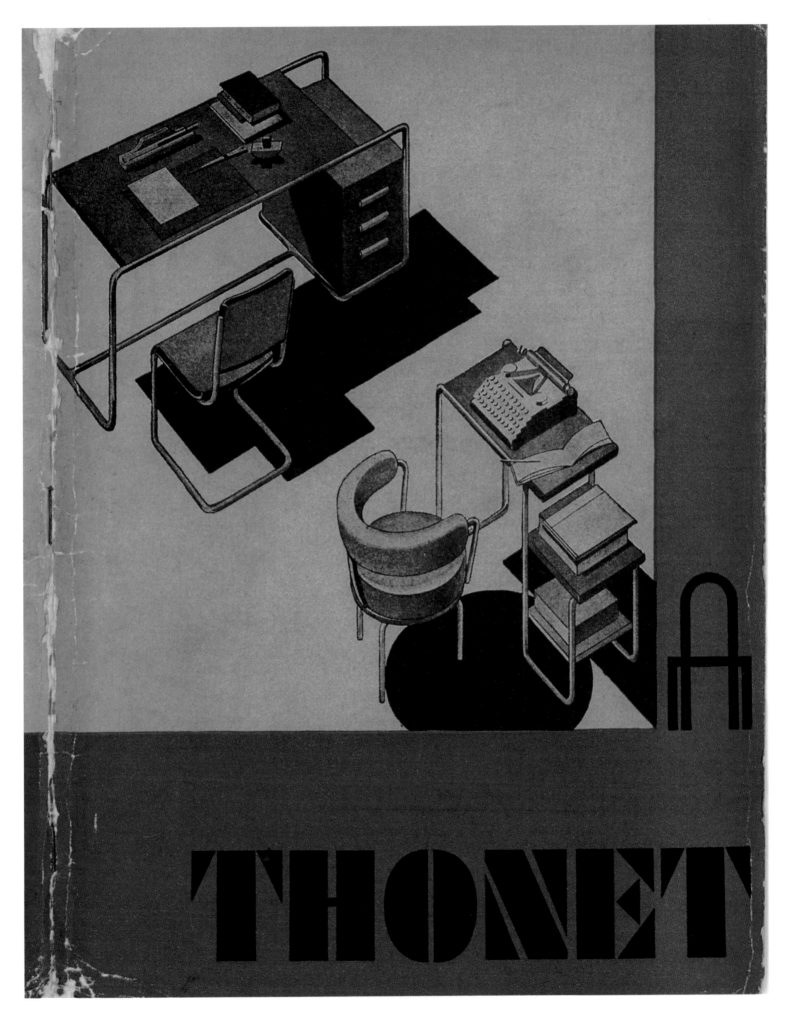

remained in production the longest.[37] The famous Thonet catalogue with a yellow and blue cover (c. 1930–31) expanded the Thonet assortment of tubular steel furniture by including models by other designers. It also contained Breuer's cantilevered chairs with model numbers B30, B46, B55 and B64. The supplementation of the cantilevered series with the B46 and the B55 may be regarded – notwithstanding the quality of Breuer's designs – as a symptom of the growing popularity of tubular steel furniture.

"... une lumière comme spiritualisée"

In 1930, on the invitation of Walter Gropius, Marcel Breuer – together with László Moholy-Nagy and Herbert Bayer – designed furnishings for the exhibition of the German Werkbund in the 20e Salon des Artistes Décorateurs Français in Paris. Breuer designed a model apartment, in which a "room for a woman" was separated from a "room for a man" by the bathroom and kitchen. Entirely in the spirit of his earlier interiors, these rooms were furnished only sparingly with tubular steel furniture and typical horizontal wall shelving or wall cabinets based on a standardised module measuring 33.3 cm. Brightness, openness and sobriety characterised these rooms, which comprised an interior wholly in thrall to the machine aesthetic. Reactions to the exhibition in the French press were critical[38] and reflected the disparity between French and German tubular steel furniture: in France individualised solutions, in Germany matter-of-fact standardisation.

Breuer's model apartments at the Berlin Building Exhibition of 1931 are barely distinguishable formally from his Paris interior. The most remarkable in appearance was his House for a Sportsman, which recalls the design of the Piscator bedroom, and which testifies

37 In the Thonet catalogue No. 161, presumably from 1961, appear the last two pre-war models.

38 See Robin Krause, "Die Ausstellung des deutschen Werkbundes von Walter Gropius in '20e Salon des Artistes Décorateurs Français'" and Matthias Noell, "Zwischen Krankenhaus und Mönchszelle. 'Le nouveau visage de l'Alemagne' – Die Werkbundausstellung 1930 im Spiegel der französischen Tagespresse", in Isabelle Ewig, Thomas W. Gaehtgens, Matthias Noell, eds., Das Bauhaus und Frankreich. Le Bauhaus et la France (Berlin, 2002), pp. 275–96, 313–346.

Marcel Breuer, apartment of a residential hotel, general view, exhibition of the German Werkbund, Paris, 1930.

▼ Apartment of a residential hotel,
   room for a lady.
▼▼ Apartment of a residential hotel,
   workroom (office).
▶ Apartment of a residential hotel,
   room for a gentleman.

96

▾ Walter Gropius, exhibition of the German Werkbund,
Paris, 1930, lounge.
▾▾ 70 sq m apartment, plan.
▸ Marcel Breuer, 70 sq m apartment, building
exhibition, Berlin, 1931.

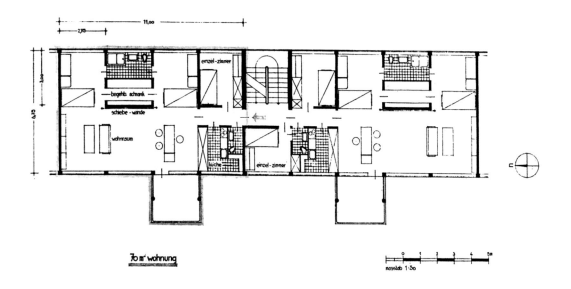

70 m² wohnung

marcel breuer
mitarbeiter hassenpflug
70 qm wohnung   1931

▶ House for a Sportsman, building exhibition,
Berlin, 1931, plan and section.

▼ House for a Sportsman, entry area.

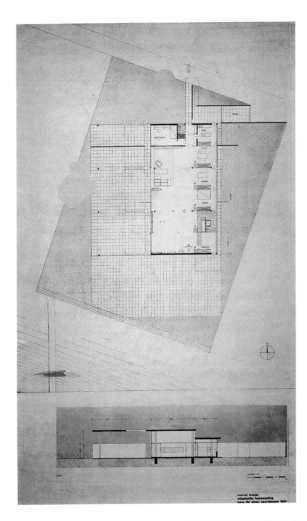

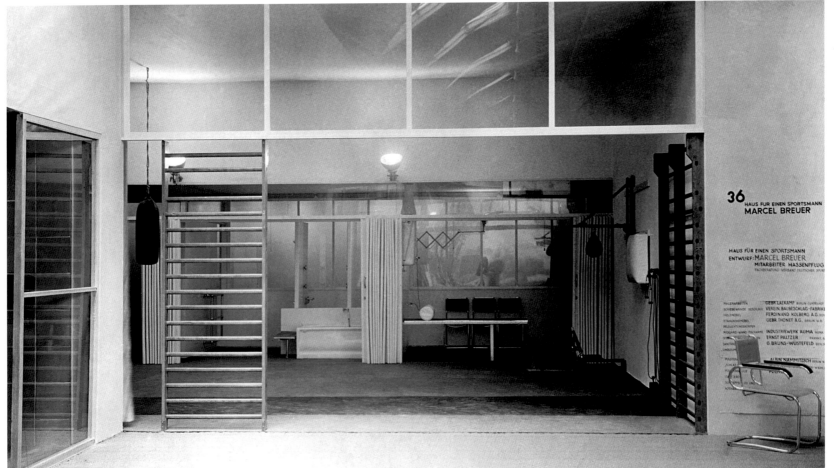

◄ House for a Sportsman, gymnasium with view into the cubicles for various residential functions.

▼ House for a Sportsman, living area with gym.

to a phenomenon typical of the times: a fascination for sobriety and healthy lifestyles. The apartment consisted essentially of a large combination of living room and gymnastics hall, on whose long side were arranged smaller side rooms for other residential functions.

Breuer's last important project in Germany was the realisation in 1932 of the Harnischmacher House in Wiesbaden – his first executed architectural design. The freestanding house, consisting of a rectangular core joined to two smaller volumes, has mainly been discussed in the context of his furniture designs (especially the club armchairs).[39] Yet it also heralded the beginning of Breuer's second career as an architect. The interior of the house – later destroyed in the war – incorporated furniture from the Harnischmacher apartment, which Breuer had decorated in 1929. Among these items were unique pieces such as the armchair with wooden runners and the tubular steel chaise longue in the library, which are now regrettably missing.

Aftermath

On 1 June 1932, the Supreme Court of the Reich resolved the litigation between Thonet and Lorenz in favour of the latter. Mart Stam was awarded the artistic copyright for the cubic chair without back legs, and Lorenz acquired the manufacturing monopoly for Germany. The Supreme Court protected the principle of the chair, moreover, not just specific individual models dependent upon it. This meant that beginning in 1933, all cubic chairs without back legs suddenly fell under the copyright of Mart Stam, even those not designed specifically by him. In the catalogues, Mart Stam now surfaces as the designer of the models B32, B33, B43 and so on. Control of all chairs without back legs but with armrests fell to Lorenz. Little

39 Gabriele Diana Grawe, "Unité et Diversité. Ein imaginärer Dialog zwischen Eileen Gray und Marcel Breuer über Innenräume", in ibid., p. 141 ff., footnote 21.

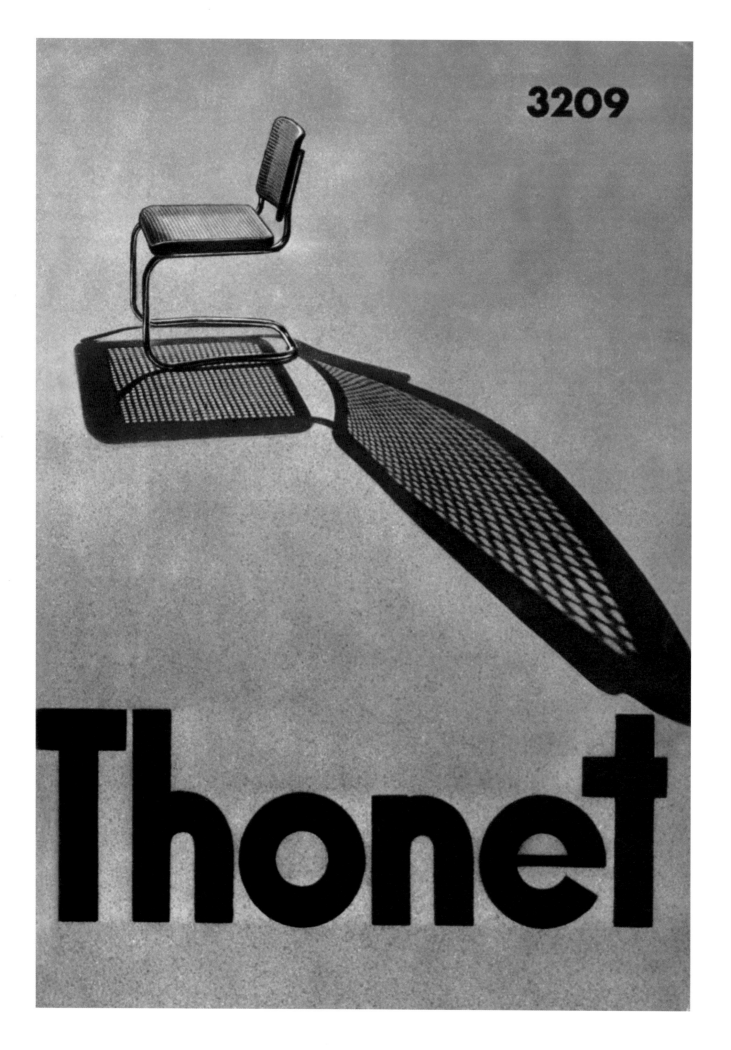

3209

Thonet

◄ Thonet catalogue, 1932.
▼ Writing table from the Ventris apartment, London, 1935–36.

remained of Breuer's authorship at Thonet. Only in the cases of the stools B8 and B9, the chairs B5 and B11, and the cantilevered armchair B35 was he still mentioned as the designer.[40] This had consequences for Breuer's income. According to research by Wilk, Thonet continued paying royalties only for several cantilever models (B32, B46, B55, B64). It should be added that Lorenz – who had terminated his own furniture manufacturing operation and subcontracted his rights to Thonet in a sublicence – worked for Thonet as a patent specialist from 1933 to 1935. In this capacity, he awarded Stam contracts for the "formal examination" of Breuer's models. About the B33, Stam wrote in a letter to Lorenz: "Given its present proportions, the chair is somewhat unsatisfactory. By virtue of the minimal curvature of the backrest (plus 10 cm beyond the seating surface), the chair has lost its severe clarity . . ."[41] Reason enough for Stam to have the gentle curve in the backrest – so characteristic of Breuer's design – eliminated. Not only, therefore, did Breuer lose authorship of his own designs, along with his royalties, but he also saw his designs altered in this high-handed manner. For Breuer, the chapter on tubular steel furniture was by this time largely a closed one.

In the mid-1930s, when these events were unfolding, Breuer was already in Great Britain, where he was intensively occupied with plywood furniture.[42] He left Berlin in late 1932 and spent the intervening period in Budapest and Switzerland, where he occupied himself with the design of houses at Doldertal; with the interior decoration of stores for Wohnbedarf in Zurich and Basel; and with working up his aluminium furniture.

By 1932, Breuer had already developed a new variant of the cantilever principle, and patented it in Germany in November that year. The front legs of the seat, still without back

40 See the Thonet catalogue Meubels en tubes d'acier, Nr. 3311 (1933) by Thonet Frères, and Thonet Stahlrohrmöbel (1935).

41 See Mácel 1992, p. 61f.

42 Breuer continued to design tubular steel furniture sporadically, for example for Dorothea Ventrix in London; see Wilk 1981, p.144 f.; Andrew Robinson, The Man who Deciphered Linear B (London, 2002), p. 28 f.,77.

▾ Living room of a model apartment, Doldertal Houses,
Zurich, 1936, with furniture by Aalto, Breuer and
Alfred Roth.
▸ Wohnbedarf shop, Zurich, c. 1934.

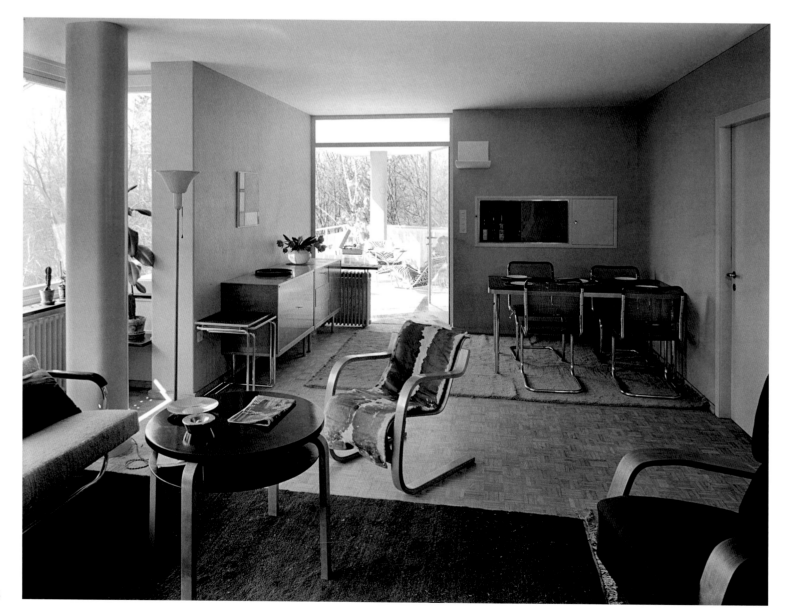

Living room of a model apartment, Doldertal Houses, Zurich, 1936, with furniture by Aalto, Breuer and Alfred Roth.
Wohnbedarf shop, Zurich, c. 1934.

◀ Prototype for an aluminium chair, competition announced by Alliance Aluminium Cie, Paris, 1933.

▼ Marcel Breuer, new design for the Wohnbedarf shop, Basel, 1933.

▶ Studio of Henri Matisse in the Hôtel Régina, Nice, 1953, with aluminium chaise longue by Breuer.

▶▶ Next page: Herbert Bayer, catalogue for aluminium furniture by Breuer, 1934.

legs, were supported laterally by a (usually) curved auxiliary structure. In several of the patent drawings, this auxiliary structure is extended to form armrests. Such a constructive solution would have permitted the use of thinner steel tubing. Breuer's search for an alternative to the commonly used cantilever principle may have been motivated by the patent dispute about the cantilevered chair, then evolving so unfavourably for him. In any event, these designs were not realised at the time. Still, they constitute the essential groundwork for the aluminium furniture Breuer would present soon thereafter.[43] At that time, the idea of improvements or changes in the cantilever principle occupied many designers across Europe. In 1930, for example, the Bohemian architect Antonín Heythum designed a cantilevered chair with a supporting tube construction attached to the rear.[44]

In further developing his design ideas, Breuer concentrated on ribbon-shaped materials, whether of aluminium or steel, and attempted to devise constructions especially suited to them.[45] The solution he discovered was well considered, simple, and practicable for aluminium, strip steel or plywood. Chairs were supplied with a springiness comparable to that of a cantilevered chair. The fundamental constructive idea was to slice through nearly the entire length of the ribbon segment. The two strands thus created comprised the front legs of the chair, on the one hand, and the stabilising auxiliary construction on the other, from which either the back or the armrests would emerge. The stiff seating surface produced the lateral connection between the parallel strands and provided for the stiffening of the construction. The elaboration of this design, which Breuer patented in Switzerland on 31 October 1933, was related to an international competition for aluminium chairs which had been announced by the aluminium combine Aluminium Cie in Paris and was decided in November 1933.

43 The chair illustrated in Wilk's book (cf. Wilk 1981, p. 119) is not, as claimed by the author, a Belgian licensed product of Breuer's patents from the S.I.D.A.M. company, but instead an anonymous operational design owned by the metal furniture company Usines Annoye in Chastre from 1931 (or possibly earlier). The chair is known from an advertisement that appeared in the journal Technique des Travaux in March of 1931. See Marc Dubois, Buismeubelen in België (catalogue, Museum voor Sierkunst Gent, 1987), p. 19 ff.

44 Antonín Heythum, O nové konstrukci pru_ného sedacího nábytku (Stavba, 1932), vol. X, No. 8, pp. 131 f.; Geest/Máčel, 1981, p. 156; Gerhard Bott and Claus Pese, eds., Sitz-Gelegenheiten. Bugholz- und Stahlrohrmöbel von Thonet (catalogue of the Germanisches Nationalmuseum Nuremberg, 1989), p. 85.

45 Wilk 1981, p. 119.

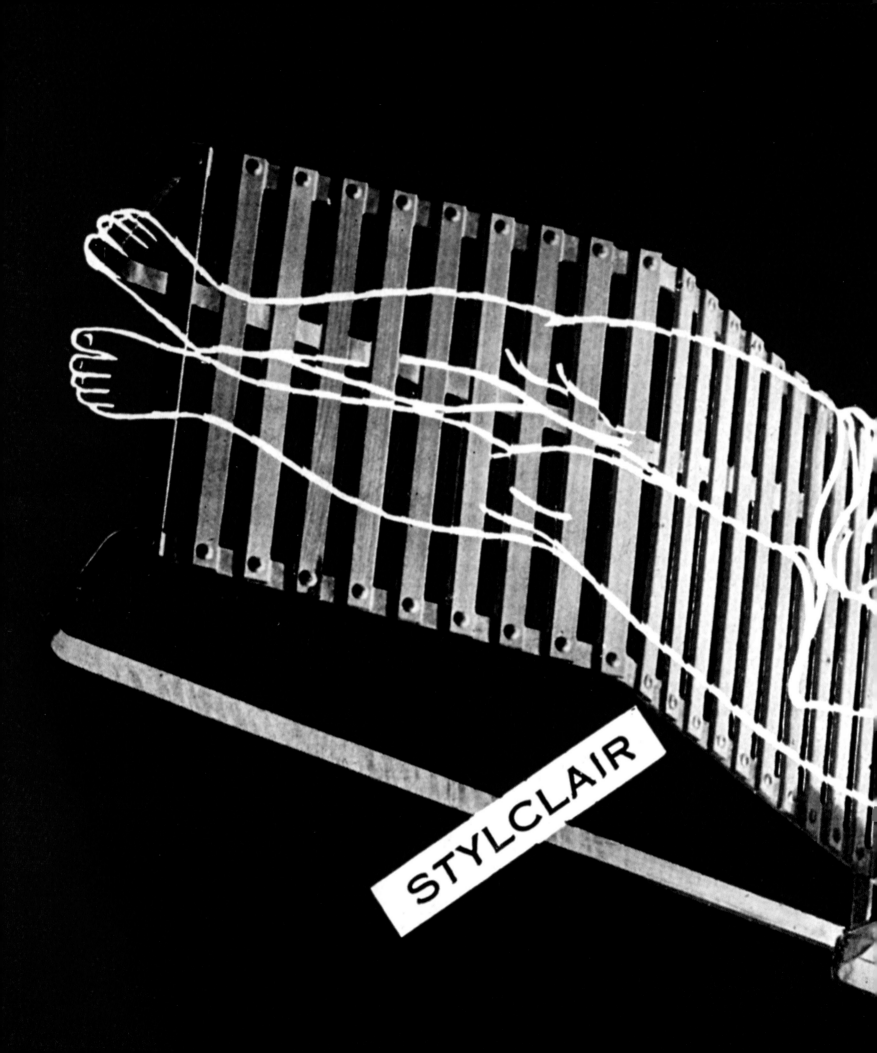

STYLCLAIR

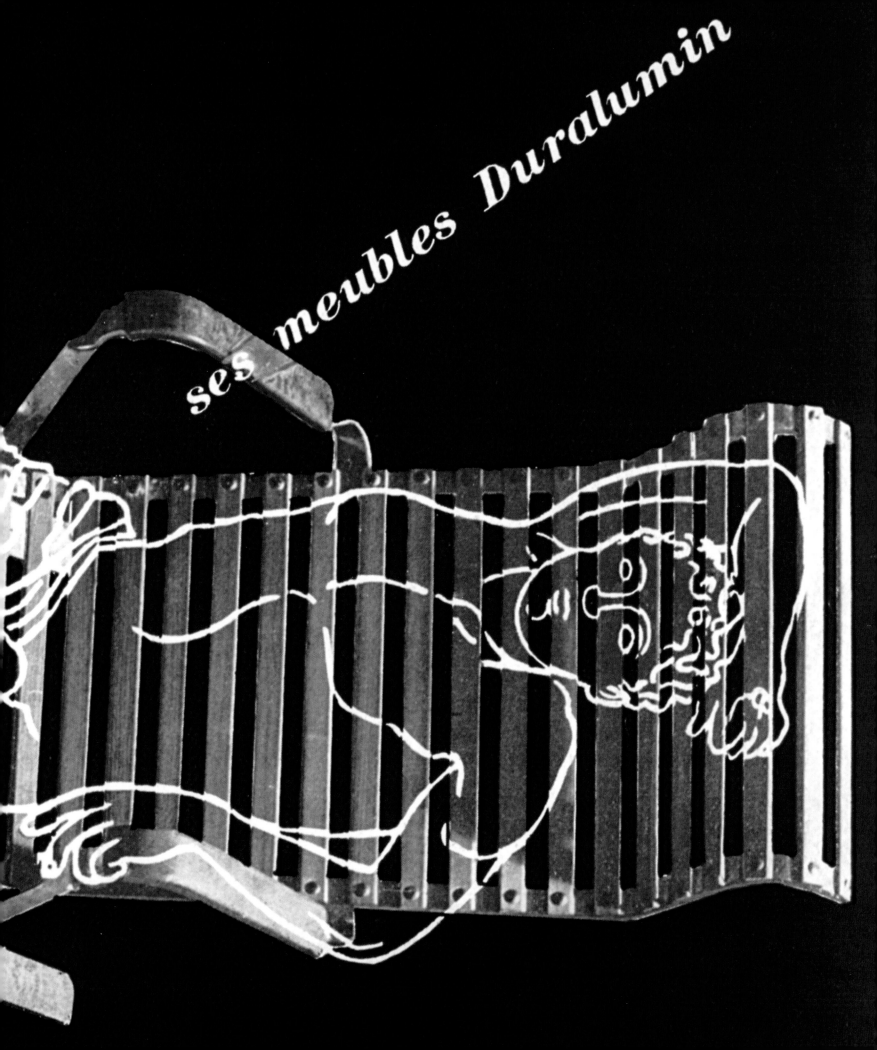

Hans Finsler, advertising photographs for
Breuer's aluminium furniture
◀ Aluminium chaise longue with upholstery
removed, 1934.
◀▾ Aluminium chair with laminate seat, 1934.
◀▾ Aluminium chair with caned seat, 1934.
▾ Aluminium flower stand, 1934.

◄ Advertising photographs with garden furniture by Wohnbedarf, Zurich, c. 1934, including aluminium furniture by Marcel Breuer.

Breuer received both first prizes: one from the jury of architects, prominently occupied by his friends Giedion and Gropius, and one from the manufacturer's jury.[46]

The aluminium furniture signalled a new stage in Breuer's creative efforts, and testified once again to his design talent. Both in terms of construction and of the exploitation of materials, he succeeded in finding an alternative to the principle of the tubular steel chair without back legs. In the role of manufacturer, the Swiss company Embru in Rüti made an essential contribution to realising these designs. The company Wohnbedarf took charge of sales. Embru was the main supplier for Wohnbedarf and, besides the aluminium furniture, had also manufactured Breuer's tubular steel chairs that were covered by Thonet's license. To accelerate sales of his new designs, Breuer personally established contacts with various European furniture manufacturers. During a search for skilled producers in the Netherlands, for example, he also requested the assistance of Cor Van Eesteren, the secretary of CIAM.[47] Outside Switzerland, the furniture was also manufactured by Gebrüder L. & C. Arnold in Schorndorf, Stylclair in France and A. L. Colombo in Italy.[48] The selection of furniture fashioned from the aluminium alloy Anticorodal included chairs with or without armrests, armchairs, chaises longues, stools and flower stands. Despite the originality of the constructions, and their relatively low prices and minimal weights, sales were sluggish. Only when marketed as patio and garden furniture did revenues climb, albeit remaining below Breuer's expectations on the whole. Yet even with the plywood furniture realised by Breuer in England in the mid-1930s in collaboration with Isokon, he was unable to reproduce the success associated with the discovery of tubular steel furniture.

46 Sigfried Giedion, "Schweizer Aluminiummöbel", in Mehlau-Wiebking, Rüegg and Troppeano, eds. 1989, p. 64.

47 See Breuer's letter of 9 September 1934 to Van Eesteren, and Van Eesteren's reply of 20 September 1934, Archive NAI, Rotterdam.

48 On Colombo, see Anty Pansera, ed., Flessibili splendori. I mobili in tubolare metallico. Il caso Columbus [NOT COLOMBO?] (Milan, 1998), pp. 157, 162.

◄ Isokon chaise longue, 1935, Collection of the
Vitra Design Museum.
▼ Ventris apartment, London, 1936, living room.

MARCEL BREUER FURNITURE

Furniture for Galerie Nierendorf, Berlin, 1924,
chair ti 2 (1924), Private Collection (courtesy Galerie
Ulrich Fiedler, Köln).

▼ Furniture for Galerie Nierendorf, Berlin, 1924,
stool ti 13 (1924), Private Collection (courtesy Galerie
Ulrich Fiedler, Köln).

▸ Furniture for Galerie Nierendorf, Berlin, 1924, detail
  of gallery bench, Private Collection (courtesy Galerie
  Ulrich Fiedler, Köln).
▾ Furniture for Galerie Nierendorf, Berlin, 1926,
  gallery bench, Private Collection (courtesy Galerie
  Ulrich Fiedler, Köln).

▾ Dressing table ti 60 with mirror, 1925–26,
Die neue Sammlung, Staatliches Museum für
angewandte Kunst, Munich.

▾ Display cabinet ti 66b, 1926,
Die neue Sammlung, Staatliches Museum
für angewandte Kunst, Munich.

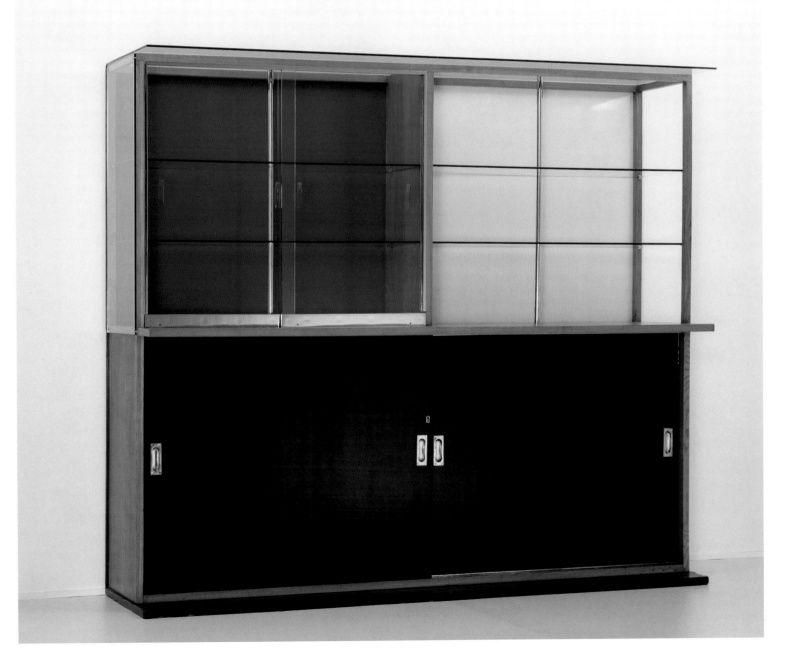

Work table from the Bauhaus Dessau, 1926,
Private Collection
(courtesy Galerie Ulrich Fiedler, Köln).

▼ Chair B5, 1926,
Alexander von Vegesack Collection.

▼ Isokon stacking tables, 1936,
  Alexander von Vegesack Collection.

◄ Isokon table and chairs, 1936,
Collection of the Vitra Design Museum.

▼ Writing desk and chair, Bryn Mawr College,
Philadelphia, USA, 1938,
Collection of the Vitra Design Museum.

ESTABLISHED MODERNISM – THE FURNITURE OF
MARCEL BREUER IN PRODUCTION BY GAVINA AND
KNOLL INTERNATIONAL

ESTABLISHED MODERNISM – THE FURNITURE OF MARCEL BREUER IN PRODUCTION BY GAVINA AND KNOLL INTERNATIONAL

DONATELLA CACCIOLA

In 1925, Marcel Breuer designed a piece of furniture that would make history: a club chair in bent tubular steel that has become a familiar icon of classical modern design under its later name "Wassily". It was soon seen by the public, in January 1926, in an exhibition devoted to the designer in Dessau's Kunsthalle, then under the directorship of the art historian Ludwig Grote (1893–1974). When the Bauhaus opened in Dessau in late 1926 it was the featured display, and created a sensation.

Initially, from 1926 to 1928, it was produced by Standard Möbel, Berlin, under the model name B3. Later, production was taken over by the German branch of Thonet. This innovative furniture design was disseminated in numerous countries – not least through Fratelli Thonet in Milan. At first, its success was of brief duration: its presence in the brochures of commercial firms can be documented only up to the 1930s. Back then, it was still far from attaining the status it would acquire later as an item of furniture that seemed at once contemporary and timeless.

The first step in the elevation of the design to the rank of a classic came in 1962, when the Italian firm Gavina SpA, founded at San Lazzaro near Bologna in 1960, launched a new edition of B3. The company's head, the lively entrepreneur Dino Gavina, met Marcel Breuer that year in New York through Andreas Grote, son of Ludwig Grote. A relationship developed that was private and friendly rather than business-like in nature, as their wide-ranging correspondence attests. Their letters continued until at least 1979, by which time Breuer had withdrawn from professional activities for reasons of ill health.[1] He often expressed his fondness for Gavina, and insisted on evaluating the prototypes for the new editions of his tubular steel furniture personally and on site.

Between 1925 and 1928 Breuer had developed five versions of this armchair; Gavina's re-edition was based on the second Standard version of 1927, in which the back rest is strengthened by a backward-curving tubular steel strut.[2] In contrast to the other variants of

1 This correspondence, consisting of 111 letters – along with the technical drawings and blueprints for the Breuer furniture designs – is held in the private archive of Dino Gavina, housed in his studio in the former headquarters of Gavina SpA in San Lazzaro di Savena; it is not open to the public. Other letters from the Breuer studio, along with the remainder of the estate held by his widow Connie, went to the Smithsonian Institution, Washington, D.C., in 1999 (Marcel Breuer Papers 1920-1986).

2 Alexander von Vegesack, Deutsche Stahlrohrmöbel (Munich, 1986), p. 31; the indication in this book that the new editions by Gavina and Knoll were based on different models is mistaken (pp. 37, 72). A photograph entitled "First bent continuous tubular steel furniture – 1925" (Marcel Breuer Papers) in fact documents a leather version of the "Wassily" chair, further contributing to the continuing confusion about the as yet unclear developmental sequence of B3 in the 1920s.

▼ Marcel Breuer, Dino Gavina and Achille Castiglioni in the Gavina shop in Milan, spring 1963.
▶ Marcel Breuer, Constance Breuer and Achille Castiglioni in the Gavina shop in Milan, spring 1963.
▶▶ Disassembled "Wassily" armchair, marketing photograph by Knoll International.

this model, this particular version has no welding: the six structural members are connected simply by screws. Gavina lent the armchair a new identity in various ways: the tubular steel construction was chromed instead of nickel-plated, and featured strengthened tube walls; the familiar textile seat was replaced by leather. At 11 kg, the new version weighed a full 5 kg more than the original B3. At Breuer's suggestion the chair was renamed "Wassily" in honour of the painter Kandinsky, one of his first admirers at the Bauhaus.[3] Catchier than a simple model number, the name would henceforth be associated with this legendary chair, just as a name is associated with a famous face. It is likely that Breuer had been considering a new edition of his furniture designs several years before he met Gavina, since there is a technical drawing from 1958 of the exact version of B3 that was used.[4]

Notwithstanding legal battles affecting cantilevered tubular steel furniture outside Italy, which remained unresolved into the 1980s,[5] several other tubular steel designs developed by Breuer in the 1920s were included in the Gavina programme. The company produced the models B32 and B64 (both named "Cesca" after Breuer's daughter Francesca). In addition to models with or without arm rests and with caned seats and back rests, upholstered and leather variants were also scheduled. In 1964, a chaise longue in laminated wood, designed in 1935 for the English furniture manufacturer Isokon, was added to the range.

The new editions were developed in a creative partnership between Gavina and Breuer, with model names discussed and decided upon by both. With advances in production technology, Gavina strove for a "Wassily" armchair that could be simply disassembled and

3 Arthur Rosenblatt, ed., Marcel Breuer at the Metropolitan Museum of Art (New York, 1975), p. 6. The official designation was "Wassily 1925", but this appears only in documentation used within the firm, for example in the Gavina–Breuer correspondence and in the drawings; it does not appear in the brochures, pamphlets or catalogues.

4 Drawing dated 25 March 1958, Dino Gavina Archive.

5 The Lorenz–Thonet trial was concluded on 1 June 1932. The verdict of the Higher Regional Court, Düsseldorf, on 12 June 1961, ending the ten-year proceedings between the tubular steel furniture producer RASTA, Ratzeburg-München, and Thonet, awarded Mart Stam the artistic copyright for the chair without back legs. This was, however, not the final litigation; two subsequent verdicts, in 1981 (Federal Court, Karlsruhe) and 1989 (Higher Regional Court, Cologne) confirmed this decision. Summa

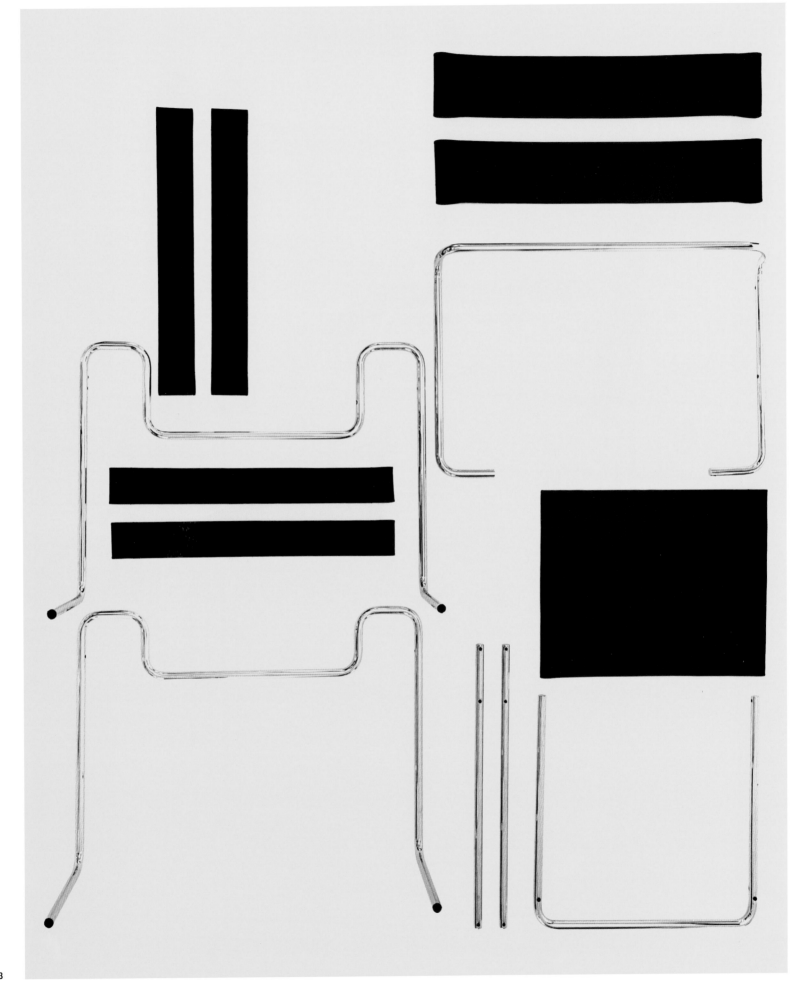

reassembled by the customer. Viewing the first finished copies, Breuer is supposed to have declared them the most beautiful he had ever seen. Still, upon examination, he had to concede that the chair might prove impossible for ordinary people to assemble: even professionals required a good two hours to accomplish this task![6]

Gavina's production was initiated in 1962, when tubular steel furniture in general was experiencing a cyclical low. Thonet had substantially reduced its selection of tubular steel furniture in the post-war era; by the beginning of the 1960s, only two variants of a cantilever chair were being offered. The 1960s saw a boom in the development of polymer plastics and their application in furniture manufacture; industrial production became simplified, and furniture could now be produced from moulds in a single pour. Firms such as Kartell and Danese in Italy succeeded in fusing the most advanced plastics technology with a new aesthetic (as had been the case in the 1920s, of course, with tubular steel furniture). Against this background, it is all the more astonishing that "Wassily" and other models by Breuer enjoyed such an extraordinary commercial and image success.

Gavina was a far-sighted entrepreneur with a pronounced business sense. He exploited the most advanced industrial processes, putting into practice serial production methods that were unattainable in the pre-war years. He was obsessed by the "machine aesthetic" and saw himself as a patron of the arts.[7] Gavina conceived of serial production as a mode of copying inseparable from the production of *multiples d'art,* in which he had become involved several years earlier with the serial production of sculptures by Lucio Fontana. Gavina's goal was to exploit industrial production for the sake of the multiplication and mediation of culture, in connection with an emphasis on the personality of the individual artist. Because Breuer's

summarum, a series of tubular steel chairs – S32, S32N, S64N, S32PV, S64PV– appeared in 1999 in the volume Stahlrohrmöbel, edited by the Thonet firm, with the designation "Design: Marcel Breuer; artistic copyright: Mart Stam". His copyright in the club armchair B3, on the other hand, was never questioned. The decades-long legal battle about the chair without back legs has been meticulously documented in Werner Möller-Otakar Máčel, Ein Stuhl macht Geschichte (Munich, 1992) and Otakar Máčel, "Der Freischwinger. Vom Avantgardeentwurf zur Ware" (dissertation, Delft Technical University, 1992), using material from the estates of Anton Lorenz (Vitra Design Museum, Weil am Rhein) and Mart Stam (Deutsches Architekturmuseum, Frankfurt am Main).

6 Marcel Breuer to Dino Gavina, New York, 4 January 1963, Dino Gavina Archive.

7 Also significant is that directly after the closing

furniture designs were ideally adapted technically to mechanical manufacture, he assumed a special status for Gavina among the "artists and poets of rationalism".

Gavina's aesthetic orientation is reflected in his advertising brochures and catalogues, spare in design, which contained, alongside illustrations of products, detailed measurements and information about the materials used in each individual piece.[8] However, there was nothing over-refined about Gavina's marketing strategy – shops in Barcelona, Paris and New York ensured the distribution of his products among an interested public.

Gavina's success with his re-editions of Breuer's furniture (he produced 1,000 pieces annually of both "Wassily" and "Cesca") emboldened other firms to bring historical re-editions of furniture into production, a trend that became increasingly pronounced throughout the 1970s. Gavina regretted this tendency, which he himself had unleashed: he regarded Breuer's furniture not as historical, but instead as contemporary in relation to the 1960s. In 1964, he rejected a proposal to produce furniture designed by Le Corbusier.[9] Just how little Gavina was concerned with re-editions of "historical" furniture for its own sake is clear from the example of Breuer's Canaan desk, designed in 1951 for his own home in New Canaan, Connecticut. This went into production by Gavina in 1963; it was offered in two sizes, and was faithful in all details to the original specifications, yet it rarely appeared in Gavina's advertising brochures.

Gavina's growing fame prompted the American furniture manufacture Knoll Associates, Inc.[10] to enter into negotiations on a possible close collaboration. These failed, and Knoll finally took over Gavina SpA in 1968, along with its entire product list.[11] As time

of Gavina SpA, he founded the Centro Duchamp in its former headquarters at San Lazzaro, a meeting place and facility to promote the latest artistic tendencies, for instance Gruppe N and the kinetic artists.

8 Virgilio Vercelloni, Das Abenteuer des Designs (Gavina, Milan, 1985; German edition 1987), pp. 223–52.

9 Heidi Weber had been producing this furniture since 1959. Her growing success meant that the hand-made copies from her small factory in Zurich soon failed to meet demand, and she was seeking a furniture enterprise as a business partner to engage in serial production. The firm finally chosen was Cassina in Meda near Milan (conversation with Heidi Weber in Zurich, 29 September 2002).

10 From 1969, Knoll International, Inc.

11 All models in the collection were taken up by Knoll as "The Gavina Group"; several years

MARCEL
BREUER
1924
GAVINA
1962

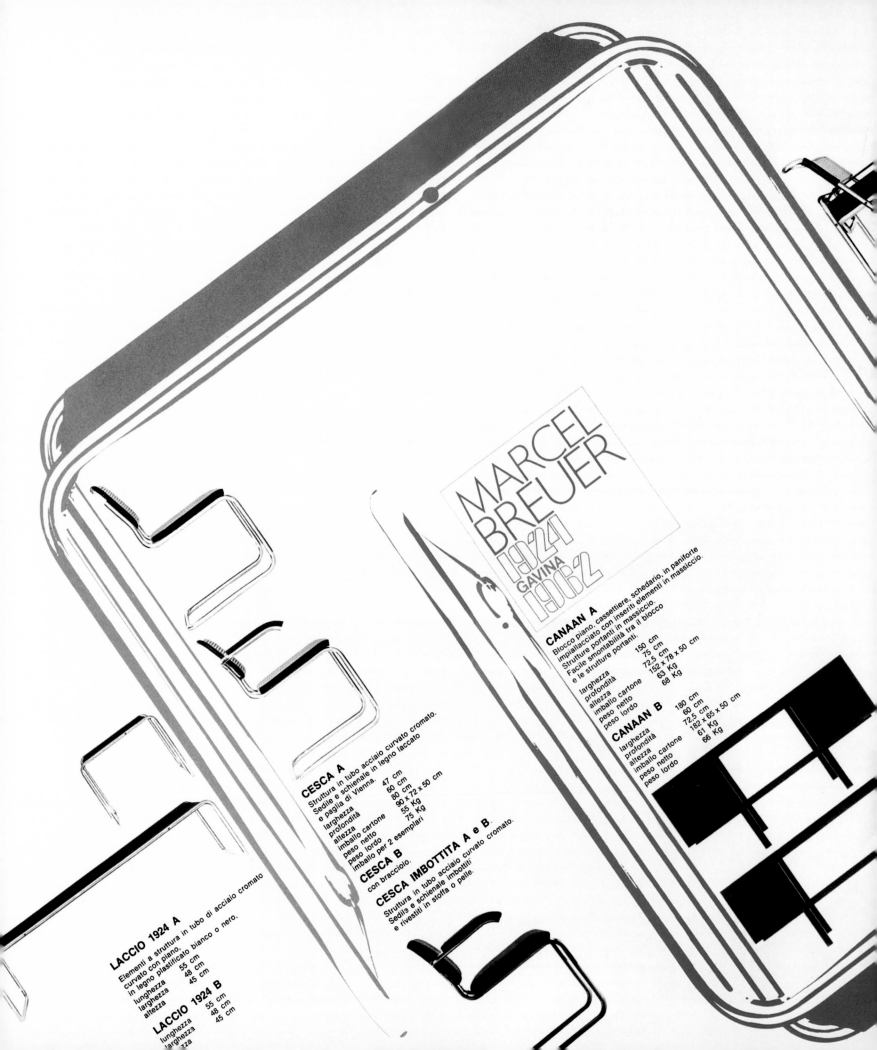

MARCEL BREUER 1924 GAVINA 1962

CANAAN A
Blocco piano, cassettiere, schedario, in paniforte
impiallacciato con inseriti elementi in massiccio.
Strutture portanti in massiccio.
Facile smontabilità tra il blocco
e le strutture portanti.

larghezza	150 cm
profondità	75 cm
altezza	72.5 cm
imballo cartone	152 x 78 x 50 cm
peso netto	63 Kg
peso lordo	68 Kg

CANAAN B

larghezza	180 cm
profondità	60 cm
altezza	72.5 cm
imballo cartone	182 x 65 x 50 cm
peso netto	61 Kg
peso lordo	66 Kg

CESCA A
Struttura in tubo acciaio curvato cromato.
Sedile e schienale in legno laccato
o paglia di Vienna.

larghezza	47 cm
profondità	60 cm
altezza	80 cm
imballo cartone	90 x 72 x 50 cm
peso netto	55 Kg
peso lordo	75 Kg
imballo per 2 esemplari	

CESCA B
con bracciolo.

CESCA IMBOTTITA A e B
Struttura in tubo acciaio curvato cromato.
Sedile e schienale imbottiti
e rivestiti in stoffa o pelle.

LACCIO 1924 A
Elementi a struttura in tubo di acciaio cromato
curvato con piano,
in legno plastificato bianco o nero.

lunghezza	55 cm
larghezza	48 cm
altezza	45 cm

LACCIO 1924 B

lunghezza	55 cm
larghezza	48 cm
zza	45 cm

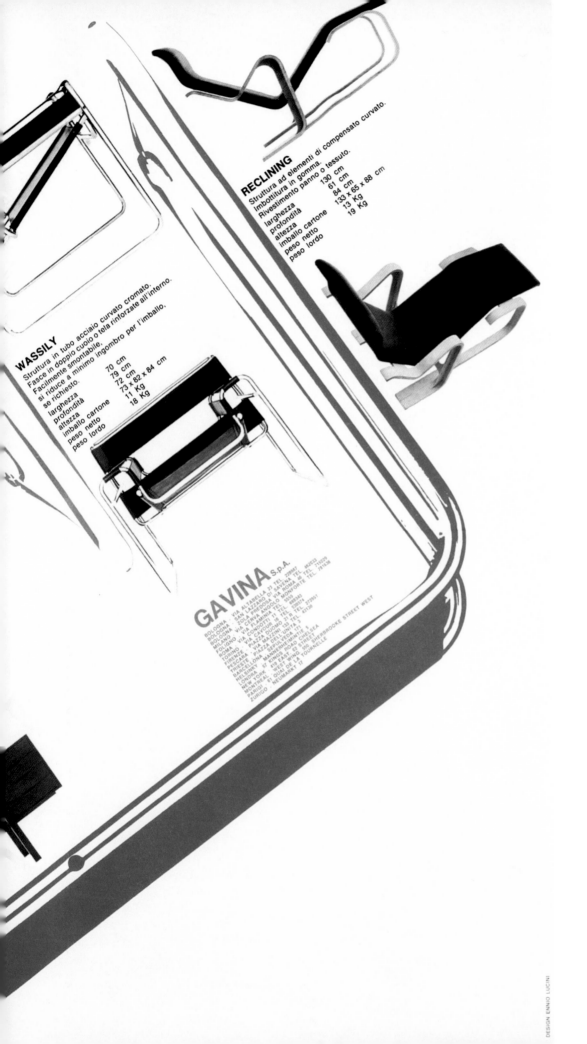

RECLINING
Struttura ad elementi di compensato curvato.
Imbottitura in gomma.
Rivestimento panno o tessuto.
larghezza 130 cm
profondità 61 cm
altezza 84 cm
imballo cartone 133 x 65 x 88 cm
peso netto 13 Kg
peso lordo 19 Kg

WASSILY
Struttura in tubo acciaio curvato cromato.
Fasce in doppio cuoio o tela rinforzate all'interno.
Facilmente smontabile.
si riduce a minimo ingombro per l'imballo,
se richiesto.
larghezza 70 cm
profondità 79 cm
altezza 72 cm
imballo cartone 73 x 82 x 84 cm
peso netto 11 Kg
peso lordo 18 Kg

GAVINA S.p.A.

BOLOGNA · VIA ALTABELLA 27 TEL. 229847 263533
BOLOGNA · SAN LAZZARO DI SAVENA TEL. 710026
BOLOGNA · ZOLA PREDOSA VIA RIVANA 8 TEL. 715136
MILANO · VIA CERVA ANGOLO VIA CONSERVATORIO MONFORTE
FOLIGNO · VIA CAVOUR 16 TEL. 80549
TORINO · VIA CONDOTTI 31 R. TEL. 82841
ROMA · PIAZZA DUOMO 132 TEL. 50674
FIRENZE · PIAZZA DELL'UNITÀ 1
TRIESTE · VIA MAZZINI 1/3 TEL. 773551
BARCELONA · VIA SESPRENENTINTLE 5
HELSINKY · MANNERHEIMINTIE 17/5
LONDRA · KINGS ROAD STREET CHELSEA
NEW YORK · 478 EAST 72nd STREET
MONTREAL · WEST SPRING 355 SHERBROOKE STREET WEST
PARIGI · 81 QUAI DE LA TOURNELLE
ZURIGO · NEUMARKT 17 43136

passed, the editions of Breuer's furniture kept growing. In peak years, 30,000 "Cescas" were produced annually. "Cesca" and "Wassily" both found their place in advertising campaigns for Knoll produced by well-known photographers, which often contained allusions to the chairs' museum status: the very same item of furniture could be mere merchandise (in the Knoll showroom) or an exhibit (in New York's Museum of Modern Art).

Knoll Associates, being active worldwide, was obliged to take account of the conditions and needs of various markets. In Germany, Knoll would have infringed the exclusive Mart Stam copyright held by Thonet for the cantilevered chair, so "Cesca" could not be marketed there. The Canaan writing desk was never imported to the USA, while in Germany production was suspended after about ten years since sales never amounted to more than a few dozen annually. The design itself was not responsible for this failure, nor was the fact that it had been conceived for the office not the home. The writing desk simply did not fit into the larger programme of "selling the avant-garde", as proclaimed by the advertising campaigns of both Gavina and Knoll. It was not marketed as bearing an innovative aesthetic, and did not appear in the Knoll brochures for the Breuer Collection. Eventually, Knoll put Breuer's designs together with those of Ludwig Mies van der Rohe, under the new heading "Bauhaus Classics".

The 1980s is said to have been the decade of "design classics", with various manufacturers offering series of older or more recent models by renowned designers who had "made history".[12] Breuer's designs were, of course, among them. The most noticeable alteration marking the transition from productions by Gavina to those by Knoll consisted of Breuer's engraved signature on the frame of "Wassily". Gavina never concerned himself with

later, the Breuer models were singled out as "The Breuer Collection". See undated Knoll leaflet in Marcel Breuer Papers, reel 5739, docs. 773–774 and 1405–1408.

12 See Klaus Jürgen Sembach, Moderne Klassiker. Möbel, die Geschichte machen (Hamburg 1983), one of the first contributions to the literature on "design classics". This work has recently been supplemented by Gerda Breuer, Die Erfindung des Modernen Klassikers. Avantgarde und ewige Aktualität (Stuttgart, 2001); a Gavina leaflet from the 1960s showing the "Wassily" armchair provides the cover image.

▼ "New Canaan" writing desk, small version, 1963.

▼ B32 in a Knoll brochure, 1981.
▷ B3 and Lacio in a Knoll brochure, 1981.

162

**Wie unterscheiden Sie
den Original Wassily Chair
von Plagiaten?**

4. Rindkernleder

1. Rohrenden

5. Inbusschrauben

6. Endkappen

2. Seitenkufen

3. Marcel Breuer-Schriftzug

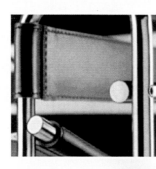

1. Die waagerechten bzw. schräg stehenden Rohrenden des Originals schließen bündig mit den senkrecht stehenden Rohren ab.

4. Das Rindkernleder des Originals entspricht höchster Qualität, ist speziell behandelt und in einer besonderen Technik verarbeitet, wodurch langjährige Formstabilität gegeben ist.

2. Die Seitenkufen des Originals haben eine leichte, gleichmäßige Wölbung nach oben, um die Standfestigkeit auf Teppichböden zu erhöhen. Für die Anbringung von transparenten Einschnapp-Gleitern (bei harten Böden) sind Bohrungen vorhanden.

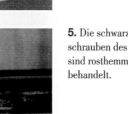

5. Die schwarzen Inbusschrauben des Originals sind rosthemmend behandelt.

3. Der Original Wassily Chair weist im Gestell-Unterteil eine Gravierung mit der Signatur Marcel Breuers auf.

6. Die Endkappen der Rohre des Originals sind angeschweißt, geschliffen und mit dem Rohr verchromt. Sie sind nicht eingesteckt.

Was Sie sonst noch über den Original Wassily Chair von Knoll International wissen sollten:

• Die Abmessungen des Originals sind das Endergebnis der von Marcel Breuer erstellten Prototypen.
• Beim Original Wassily Chair ist ein Präzisions-Stahlrohr eingesetzt, wodurch auch bei langjährigem Einsatz eine Verformung vermieden und Stabilität garantiert wird.

• Der mehrstufige Verchromungsvorgang des Originals (mehr als zwölf Arbeitsgänge) garantiert Ihnen höchste Qualität.

Knoll International GmbH
Gottlieb-Daimler-Straße 35
D-71711 Murr
Tel.: (07144) 201-0
Fax: (07144) 201-211

◀ Advertisement, Knoll International, in Der Spiegel, 1984, vol. 51, p. 185.

copyright protection, although he was fully aware that illegal imitations of his editions were being offered for sale. The advertising campaigns by Knoll and many other leading manufacturers around the world, by contrast, called attention to it, often using the battle against forgeries as a theme. "How does the original 'Wassily' Chair differ from forgeries?" asked a German campaign by Knoll in the mid-1980s. The answer: six characteristics make the first tubular steel armchair unmistakeable. They are: 1. the connections between horizontal and vertical tubing; 2. the bottom runners, which do not sit flat on the ground but are slightly arched; 3. the engraved signature "Marcel Breuer"; 4. the cowhide seat and back rests; 5. the socket head cap-screws, and 6. the welded tube caps. Features 3, 4 and 5 were introduced only with the new Knoll edition. In 1982, "Wassily" was accorded artistic copyright protection in Germany. A 1984 advertising campaign, appearing among other places in the weekly magazine *Der Spiegel,* came to a climax with the bold slogan: "This armchair is a work of art."[13]

Both of these bestsellers, "Wassily" and "Cesca" – now heavier, more elegant, and composed of finer materials than the originals – have ultimately come to stand for the avant-garde itself. Thus the movement that had such difficult early years could at last reap a hard-earned celebrity – and, even more important, enjoy at the same time a second youth, one more brilliant than ever.

13 Der Spiegel, 1984, vol. 51, p. 182.

"A SOPHISTICATED WAY OF LOOKING NATURAL"

"A SOPHISTICATED WAY OF LOOKING NATURAL"

THE ARCHITECT I. M. PEI ABOUT HIS FRIEND MARCEL BREUER

The following text is based on a conversation Alexander von Vegesack and Mathias Remmele held with I. M. Pei in his New York office in autumn 2002.

My acquaintance with Breuer dates back to the 1940s. He was a bachelor then; we both were. We became very close friends and I knew him very well. He was more than an architect I admired, he was a real friend. Later, he and his wife and I and my wife sailed together twice in Greece, each time for about two weeks. You have to be very good friends before you can suffer each other for two weeks on a boat! We had a wonderful time together.

When we went to Greece, at the outset we agreed not to talk about architecture. I guess we did hold to that. We speculated a great deal about life in Greece in the days of the Athenians and the Spartans, and even before that in Mycenae; we speculated about what these people were like, given that they created such wonderful architecture. Therefore in some ways we could not follow our original plan not to talk about architecture, because life expresses itself in architecture. He and I both believe in that. I think he was a person very much interested in life and life therefore was for him a source of inspiration. He talked very often about how people live, and the simpler the life, the better he liked it. He abhorred superficiality. Wherever we went, we drank a lot of ouzo, and he liked to observe people, very simple people. He liked simplicity in life: he remarked to me, jokingly, that he would like the life of a shepherd. He enjoyed cooking – mostly goulash – he would say it turned out different every time. His taste in food and wine was very, very simple.

I think he expressed himself in the simplest terms possible; on the other hand, he was a very sophisticated man. His work at the Bauhaus attests to that. His furniture design is comparable to that of Mies. His architecture, on the other hand, is more in tune with that of Le Corbusier. Of course Breuer has two sides, and you do not find that in Le Corbusier, you do not find it in Mies van der Rohe. That peasant side of Breuer is very endearing. Actually I should not use the word peasant, because peasant sounds like a person who is totally unsophisticated. „A sophisticated way of looking natural" is the better phrase. That side of him comes out in his architecture; it makes his work so variable, so very rich.

Some people describe him as a shy person who made a very strict separation between his private and his professional life. It is true that he did not include many of the people he worked with in his private life, and this is not surprising since he was with them for so many hours of the day. The people who worked for and with him all remember him very fondly.

He was the most popular teacher at Harvard. This was because of his method of teaching, perhaps, but also, I believe, because of his personality. He was very easy-going and he always looked at architecture from the humanistic side; he designed architecture for people, and he took into consideration how they lived and worked. His instinct for design, which as we all know was remarkable, followed this line of analysis.

I really regret that I didn't have the pleasure of studying under him at Harvard. As a graduate student I studied under Gropius. However, Breuer was a member of the design juries, and I remember his critique of my projects very well. He was a wonderful teacher. I think as a teacher, together with Gropius, he made a major contribution to architectural education.

And yet teaching was not what he wanted to do. So, he came to New York in 1946, and in the "real" world of architectural practice, he had a chance to express his architectural concepts of form and space. He had a great interest in the expressive possibilities of concrete, an interest that we shared. I like to think that back in the 1950s the two of us were probably pioneers in this field.

Because of his use of concrete, one can call Breuer a sculptor-architect. His auditorium for New York University at University Heights is a pure piece of sculpture. Some people did not like his sculptures but I liked them. I think he took his inspiration mainly from Cubism. Cubism was very important to modern architecture, and has continued to be. I should not forget to mention Le Corbusier in this connection. He started to use *beton brut,* which was very difficult for the public to accept. Ronchamps was a great success: Breuer must have admired it, as I do.

Breuer did a lot of fine buildings – for instance, his churches and monasteries. I very much admire his use of concrete. His IBM building in the south of France, for instance, is a very important work, which in my opinion is better than his UNESCO building in Paris. The IBM building seems to float above the irregular contours of the landscape on its *pilotis.* There, I think, he showed genius. It is a very fine building.

The Whitney Museum remains one of the best buildings in New York, in spite of the fact that it was selected as an object of scorn by the Post-modernists. But perhaps Breuer was considered to be out of fashion back in the 1970s. When Michael Graves proposed to add on to the building, I was one of the very few who were very vocal against the change. At Connie Breuer's home a few of us met to try to find a way to save the Whitney. We protested – voices in the darkness, perhaps, but it did do some good. The community finally voted against the change. When I look at the building today, I still think it is a brilliant piece of work. The wave of Post-modernism lasted about ten years, but this fashion has faded. Architecture has indeed become like fashion: if you want your project to be successful, it has to be novel, has to be something new.

Breuer's work in the field of domestic architecture is also very important. Before he came to America, he designed some important three storey apartment houses, which were widely copied in Europe. After he came to the U.S. in 1937, he designed a number of beautiful houses. One of the houses he built for himself in Lincoln remains one of my favourites. It is a split-level house – when you walk into that living room it is just a wonderful space that flows from one level to another, and seems to be much larger than it is. It is no longer the same now – it has been remodelled. But it was a wonderful house.

The second house that he built in Massachusetts is the Chamberlain Cottage – small, but important. The cantilever, the balloon frame, was done with wood. It is very much like his furniture – simple and elegant.

He designed many houses after he came to New York. Later he did several houses for himself – experimental. My wife and I spent a lot of time at his house in New Canaan with the large cantilevered terrace. We met many of his friends from Europe, from the Bauhaus – Arp, Bayer and others – and we had dinner on that deck. He did a house in Williamstown, Massachusetts, which I particularly like.

In the domestic field I mention just those four, each done at a different period of his life. In his later period he favoured a binuclear approach to house design – separating social and private – but I do not consider that this is as important as his earlier work.

Breuer's furniture remains a very important part of his work. Vitra Design Museum has many examples. Breuer used tubular steel in the simplest, most logical way, and it is here that you see his talent in design. The "Wassily" is one of the most important chairs ever designed.

In his later years he was reticent about furniture design and would not talk of it, saying that he was not doing it any more; he was more interested in architecture. He wanted to be recognised as one of the most important architects of his time. In the 1950s Mies van der Rohe's reputation was pre-eminent in the U.S., which contributed to Breuer's frustration.

In retrospect, his fondness for natural material such as wood, stone, and even concrete, both enriched and limited his work. I cannot recall that he ever built a glass and steel curtain wall building. Perhaps that was because he had little opportunity to design high-rise buildings. By contrast, his reputation suffered a great setback from his proposed design for a tower over Grand Central Station in New York, which was criticised and rejected. Still, when I look at his work in its totality, Breuer's position in the field of design and architecture is secure. This is my opinion.

BAMBOS – THE YOUNG MASTER HOUSES BY MARCEL BREUER

BAMBOS – THE YOUNG MASTER HOUSES BY MARCEL BREUER
LUTZ SCHÖBE

Dwelling at the Bauhaus

At the Bauhaus in Dessau in the 1920s, domestic architecture was one of the main themes in the creation of objects and buildings. New concepts, often avant-garde, were developed and tested in designs for appliances, houses and cities with far-reaching impact. The solutions, intended to have an educative effect and provide exemplary models, revolved around an orientation (not always free of social contradictions) between the "minimum subsistence dwelling" (the Törten Estate in Dessau, the Studio House of the Bauhaus building) and the villa-like artist-created Master Houses. Whereas the former category was a committed attempt to solve the acute housing problem of the time, the more generously appointed Master Houses were declared by their architect Walter Gropius to be a blueprint for the future: "Many things seem like luxuries today that will become the norm of tomorrow."[1]

The plan to erect residences for the Bauhaus teaching staff – in the form of studios, and dwellings for teachers, artists and masters – went back to the Weimar era of the Bauhaus. In Dessau, the aim of combining an experimental instructional model with an ideal shared community of designers and artists was realised for at least some of the instructors. The higher-ranking teachers, the "masters Kandinsky, Klee, Feininger, Moholy-Nagy, Muche and Schlemmer, enjoyed comparatively exclusive accommodation, while the "young masters" were assigned "the welfare institutions for the students"[2] in the Prellerhaus.[3]

1 Walter Gropius, Bauhausbauten in Dessau, 1930, p. 112.

2 Ibid., p. 15.

3 Modelled on the student dormitory at the Bauhaus in Weimar, former residence of the painter Friedrich Preller, the Studio House of the Bauhaus building in Dessau was called the "Prellerhaus".

◀◀ Model apartment, Dessau-Törten Estate, 1926,
   with furnishings by Marcel Breuer.
◀ Master Houses, Dessau, Moholy-Nagy's living room,
   1927–28.
▶ Walter Gropius, Director's House, Dessau, 1926.

The Master Houses by Walter Gropius and the Young Master Houses (BAMBOS) by Marcel Breuer are among a series of designs concerned with the demands of more exclusive and of middle-class housing. Both are manifesto-like, designed by the two architects as avant-garde demonstration buildings. In their structural honesty, functionalist orientation and formal logic, they uphold the main dictates of the new architecture. They are shaped by the housing estate concept, the idea of collective living, the mixture of functions (living and working), the combination of various storey units and the application of a system geared towards standardisation or reproducibility of building components.

The BAMBOS project

Created for the Bauhaus masters, following the school's relocation from Weimar to Dessau, the Master Houses by Walter Gropius provoked considerable opposition among both the students and the "young masters"[4] even at the design phase; they were criticised for being "unsocial" and overly "bourgeois". Young teachers such as Marcel Breuer, Hannes Meyer, Josef Albers, Hinnerk Scheper, Herbert Bayer, Otto Meyer-Ottens and Joost Schmidt considered themselves equal to their more senior colleagues and demanded comparable houses. The studios they were assigned in the Prellerhaus provided a certain comfort, but they felt discriminated against and expressed this in no uncertain terms.[5]

Marcel Breuer, head of the cabinet-making workshop and an ambitious architect, and his colleague and competitor Georg Muche hoped to take part in the design of the Master Houses, but this was a wish Gropius denied to both men. The conflict over the marketing of

4 Beginning in 1925, former students were appointed to serve as "young masters" at the Bauhaus and entrusted with taking charge of individual workshops, thus removing the distinction between craftsman and artist which had been practised earlier in Weimar. According to entries in Ise Gropius's diary, these younger teachers were sometimes also unofficially referred to at the Bauhaus as the "small masters". See note 5.

5 "topping-out ceremony for the master houses. several of the small masters stayed away, apparently to show that they take no interest in these houses ..." Diary of Ise Gropius, 21 November 1925. "small masters" petition to gropius. complaints about discrimination and quite arrogant demands. a tone worse than a citizens association ... deeply offended that they aren't getting housing themselves." Diary of Ise Gropius, 8 November 1926, Bauhaus Archive Berlin.

Breuer's tubular steel furniture finally sparked the so-called "Breuer crisis",[6] which peaked when Breuer gave in his notice.[7] Gropius acquiesced and, to appease the young masters, pledged his support for the construction of experimental buildings. These were called the BAMBOS Houses, after the first letters of their future occupants: Breuer, Albers, Meyer, Bayer, Meyer-Ottens, Schmidt. (It is unclear why the young masters Stölzl and Scheper were left out of this scheme, which could be expanded to accommodate any desired number of units.)

In July 1927, funds for the project were approved: "meeting in the bauhaus about the 350,000 marks provided by the research society of the german reich, typenausschuss (type committee). gr. [gropius] finally returned with the signature from berlin ... general relief at the bauhaus that the coup succeeded. hannes meyer is to get 50 houses and breuer is to build a small housing estate across from the bauhaus for the younger teachers."[8]

Apparently Breuer had developed the conceptual framework for the Young Master Houses in July 1927 and worked out the actual designs in August. When the houses were in the planning phase, it seems that reservation requests and neighbour preferences were already being put forward, as can be inferred from a site sketch by Oskar Schlemmer from the summer of 1927.[9] There is no record, however, of whether the project name BAMBOS also reflected the original order in which the houses were to be assigned.

Realisation of the scheme was put on hold, however, initially because the Mayor feared resistance from the public over the erection of a "second Bh colony" (Oskar Schlemmer). Then, in October, problems emerged with the financing; finally, a ministerial official with ties to the National Conservative Heimatschutz heritage preservation movement

6 Oskar Schlemmer, letter to Tut Schlemmer, May 1927, Oskar Schlemmer Briefe und Tagebücher, Stuttgart 1977, p. 92. For background details on the "Breuer crisis", see the essay by Otakar Máčel.

7 "breuer gave notice ..." Diary of Ise Gropius, 6 April 1927, Bauhaus Archive Berlin.

8 Diary of Ise Gropius, 13 July 1927, Bauhaus Archive Berlin.

9 Oskar Schlemmer, letter to Gunta Stölzl with a site sketch of the second "Bh colony" from the summer of 1927, Estate of Gunta Stölzl, published in Leben am Bauhaus. Die Meisterhäuser in Dessau, Munich 1993, p. 49.

◄ Walter Gropius, Master House, Dessau, 1926.
▶ BAMBOS Type 1, 1927, perspective.
▶▼ Urban planning model with Bauhaus Building and "Young Master House", BAMBOS Type 1, reconstruction (Model Workshop of the Bauhaus Dessau Foundation, 2002).

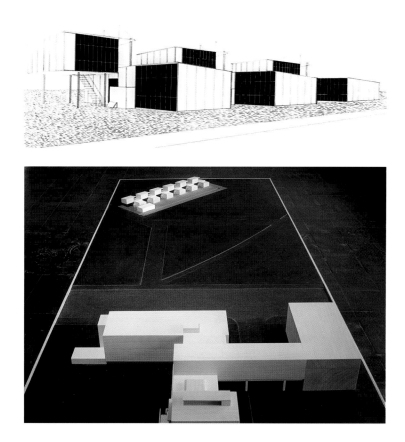

obstructed payment of the pledged funding.[10] The Young Master Houses project was evidently abandoned for good after Breuer conclusively terminated his contract with the Bauhaus in January 1928.

The original drawings for the project are believed to have been lost. Only eight photographs have been preserved, along with a brief presentation of the project on the basis of these photographs in the magazine *bauhaus*.[11]

Design, construction and concept

Intended for a site to the west of the Bauhaus building, the BAMBOS Houses were based on a system of prefabricated elements. A total of three variants were designed, with BAMBOS 1 as the one meant for execution.[12] All the structures were planned as a "steel skeleton structure with dry-mounted in-fill panels"[13] or with asbestos cement panels using a standard unit of measurement corresponding to that of the Small Metal House. In this earlier project from 1926, Breuer had explained what was special about his system: "Construction: In general, a wall has to support (itself, the roof, the people, the furnishings) and to insulate (against heat, cold, moisture and danger). The conventional stone wall supports and insulates simultaneously. With the 'Small Metal House, 1926 model' [as well as with the BAMBOS Houses, L.S.], another approach is pursued: supporting and insulating; corresponding to these two different functions, two different structural elements are employed: 1. a separate iron frame, 2. the insulating parts mounted on this frame, hence all the exterior and interior walls, doors and windows. This structural principle is intended to achieve the following results: [...] An expression of maximum lightness. Neither columns, pillars nor thick walls.

10 Diary of Ise Gropius, 10 August 1928, Bauhaus Archive Berlin.

11 Marcel Breuer, "Kleinwohnungen vom Typ BAMBOS", in bauhaus, zeitschrift für gestaltung, 3 (1928) 1, pp. 12–13. Photographs now held by the Smithsonian Institution, Archives of American Art, Washington, D.C. The reconstruction of how the project was to be sited derives from the few street names Breuer noted on the drawings for BAMBOS 2, the layout of the houses on the ground plans, the statements by Ise Gropius in her diary as well as contemporary land use allocation plans and documents recording detailed land sales by the Leopold-Dank Foundation to the City of Dessau and others now stored in the Dessau City Archive.

12 See Joachim Driller, Marcel Breuer. Die Wohnhäuser 1923–1973, Stuttgart 1998, p. 43.

13 Breuer, op. cit.

▾ BAMBOS Type 1, ground plan.
▸ BAMBOS Type 1, axonometric and section of a
  detached house.

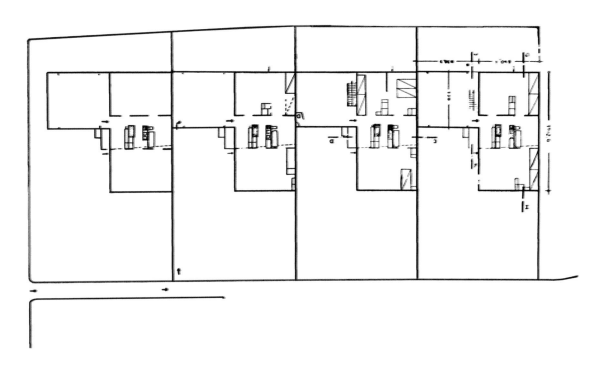

The load-bearing structural components are lines – the closer their expression comes to their structural symbol, an absolute line, the better. The lightweight insulating panels are no longer elements of a heavy wall – the closer their expression comes to their practical symbol, an absolute plane, the better."[14]

The "additive principle" adopted from furniture construction and the use of the closed box – typical characteristics of Marcel Breuer's architecture[15] – were thus already clearly present in the BAMBOS studies. As autonomous individual elements, box-shaped living and studio units were to be joined together to form a dynamic overall composition. Common to all three designs was a relatively schematic spatial organisation according to functionality (clearly defined living and working areas, short interior distances, etc.).

Breuer described the BAMBOS 1 model in the magazine *bauhaus* as follows: "ground plan: 2 main rooms for husband – wife, or parents – children, or day – night. separated and connected by bath – kitchen – heating – entrance. the main rooms can be divided with lightweight walls or curtains if necessary. site: the light openings of the living unit to the southeast and southwest, those of the work space to the northeast ... storerooms, laundry and garage separated at the entrance of the site."[16]

In fact, BAMBOS 1 seems to be the most interesting and rigorously consistent design in the series of Young Master House studies. The principle of the clear, bipolar division of living and working is uncompromisingly implemented.[17] The house consists of a 70-square-metre rectangular living unit at the garden level and a distinctly offset studio space raised on supports, like a floating upper-storey box. In reference to this part of the structure, Oskar Schlemmer spoke of "well ventilated studios", not without ironic undertones. The idea

14 Marcel Breuer, "Das Kleinmetallhaus Typ 1926" in Offset Buch und Werbekunst, no. 7, 1926, pp. 371–74.

15 See Driller, p. 21

16 Breuer, op. cit.

17 Driller, op. cit.

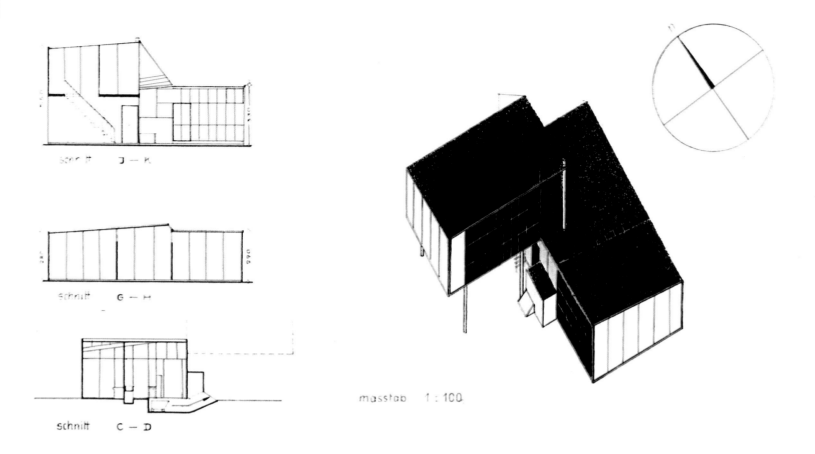

schnitt   J — K

schnitt   G — H

schnitt   C — D

masstab   1 : 100

of a house propped up on supports can perhaps be partly traced back to Le Corbusier who had just realised, among other designs, a "house on pillars" for the Stuttgart Weissenhof estate in 1927. Breuer, too, turned to this structural principle to achieve multiple effects, enlarging the garden area while making the roof of the living unit accessible as a terrace. He also listed psychological reasons in his arguments for the form of this house type: "In our modern houses, the relationship to the landscape is an important aspect of planning. There are two fundamentally different approaches, both of which are quite capable of solving the problem: on one hand, the house resting directly on the ground, allowing one to enter the outdoors on all sides and from each room – a good solution, especially for children – and on the other, the house on supports raised up above the landscape like a camera on a tripod. This gives the occupant a better view and conveys the impression of floating over the landscape or standing on the bridge of a ship. It provides a feeling of freedom, a certain élan and boldness, while the notion of being in a house located near the ground heightens the sense of security. The solution I prefer combines these two sensations ..."[18]

18 Marcel Breuer in 1955, cited from Driller, op. cit., p. 146.

With BAMBOS 1, the roofs are all slightly inclined, sometimes juxtaposed against one another. Projecting in the direction of the living unit, the sloping roof of the studio container – accessible only via a filigree exterior staircase – is stabilised by steel cables. Both the living unit – whose two main rooms are separated from one another by the central configuration of bath, kitchen, heating and entrance – and the studio container are furnished with large window openings.

As for all other design intentions, such as the interior spaces (use of materials, colour, etc.), one can only engage in speculation, since differentiated information about these details is lacking for the three BAMBOS House variants.

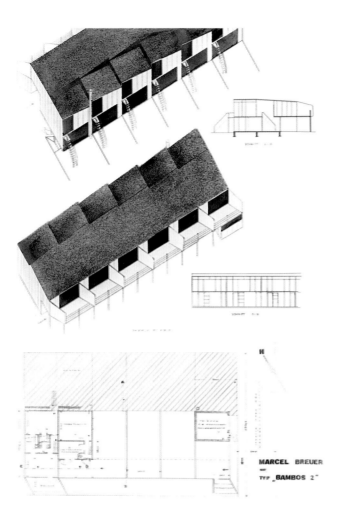

MARCEL BREUER
TYP „BAMBOS 2"

BAMBOS 2 is a two-storey structure. The studio space is contained in the lower level with the living area located above, laid out with two main rooms, kitchen and bath. The ground plan corresponds to that of BAMBOS 1. To the southwest, the living unit – likewise accessed from the exterior via a steel staircase – is finished off with a wide balcony. Here as well, the houses are set close together and form a uniform closed-off front. Like the other designs, this variant is built without a cellar, perhaps for cost reasons.

BAMBOS 3 contains a ground-level living area with a main room and integrated bunks for sleeping. The studio unit is placed on the same level with a shed roof and large north window. In this design, Breuer worked through different ground-plan solutions, demonstrating a variability based on simplicity. The angular houses form a closed-off row. The juxtaposed sloping roofs counteract the monotone uniformity and add a certain dynamisation to the roof zones.

The technically demanding BAMBOS project was part of the development of serial housing construction systems with industrially fabricated components which were promoted at the Bauhaus. From 1924 onwards, a number of experimental projects were elaborated including the Small Metal House by Marcel Breuer and the Kugelhaus am Meer by Siegfried Ebeling, neither of which was realised, and the Steel House, executed by Georg Muche and Richard Paulick in Dessau. The small house studies from 1927, likely produced just prior to the BAMBOS Houses, reveal a comparable design intention and demonstrate the variability and flexibility that could be achieved with the standardisation advocated by Breuer.

BAMBOS versus Master Houses

The BAMBOS Houses by Marcel Breuer can also be interpreted as an antithesis to the Master Houses by Walter Gropius. The former are the expression of an increased self-confidence and an emancipatory ambition with which the generation of younger architects and designers confronted their teachers and instructors. They articulate a radical conception of architecture, combining a social aim with experimental architectural solutions – a terrace house conceived as a serial construction, Breuer's own residence was not to be distinguished from the houses of its neighbours or given any special prominence. The social convictions behind the housing estate scheme are evident in the close alignment of the houses, which can be read as a resolute demonstration of collective unity. The social-mindedness is further manifest in the joint usage of utility and garage rooms, the absence of servants" quarters, the comparatively low building costs and the more modest construction volumes.

The "avant-gardism of the collective",[19] later postulated by Hannes Meyer as the second director of the Bauhaus, was already present here in an incipient stage. While Breuer designed radically functional "machines for living", Gropius realised exemplary functionalist artist dream-houses of the Moderne. In different ways, the functionalism then in vogue was "staged" by the two architects as a principle of design practice. Constructively as well as architecturally, the differences outweigh the common aspects. Breuer rigorously applied the additive principle and used a modular system transferred to a steel skeleton structure determining both the body of the building and the interior design. Conversely, Gropius developed his solidly built plastered brick buildings with a load-bearing wall shell, modelled on his variably adaptable "large-scale building block" principle. Depending on the

19 Jörg Stabenow, Architekten wohnen. Ihre Domizile im 20. Jahrhundert, Berlin 2000, p. 132.

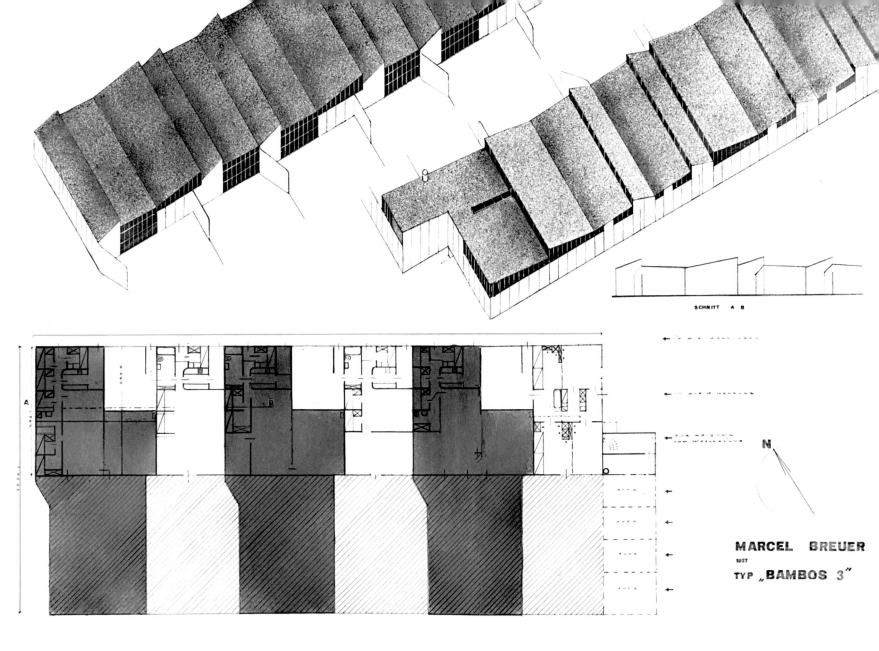

MARCEL BREUER

1927

TYP „BAMBOS 3"

SCHNITT A B

interior configuration of the rooms, itself following certain functional sequences, the cubes seem to interpenetrate one another. The individual building elements are not additively aligned but interlock and intersect, which also determines aspects of the façade organisation. The often invoked precepts of the Moderne, favouring building from inside to the outside and making internal processes readable in the exterior appearance, apply only partly to Breuer's houses. The organisation of the façades does not conform to the inner disposition of rooms, radically modern in their openness, but rather to the integrated support system, though this comes to light only where one building section is attached to another.

The BAMBOS project's failure to be realised was due to the circumstances of the time. Its structural presence would have provided a spectacular complement to the unique ensemble of Bauhaus buildings in Dessau, not least as a response to the Master Houses by Gropius, and would moreover have represented a notable contribution to the history of dwellings for artists.

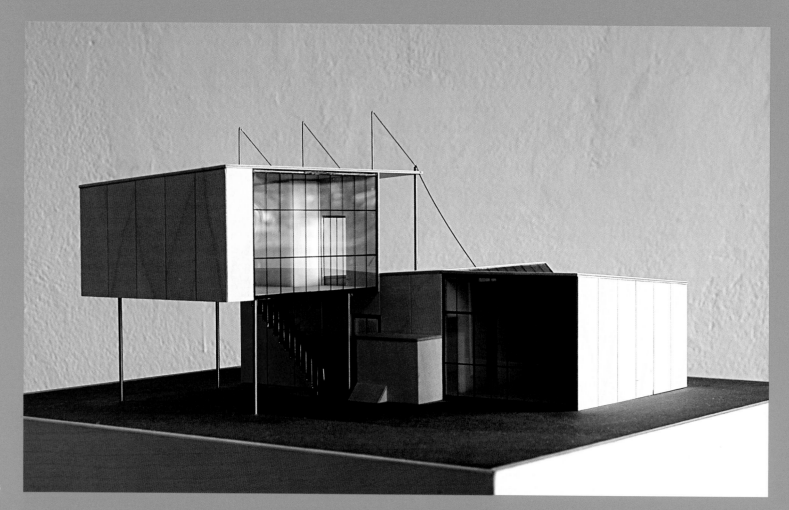

◄ Model detached house, BAMBOS Type 1, reconstruction (Model Workshop of the Bauhaus Dessau Foundation, 2002).

None the less, Breuer's BAMBOS designs were not without consequence, particularly for the architect himself. In later interior designs, such as in the apartment for a boarding house hotel (Werkbund Exhibition, Paris 1930) or the House for a Sportsman (Bauausstellung exhibition, Berlin 1931), he was able to apply or vary the principle of clear division of functions in the organisation of the living space, which is especially pronounced in BAMBOS 1. The differentiation of the functional zones constituted a foundation for his later development of so-called "binuclear houses" in the USA. Moreover, certain individual design elements elaborated in the BAMBOS project, such as the placement of individual building sections on supports and the use of exterior stairs and projecting roofs, re-emerge in many of Breuer's subsequent buildings.

ON HOUSES AND PALACES: REMARKS ON
MARCEL BREUER'S RESIDENTIAL HOUSES

ON HOUSES AND PALACES: REMARKS ON MARCEL BREUER'S RESIDENTIAL HOUSES

JOACHIM DRILLER

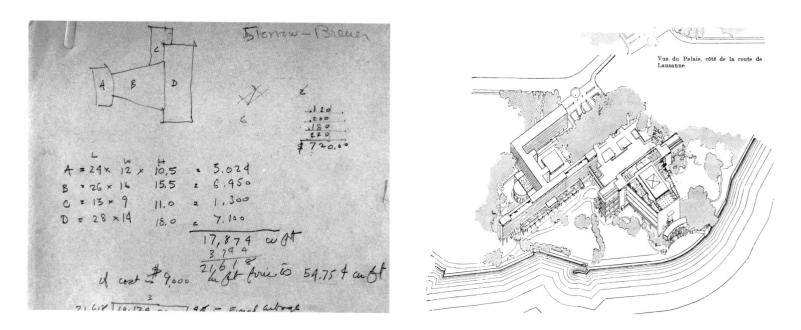

Pénétrons encore, l'œil bien ouvert, dans le plus simple attirail d'une vie champêtre d'aujourd'hui et, passant sur le paradoxe apparent, nous y retrouverons encore et toujours cette maison-palais, produit synthétique de l'esprit et du cœur ... ces maisons ont une mesure commune: l'échelle humaine. Tout est à l'échelle; on mesure le pas, l'épaule, la tête. L'économie est au maximum. L'intensité est au maximum. Un beau jour, après les avoir tout à coup comprises, on s'est écrié: "Mais ces maisons sont des palais!"

Le Corbusier, Une Maison – Un Palais, 1928

In the autumn of 1938, Marcel Breuer was granted a quite exceptional opportunity: the chance to build a small house for himself in the New England colonial town of Lincoln near Boston, and – as he enthusiastically reported at the time – "in any way I like, without having to pay for it!" Thirty-six years old and cash-strapped following professionally disappointing stints in Berlin, Budapest, Zurich and London, Breuer had left England the year before and followed his mentor Walter Gropius to the United States. Here in his newly adopted country, he had accepted a teaching position on the architecture faculty at the elite Harvard University and opened an architectural practice together with Gropius in the university city of Cambridge. Now the rich widow Helen Storrow opened up the unexpected possibility of designing and building his own house by offering to furnish the plot of land and underwrite the construction. The previous year, the philanthropist had made the same arrangement with Gropius, providing him with the financing and land to build his own house on her extensive

◄ ◄ Breuer House I, architect's preliminary sketch giving measurements.

◄ Le Corbusier's competition design, Palace of the League of Nations, Geneva, 1927, axonometric.

▼ Marcel Breuer and Walter Gropius, Breuer House I, Lincoln, Massachusetts, 1938–39, present condition.

estate in Lincoln.[1] Breuer immediately set about the planning and execution of his new abode, and by the summer of 1939 was able to move into his "house for a bachelor". Like the house of his mentor, which was located within sight, Breuer's was meant as a "calling card" with which he aimed to present his conception of architecture to the American public. And, as with Gropius's design, Breuer's house was deeply rooted in the preceding European oeuvre of its architect/occupant, whether through direct adoption of tried-and-tested solutions or through hidden allusions. But Breuer proved himself even more imaginative than Gropius, the allusions in his house reaching beyond his own earlier work. In fact, Breuer's small house was actually a "palace", which will be considered in more detail below. First, it is necessary to make a few general observations on Breuer's houses and take a brief look at their development prior to the architect's arrival in the New World.

For many years, residential architecture held pre-eminent importance in Breuer's oeuvre. On one hand, a combination of adverse circumstances long kept him from receiving any other types of concrete architectural commissions. On the other, residential architecture was particularly well suited to an inseparable unity of architecture and interior design, an ideal Breuer had always upheld, albeit with a varying degree of intensity. Finally, houses seemed to be close to his heart: even when prestigious commissions for large-scale public projects opened up to him later in his career, he never fully abandoned domestic architecture despite announcements to the contrary. In the planning of private residences, Breuer found a field for experimentation with formal and technical innovations but also a domain for an architecture where he could seek solutions that would be valid once and for ever. Considered as a whole, his houses were distinguished by astonishing stylistic continuity over a fifty-year

1 Helen Storrow went on to sponsor the construction of two more houses in Lincoln, one of which was produced from a design by Gropius and Breuer. These two subsequent buildings are located close to the original houses by Gropius and Breuer. Each year that Breuer lived in his house, he was to pay back as rent 10 per cent of the amount Mrs Storrow had provided for its construction. Breuer was later granted an option to purchase the house, but ended up declining the offer.

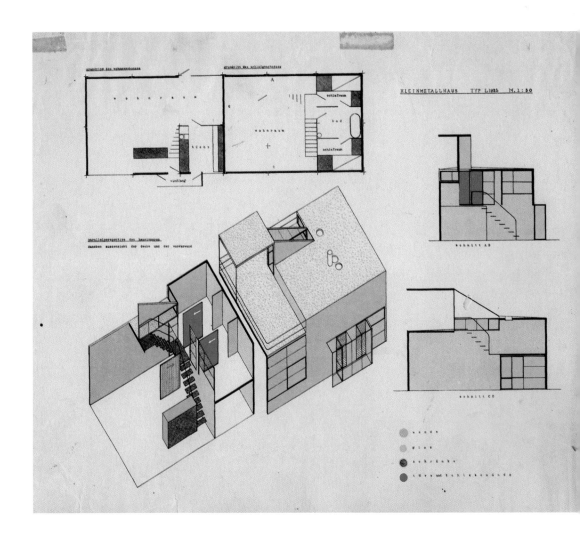

time frame. All told, Breuer designed a good hundred houses in this period – from "minimal houses" for prefabricated mass-produced housing to single-family homes up to villas for the haute bourgeoisie.[2] This part of his oeuvre has long been overshadowed in the public consciousness, at least in Germany, by his furniture design, even though more than sixty of his house designs were actually built. Most of these have survived to the present day, though in some instances with substantial alterations. This is also the case with Breuer's own house in Lincoln. In addition, there are a number of lamentable total losses. Some of the destroyed houses exhibited grave structural and technical defects, while others were victims of the ignorance of their new owners.

Early house designs

The first known house design by Breuer dates from 1923, when the young Hungarian carpentry apprentice was still a student at the Bauhaus in Weimar. Breuer had no formal architectural training of any sort, and later only picked up the relevant knowledge through his work in various architects' offices. He developed a variant (not realised) of the "Haus am Horn", a Bauhaus experimental house erected that year in Weimar, based on the concepts of the painter Georg Muche.

There being then no regular instruction in architecture at the Bauhaus, Breuer and Muche were among the members of the school who formed a loose study group in the autumn of 1923 in which questions of architecture were addressed on a more or less amateurish level. Through this involvement, the two seem to have become locked in a pattern

2 For a wide-ranging discussion of Breuer's residential architecture and further information on the buildings and projects addressed here, see Joachim Driller, Marcel Breuer. Die Wohnhäuser, 1923–1973 (Stuttgart, 1998); English edition Breuer Houses (London, 2000); and Isabelle Hyman, Marcel Breuer, Architect: The Career and the Buildings (New York, 2001). For a treatment of Breuer's American houses, see also 2G Revista Internacional de Arquitectura/ International Architecture Review, no. 17: Marcel Breuer. Casas americanas/ American houses (Barcelona, 2001).

of competition with one another, which intensified after the relocation of the Bauhaus to Dessau in 1925 and Breuer's designation as a "young master". Against the background of the school's reorientation away from a cult of handicrafts to the "new unity of art and technology" propagated since 1923, Muche and Breuer each developed proposals for model housing types intended to pave the way for serial housing construction with industrially prefabricated components. Their designs were founded on the idea of a metal frame construction with in-fill panels for the interior and exterior walls. In contrast to Muche, Breuer was never given the opportunity to execute a prototype. Nevertheless, two of the prefabricated house studies he presented at the time – the Small Metal House from 1925–26 and the BAMBOS Houses from the following year – had a sustained influence on the formal language of his residential house designs, specifically in terms of the formal and aesthetic interpretation of the structural system and the nature of the compositional technique.

With the Small Metal House, the wall panels were to be directly mounted on the load-bearing iron frame. Breuer remarked on the system employed here: "This structural principle is intended to achieve the following results: ... An expression of maximum lightness. Neither columns, pillars nor thick walls. The load-bearing structural components are lines – the closer their expression comes to their static symbol, an absolute line, the better. The lightweight insulating panels are no longer elements of a heavy wall – the closer their expression comes to their practical symbol, an absolute plane, the better. The monumentality of masses, this architectural principle that continues to hold to the present day, is overtaken by a bold play of forces under maximum tension, by the monumentality of the intellect."[3]

3 Marcel Breuer, "Das 'Kleinmetallhaus Typ 1926'", in Offset Buch und Werbekunst, no. 7, 1926, pp. 371–74; pp. 371 f.

To formulate this in less lofty words: in the appearance of his houses, from the mid-1920s onwards Breuer sought to realise the same aesthetic of lightness he strived for in the parallel development of his tubular steel chairs. Yet there was a decisive difference, stemming from the function at hand: while the chairs form "open" volumes, outlined by the metal rods as "lines in space", the house requires a protective external encasement. The solution Breuer here proposes is of special significance. In renouncing a spatial division of load-bearing frame and applied panels, hence an absolute avoidance of freestanding "columns" and "pillars", he ends up with the negation of a visibly tectonic system in favour of an emphasis on the "absolute plane". The wall's resulting appearance as a volume shell of maximum lightness and rigidity is not unlike the walls of a free-standing cabinet, with the building giving the overall impression of a self-contained cabinet-like box. This is especially evident in the axonometric drawing of the Small Metal House that Breuer published in 1926.

A comparable analogy to furniture design principles is also evident in the BAMBOS Houses, planned as apartments for the "young masters" of the Bauhaus, for which Breuer developed three design variants. They each consist of a living unit and separate studio container, which is either elevated and set in front of the living unit, attached to it at ground floor level or set under it as a basement storey. This purely additive compositional technique of variously combined cabinet-like boxes is directly related to Breuer's flexible systems for so-called Anbaumöbel (unit furniture), built from individual interchangeable elements. Varying heights and pitches of the roofs make it possible to read from the exterior the various functional areas, which are marked by a further clear differentiation within the boxes.

▼ Schneider House, probably planned for Wiesbaden,
   Germany, 1929, model (unrealised).
▶ Harnischmacher House I, Wiesbaden, Germany,
   1932, view from south-east.
▶▼ Harnischmacher House I, view from south-west.

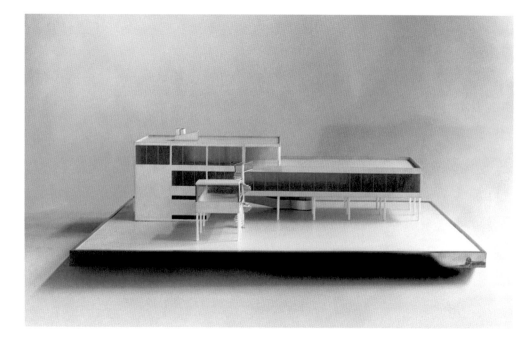

Harnischmacher House in Wiesbaden

In April 1928, Breuer took his leave of the Bauhaus and settled in Berlin to work as an independent architect. His practice struggled financially. Over the next years he sent out a series of submissions to design competitions for large-scale architectural projects, none of which had even the slightest chance of being realised. These were joined by a small number of plans for residences, though to date very little is known about the background of these projects. Here, as well, none of the proposals led to concrete commissions. Breuer would have to wait until 1932 before finally getting the opportunity to realise one of his designs: the Harnischmacher House in Wiesbaden for the general manager of the Erdal Company (shoe care products) and his wife. To this unanticipated opportunity Breuer reacted with understandably strong enthusiasm: "After all, I thought I would never get the chance," he wrote in a letter. And after nine disheartening years without realising a single one of his architectural designs his will must have been exceptionally strong as well to deliver a bold manifesto of his personal conception of architecture and formal language.

The Harnischmacher House, destroyed in World War II,[4] consisted of a main central structure, facing south towards the city and Rhine Valley, with two attached verandah wings, the west wing also including a study over the garage. Standing like a signal beacon among the historicising neighbouring homes with its white coat of paint and elevated sections, the house corresponded to then-current design archetypes of modern architecture. In particular, special mention should be given to the houses of Le Corbusier: his famous villa in Garches is likely to have given Breuer the idea for the flight of outdoor steps. Yet Breuer managed to achieve a design entirely his own, with the disposition of the sections of the building more akin to his

4 Breuer designed another house for the Harnischmachers in Wiesbaden after the war; completed in 1954 and still in existence today, it was the last Breuer house to be built in Germany.

architectural projects from the Bauhaus, especially the BAMBOS Houses, than to the formal language of Le Corbusier. For instance, the roof level of the verandah wings is considerably lower than that of the main structure, which provides clear visual demarcation of the different sections. Breuer's compositional system here is again additive and visible on the exterior: the main structure constitutes the dominant building element in the floor plan and elevation, and around it – comparable to the variable modules of an Anbaumöbel system – the verandah wings are grouped to form a coherent overall composition.

    With this house, Breuer was also able to realise his ideal of integral, harmonised planning of architecture and practical interior design. However, apart from the obligatory built-in closets and shelving, a good part of the furniture was simply taken over from an apartment Breuer had remodelled for the Harnischmachers earlier, in 1929. The resulting interior was typified by the contrast between white walls and the black polished surfaces of most of the wood furnishings as well as by tubular steel furniture.

    In their stringent functionality and the coolness of the materials, Breuer's interiors from this period do not exactly radiate an atmosphere of comfortable domesticity. Taking extant photographs as evidence, the interior of the Harnischmacher House was no exception. The halls and bedrooms, at least, still evoke an association with dentists' rooms which had struck critics of his earlier apartment interiors. Of course, the house was fully intended to convey an uncompromising statement of a new "healthy" form of architecture and way of living, quite in keeping with the demand for "liberated living" put forward three years earlier by Breuer's good friend Sigfried Giedion.[5] "Light, air, movement, opening," the Swiss art

5 Sigfried Giedion,
Befreites Wohnen
(Zürich / Leipzig, 1929).

198

▶ Harnischmacher House I, work room.
▼ Harnischmacher House I, Marianne Harnischmacher
 in the living room.

historian had called for, and it was to these maxims that the building was radically committed, with its verandahs, large windows and sparse furnishings.

Buildings and projects in England

Breuer, who was of Jewish descent, left National Socialist Germany in late 1933. Over the next two years, he worked mainly in Budapest and Zurich, before moving to London in October 1935. Only a small number of buildings and architectural projects were produced during his time in England, although a number were of formative significance for the development of his American residential architecture – not least because the canon of utilised materials had expanded during this time, which tempered the appearance of his buildings.

Of utmost importance was a small temporary exhibition pavilion in Bristol that Breuer designed in 1936 for the furniture producer Crofton Gane. Massive wall structures using local Cotswold stone, in combination with large inset window sections and a lightweight roof construction in wood, provided for a striking composition. The interior was predominantly done in plywood with birch veneer. As such, the pavilion constituted the first manifestation of interest in the use of natural and, in part, local building materials which henceforth would be asserted in Breuer's architecture. This was thoroughly consistent with general tendencies of modern architecture in the 1930s – a few years earlier, for instance, Le Corbusier had built a house for Hélène de Mandrot in southern France with a wall structure composition similar to the one employed for Gane's Pavilion.

In Breuer's case, however, such general new trends and developments were combined with his special Bauhaus background. At the Bauhaus, great importance had been attached in both the preparatory course and the workshops to experiments with the textural qualities and with the (new) applicational and technical possibilities offered by different materials, even natural ones. This is clearly the source for the material contrasts and use of plywood in Gane's Pavilion.

The floor plan shows that Breuer's wall structures exactly circumscribe the volume. Hence it is not a configuration of planes in the manner of buildings by Mies van der Rohe, developing from inside to outside; rather, it is a box, albeit one featuring oblique angles, made of stone, glass and wood around which additional freestanding wall structures are grouped. The plastic detailing of Gane's Pavilion and the appearance of the materials had changed considerably compared with Breuer's house designs from the Bauhaus era, yet the fundamental idea of a self-contained box remained.

The same holds true for a 1937 design for a ski lodge in the Austrian town of Ober-Gurgl which Breuer produced for a ski instructor friend while in London. An innovation over the pavilion in Bristol, the wall segments of this unrealised construction were to be alternately combined with wood frame walls. The framing and cladding of the walls were designed to reinforce one another structurally. In its structural system – that is, in the renewed renunciation of a spatial division of frame and wall – and in visual appearance, the thin lightweight wooden walls would have approximated the cabinet-like walls of the Small Metal House.

◄ Marcel Breuer and F.R.S. Yorke, Gane's Pavilion,
Royal Agricultural Show, Bristol, England, 1936.
▼ Gane's Pavilion, view from east.
▼▼ Gane's Pavilion, exhibition hall.

▼ Gane's Pavilion, view from south.
▼▼ Gane's Pavilion, exhibition hall.

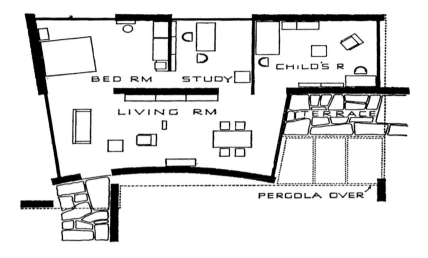

In his work in Europe, therefore, Breuer had developed the characteristic design principles, in part derived from his furniture design, which would go on to typify most of his American houses: the clearly visible additive compositional principle and the self-contained box with a rigid volume shell which might be executed in a wood frame construction or circumscribed with wall structures. All of these would again feature in the house Breuer built for himself in 1938–39.

Breuer House in Lincoln

In a description prepared for Helen Storrow, Breuer characterised his small house as a "studio-house". The principle element of the multipartite structure is a one-and-a-half storey living room area with a trapezoidal floor plan, flanked to the east by a two-storey section and to the west, separated by a curved chimney wall in natural stone, by a verandah. The module-like combination of the building's sections and the differentiation of the functional areas are again articulated on the exterior in the varying roof heights.

With his house in Lincoln, Breuer was particularly proud of the energy economics of the planning concept. For instance, the living room area is closed off to the south by a glazed wall reaching nearly from floor to ceiling. This was designed to let in the low-lying sun in winter to help heat the interior, while in summer the projecting roof would provide shade. As initially built, however, the concept was found to contain a number of serious flaws. Problems with the oil heating caused the rooms to heat unevenly in winter, thus thwarting Breuer's plans. Moreover, half a year after completion, most of the window frames were leaking; after

two years, rain began to penetrate the flat roof, a nuisance that would plague several of the architect's American houses.

As an architectural "calling card", the largely open spatial concept of the house was certainly much more convincing. The basement floor of the east section, set below the living room area, accommodates the kitchen, dining room and a room for the domestic help; above, two rooms (bedrooms or studies) are separated by a bathroom. Both storeys partially open up to the living room area. A lightweight sliding door and a curtain can be employed to shield off most of the upper level. While all the ceilings are painted a light shade, most of the walls are clad in untreated wood. The living room area thus features the same juxtaposition of natural stone, glass and wood found in the interior of Gane's Pavilion. The natural materials create an inviting domestic atmosphere, with very little remaining of the cool aesthetic of the Harnischmacher House.

Contributing to this effect are the armchairs and tables made of plywood that Breuer had developed back in England. Closets and shelves are integrated into the architecture as built-in elements and thus carry on Breuer's European concepts for living, which found a receptive audience in America with its greater tradition of built-in furnishings.

The house in Lincoln clearly exhibits a conceptual affinity with the Small Metal House. Both feature the open connection of a high-ceilinged living room area with an adjoining two-storey unit, and the levels to the rear are nearly identical in their disposition of the floor plan, even if they are mirror-imaged at the basement level. An intermediate link between the Bauhaus-period project from 1925–26 and his first house is furnished by a design Breuer produced for a small house in Budapest (unrealised). Located right on the Danube, the

◁   Breuer House I, view from south with garden.
▽   Breuer House I, view from south-east.
▷   Breuer House I, view into living room.
▽▽   Breuer House I, view from south-west.

▼ Breuer House I, south view, present condition.
▶ Breuer House I, dining room.
▶▶ Breuer House I, view from living room into two-storey area; the built-in shelves conceal stairs rising to second level.

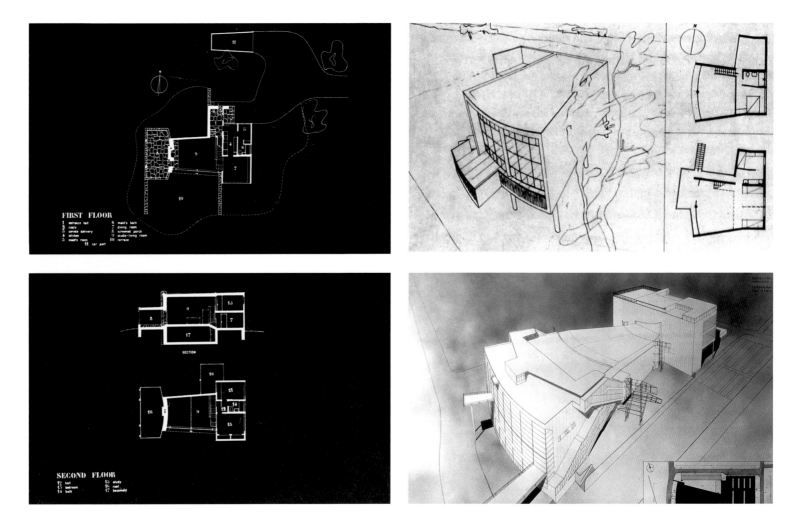

FIRST FLOOR

SECOND FLOOR

house was to stand on pillars but otherwise its spatial organisation and oblique angles, here fashionably exaggerated, definitely anticipate elements of the building in Lincoln. Ultimately, however, the first house Breuer built for himself in the United States constitutes a melding of the Small Metal House and the Budapest design with Gane's Pavilion, whose curved natural stone wall was taken over in Lincoln, acting again as the end wall of a trapezoidal living room area.

Elements of Breuer's house in Lincoln thus had ample precursors. In terms of the exterior form, there was even a forerunner design in one of the proposals Breuer submitted in competition for large-scale projects while in Berlin, namely that for a Ukrainian State Theatre in Kharkov, dating from 1930–31. For this building, whose overall shape had apparently also provided inspirations for the Budapest design, Breuer likewise proposed the joining of a trapezoidal building element closed by a curved wall with a cross section and a low annexe, albeit in a different sequence. None the less, evidence indicates that the architect might have originally envisaged a different arrangement of the sections of his American house, too. His archived papers contain numerous undated floor plan sketches for an unidentified house very similar to the one in Lincoln.[6] Some of these sketches express an "organic" architectural language otherwise atypical of Breuer. They show a high-ceilinged living room area and adjoining two-storey unit, plus a south-facing verandah. It is documented that Breuer wanted the verandah as close as possible to the adjoining woods, and perhaps it was this wish that ultimately led to its shift to the west side.

6 If these floor plan sketches do not belong to the Breuer House in Lincoln, they must refer to Fischer House I in Newtown, Pennsylvania, which was designed a short time later. It is possible that Breuer initially considered designing a house for the Fischers quite similar to his own.

◄◄ Breuer House I, ground plan and section.
◄ Weekend house on the Danube, Budapest, Hungary, 1933–34 (unrealised).
◄▼ Kharkov Theatre, Ukraine, 1930–31, perspective (unrealised).

▼ Breuer's sketch, ground plan for a single-family house.
▼▼ Breuer House I, veranda, protected by screens.

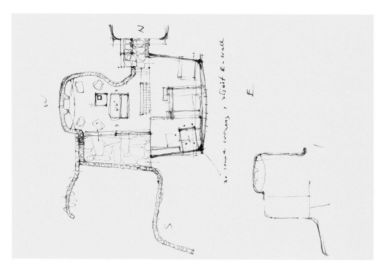

Title page of Le Corbusier's Une Maison – Un Palais.

This would mean that a connection between the Lincoln house and another large-scale project was more likely to have come about by chance. The project was not one of Breuer's, but a 1927 design competition entry by Le Corbusier: his design for the Palace of the League of Nations in Geneva. Probably Breuer recognised the opportunity to make this homage after moving the verandah, and then explicitly formulated the reference after the fact. For with that reference the scheme for the house seems to incorporate a programmatic statement.[7]

The house in Lincoln and the design by Le Corbusier both feature a rectangular block to the rear followed by a middle trapezoidal element on to which a much lower curved structure is attached.[8] Thus Breuer would have rendered the Corbusian large-scale form into miniature scale and utilised it for a new function – an approach whose origin probably again lies with Le Corbusier and his own interpretation of his Geneva design. After his competition entry lost out to conservative Beaux-Arts designs, in a dubious decision-making process, Le Corbusier wrote *Une Maison – Un Palais* in defence of his project.[9] As the book's title suggests, he established, beyond other things, a metaphorical linking of house and palace, and then proceeded to elucidate the concept of an "administrative palace", his Palace of the League of Nations. The quintessence of this suggestive line of argument was the declaration, not quite new, that functionality and beauty, regardless of a building's size, are always founded on a well thought-out fulfilment of the functions and economy of construction, the "eternal laws" of harmonic architecture and the consideration of human scale, not on the dead rules and regulations of academic architecture. Pursuing this line, Le Corbusier equated the Geneva building project with the creation of a (large) house, which could be turned around to claim: where a small house succeeds in fulfilling the aforementioned criteria – be

7 The author earlier pointed out the correspondence in the form and disposition of the sections between the house in Lincoln and Le Corbusier's design for the Palace of the League of Nations (Driller 1998, p. 111), though at that time he was not able to offer an interpretation. Today, however, he believes the formal similarity can be construed in regard to the symbolic content. For the same reason, contrary to his original assumption, the author now considers it possible that Breuer did in fact cite Oskar Schlemmer's painting "Concentric Group" in the interior.

8 The house in Lincoln is also comparable to Le Corbusier's design in the placement of the large side window (though the assembly hall in Geneva was to be glazed on two sides); in the emphasis on a vertical element, the chimney, on the front wall of the central building section (where the Geneva design features a monumental single pilotis that was to support a sculpture group), and in the display of the

212

◀ Competition sketch by Le Corbusier for the Palace of the League of Nations in Geneva, 1927, from *Une Maison – Un Palais*.

▼ Sketch of a fishing hut from Le Corbusier's *Une Maison – Un Palais*.

it a regional fishing hut perfected as a house type over centuries, or a modern residential building – it moves the viewer through the perfect beauty yielded by the unobtrusive logic of the form and becomes elevated to the sphere of the "palace".[10] For dignity is based on a "decent bearing" – that is, on simplicity.[11]

Breuer was certainly familiar with Le Corbusier's 1928 book, *Une Maison – Un Palais*.[12] And surely he thought of his own house in Lincoln as his own personal small "palace". At last he was able to implement – with ideal furnishings and detailing – the spatial concepts and philosophies of living that he had advocated as an efficient and functional form of the small house since his time at the Bauhaus; he was even able to live it out himself as a proud homeowner, thereby setting an instructive example for others.[13] Nevertheless, the "dignified" synthesis of economy and aesthetics that Breuer undoubtedly saw fulfilled in his house can hardly be the sole reason for the miniaturisation of the "large house" (the Geneva parliament building by Le Corbusier) that he carried out in Lincoln, although Le Corbusier had himself sought to stress this synthesis in *Une Maison – Un Palais*. Rather, it is necessary to consider Breuer's personal situation at the time and his new professional environment in order to shed light on why he chose precisely this special image for his house, an image he never returned to again in his work.

Shortly after Breuer had been "commissioned" by Helen Storrow to plan his own house, he wrote to a good friend in England: "I ... am quite happy here in America. I am rushed with work, which has its difficulties, but which gives a promising outlook for the future. ... And, after all, I am glad not to be in Europe at the moment, where it seems as though everyone were planning to kill his neighbor."[14]

twin supports of the verandah (in the Geneva design the low presidential pavilion is mounted atop an open row of pilotis). Moreover, the curved natural stone wall in Lincoln, which Breuer had already used in Gane's Pavilion, goes back to a different building by Le Corbusier, the Swiss Pavilion of the Cité Universitaire in Paris (1930/31). The author thus believes that the reference to Le Corbusier is far more convincing than attempts to trace the house in Lincoln to historic British residential house typologies with which Breuer had presumably come in contact with in England. See 2G, no. 17, 2001, pp. 34–37. All the more so, considering that such attempts disregard the designs Breuer produced before his move to England which were just as decisively influential for the Lincoln house (the Small Metal House, the Kharkov Theatre, the house in Budapest).

9 Le Corbusier, Une Maison – Un Palais. "A la recherche d'une unité architecturale" (Paris,

Breuer House I, view from north-east.

On the eve of World War II, Breuer had found a new home in the United States that gave him refuge and employment. His look back at the Old World merely offered the certainty that former visions of a peaceful coexistence there would sooner or later fall victim to Nazi aggression. Here we come full circle to the Palace of the League of Nations design, which Le Corbusier had said was founded on clarity and integrity – characteristics Le Corbusier had also ascribed to the League of Nations itself in 1927–28 as the bearer of hope for a new world order.[15] Ten years later, these political hopes had been shattered. What was once meant to stand as a modern palace symbolising a modern community of nations and the peaceful resolution of conflicts could now at best be upheld in the small and private realm as a visual remembrance. And perhaps it was really the case that Breuer, after arriving in the New World, himself a victim of political circumstances in Europe, was guided by precisely this intention in the planning of his first house: to create a "palace of memory" for what could have been, but without neglecting what was demanded by the new environment.

For even if such an interpretation goes beyond Breuer's actual intentions in respect to his Lincoln house, Le Corbusier's Geneva design might still have played an important role. Reference should again be made to the neighbouring Gropius House, which was conceptually based on a dialectic allusion to the Director's House of the Bauhaus in Dessau. With his American house, Gropius wanted to supply an unequivocal, uncompromising statement of his personal formal language and thus he chose to establish a link to one of his best-known European buildings.[16] In 1938, despite his earlier breakthrough with the Harnischmacher House, Breuer did not yet have a similarly well-known project of his own to which he could appeal. What could be more obvious, then, than to make clever use of Le Corbusier's League

1928; unaltered reprint Paris, 1989). For details on the history of Le Corbusier's Geneva project, see Werner Oechslin, ed., Le Corbusier & Pierre Jeanneret. Das Wettbewerbsprojekt für den Völkerbundspalast in Genf 1927 (Zurich, 1988).

10 Along the same lines and with his characteristic rhetoric, Le Corbusier had also addressed the theme of house and palace – with reference to the "machine for living in" and the Geneva design – in the foreword of the third edition of his book Vers une architecture, also published in 1928: "since the time when we called for the 'machine for living in', we have revised our then still quite young opinion to maintain that this machine for living in could also be a palace. By palace, we wanted to make clear that each part of a house, merely through its arrangement within the whole, can have such a moving effect on us that it reveals the grandeur and the nobility of an intention. And this

of Nations scheme, a design that was virtually a synonym for the still-raging struggle against the hated Beaux-Arts tradition, and familiar to those in progressive circles in America, who knew of the outcome of the Geneva competition?[17] The houses in Lincoln prevailed as propaganda over the principles that had previously defined architectural education at institutions such as Harvard. European modernism had triumphed – with clear, manifesto-like references back to the Bauhaus and probably to Le Corbusier as well.

The houses in Lincoln were the site of frequent visits, not least by artist friends of the two architects and by Harvard students, with Breuer's house in particular serving as a place of social gathering. It seems as if Breuer had planned on this "public" function of his house from the outset, thereby also pursuing a symbolic link to European sources.

As a gathering place, the high-ceilinged trapezoidal living room area is basically a miniaturised version of the similarly designed auditorium of Breuer's Kharkov Theatre or the assembly hall from Le Corbusier's Palace of the League of Nations. Yet in the special formulation connecting it to a two-storey unit to the rear, a further gesture of reverence beyond the Small Metal House can perhaps be identified. The organisational scheme that underlies this composition calls to mind a principal work by Oskar Schlemmer: the painting "Concentric Group", produced at the Weimar Bauhaus in 1925.[18] This work shows a statuary formation of figures in a space of indeterminate height, set in front of a background that is also divided into four slightly offset rectangular fields, which seems to be partially opening up. Even the distribution of light exhibits a parallel: the figures are primarily illuminated from the right, which is where the large window is situated in the Lincoln house.

intention, for us it was synonymous with architecture. ... A house – a palace. We believed we could put the whole passion of our occupation into this contemporary task. At that point, in 1926 the League of Nations called on architects from all countries and asked them for a palace. We immediately conceived of the situation like so: a palace – a house. Such a precise programme moreover invites this formulation. For what was demanded for Geneva was a huge administrative building. Is this something other than studying 'the house for the average man', for the 'first best' ...?" Cited from Le Corbusier, Ausblick auf eine Architektur (Frankfurt am Main / Berlin, 1963), p. 18 f; translation from German.

11 On this subject and on the proximity of Le Corbusier's theses to those of Jean-Jacques Rousseau, see Adolf Max Vogt, Le Corbusier, Der edle Wilde. Zur Archäologie der Moderne (Braunschweig /

◄ Constance Breuer (above) and Dottie Noyes at a party, Breuer House I, c. 1940.

It has been noted that in his figural-spatial compositions from the Bauhaus era, Schlemmer assigned an anticipatory role for a future architecture. He wrote in 1922: "I'm not able to build houses except the ideal one that can be derived from my paintings, which serve as an anticipation of it." At the same time, these paintings by Schlemmer could have been models intended to serve the aims and objectives of the Bauhaus, creating a "symbol of community" and functioning as an artistic vision of a "New Man" in conjunction with the new concepts of building.[19]

By 1938, Breuer had certainly long moved away from the idea of the "New Man".[20] Nevertheless, the connection to "Concentric Group" may not have come about purely by chance. In creating the special composition, Breuer might have perhaps taken inspiration from precisely the model character of this and other paintings by Schlemmer, for example in regard to an ideal architecture and a community of like-minded individuals. Not that Breuer should have expected the revival of the Bauhaus and its programmatic intentions at Harvard University. But his new environment, with its spirit of optimism and possibility, and its young students – who had more immediate connection with Breuer than with the considerably older Gropius with his characteristic Prussian reserve – perhaps inspired him to reminisce accordingly.

Furthermore, Breuer and Schlemmer shared a common interest in the question of how people were to comport themselves within the new architecture. In his earlier design for the Small Metal House, the living room area was to be large enough for "six couples to dance comfortably in". And in Breuer's later houses, such as the one in Lincoln, the furnishings – at least in the published photographs of the interiors – stipulate a choreography for inhabiting

Wiesbaden, 1996), pp. 115–21.

12 Through his contact with Sigfried Giedion and work in the CIAM, Breuer would have had sufficient opportunity to become familiar with Une Maison – Un Palais.

13 For more on the idea of the architect inhabiting his own studio residence as an instructive example for others, claiming it to function as a universal house type, see Matthias Noell, "Choisir entre l'individu et le standard" – Das Künstlerhaus bei Gropius, Le Corbusier, van Doesburg, Bill", in Isabelle Ewig, Thomas W. Gaehtgens, Matthias Noell, eds., Das Bauhaus und Frankreich, 1919–1940 (Berlin, 2002), pp. 83–115.

14 Letter from Breuer to Dorothea Ventris, 16 November 1938 (Marcel Breuer Papers, Syracuse University Library).

15 Une Maison – Un Palais has this to say on the subject: "Nous ne sommes pas à la foire

the space. The near absence of human figures in these staged photographs seems paradoxical, yet also makes sense: the ideal of spatial balance and contemplative calm that distinguishes both Schlemmer's paintings and the photographs would have been likely to be disturbed by real people (who of course comport themselves quite differently from Schlemmer's figural groups) in Breuer's interiors, especially a festive group of artists and students.

Houses of the 1940s and 1950s

In May 1941, Breuer and Gropius parted ways. Presumably Breuer did not feel his contributions were sufficiently appreciated and probably also believed it necessary to assert his independence from his mentor. He maintained his own office in Cambridge, though the unfavourable conditions during wartime made business difficult. It was probably in this period – now he was married to an American – that he produced the sketch for a very simple small house apparently planned for himself and his wife. With a horizontal window band, it incorporates a common design element of modern architecture, yet its appearance is much more strongly defined by the rather conventional flat-pitch gable roof, otherwise atypical for Breuer's houses. In combination with the partly open row of posts, it distantly evokes the popular image of the primitive hut, in turn bringing to mind the remote fishing huts on the French Atlantic coast that Le Corbusier had employed in *Une Maison – Un Palais* in his laudatory illustrations of natural dignity.[21] Could it be that for his second house in the United States, Breuer initially returned to Le Corbusier's 1928 book, though this time not to the "large house" discussed there, but to the notion of "small palaces"?

où s'ébattraient des parvenus. On exige de nous des intentions claires et une pensée pure. Cette clarté et cette pureté, ... n'est-ce pas aussi comme le signe même de la nouvelle institution qui, à Genève, devrait répondre à l'espoir des sociétés nouvelles?" (1989 reprint, p. 84).

16 See Driller 1998, pp. 90–101.

17 It is very possible that Sigfried Giedion inspired Breuer to make the allusion to the Palace of the League of Nations with his house in Lincoln. Giedion had begun giving guest lectures at Harvard in 1938, in which he presumably made some mention of the Geneva competition. See Jos Bosman, "Sigfried Giedions Urteil und die Legitimation eines geringen Zweifels", in Werner Oechslin, ed., Le Corbusier & Pierre Jeanneret (1988, pp. 135–48), p. 148.

18 Illustration in Driller, 1998, p. 108.

▾ Breuer's sketch of a house for himself.
▸ Cover of exhibition brochure, Museum of Modern
   Art, 1949.

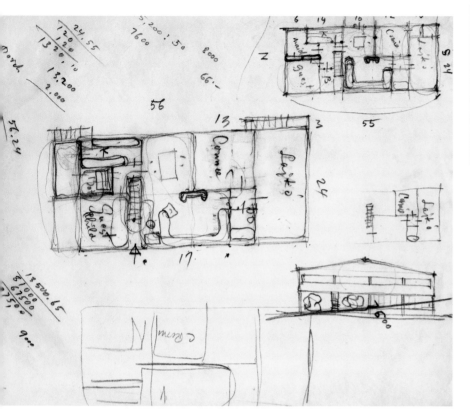

The House in the Museum Garden

Marcel Breuer *Architect*

4 West 54 Street

New York

Be that as it may, this idea was not directly realised in Breuer's residential architecture. During this same wartime period, however, Breuer developed important concepts such as the "binuclear plan", which would come to define the numerous houses that established his reputation as a residential architect on the American East Coast from 1946 onwards. In that year, Breuer moved his practice from Cambridge to New York, thus abandoning his house in Lincoln. He also gave up his position at Harvard, his attachment to teaching having markedly cooled over the years.

Breuer's success in New York was decisively aided by the city's Museum of Modern Art, which organised a travelling exhibition on his oeuvre in 1948. This was followed in 1949 by the construction of a demonstration house in the Museum Garden of MoMA as well as a monograph by Peter Blake.[22] In particular, it was by visiting the demonstration structure that numerous potential clients decided to hire Breuer as the architect for their own houses.

Breuer's American post-war houses were produced for a largely homogenous clientele: financially well-off young couples, open to new ideas and styles (not least to the prevailing taste of the day), who wanted to move out from cities into nearby countryside and build a home for themselves and their children. In these circles, Breuer's houses were considered models of "informal living", which moreover made use of familiar, natural materials and even traditional details – such as the open fireplaces that Breuer fashioned into striking "sculptures". It was precisely the fact that this was a form of "domesticated" modernism, both inside and outside, that lent the houses their particular attraction. Hence it was not solely furniture and interiors that made Breuer a member of the avant-garde in the 1950s.

The houses designed by Breuer in the 1940s and '50s exhibit a fixed typology and a

19 See Karin von Maur, Oskar Schlemmer. Monographie (Munich, 1979), pp. 131, 147.

20 A reference to the "New Man" appeared again a short time later in, of all places, an article Breuer wrote for the popular magazine House & Garden: "Tell me, what is modern architecture?", in House & Garden 77, April 1940, pp. 47, 71. The article's title and content leave no doubt, however, that the "New Man", which had lurked as a nebulous ideal of artistic-intellectual educational work in the manifestos of the 1920s, had made way for the everyday American consumer.

21 See the 1989 reprint, pp. 48–52, where the quotation at the top of this essay may also be found.

22 Peter Blake, Marcel Breuer: Architect and Designer (New York, 1949).

◄ Gagarin House I, Litchfield, Connecticut, 1953–56, view of living room fireplace.
▼ Breuer's schematic sketch showing his American domestic house types.
▶▶ Next page: Breuer House II, New Canaan, Connecticut, 1947–48, view from south-east.

strict design system. As already mentioned, this was based on the additive and clearly visible combination of self-contained boxes, the compositional technique the architect had developed back in Europe.

The simplest type is the "long house" – to all intents and purposes, a free-standing cabinet altered in scale. The best-known example of such a "single box house" is the one Breuer constructed in 1947–48 for himself and his family in New Canaan, outside New York. The upper box, which originally also supported a widely projecting balcony suspended on steel cables, juts out more than three metres in some places over a narrow base storey. Breuer's obsessive preoccupation with the American wood frame construction and his exploration of the static and tectonic possibilities (and limitations) of the balloon frame here reached their culmination. As with the lightweight wooden walls in his earlier Tyrol ski lodge design, Breuer had found this method of construction to provide an equivalent for the structural principle of the Small Metal House – the balloon frame allowed the construction of boxes with filigree-thin exterior walls that form a self-reinforcing volume shell, thus making an additional support system outside the wall redundant. Here, with his cantilevered house, it was logically consistent that Breuer would transfer the "bold play of forces under maximum tension" from the iron frame construction to a wood frame – an exercise he had already practised in his furniture design.[23] But in the New Canaan house "the monumentality of the intellect" clearly overtaxed the structural system: after just a short time, the overhangs and balcony began to sag and had to be stabilised with supporting walls.

A further American residential house type by Breuer is the "binuclear house". Here, two autonomous boxes for the living and sleeping areas of the house are joined by a narrow

23 For the British company Isokon, Breuer had developed a plywood reclining chair in the mid-1930s whose form was based on a similar armchair in aluminium he had designed several years earlier.

◄ Breuer House II, view from north-west.
▼ Breuer House II, view from north.

▾ Breuer House II, ground plan.
▾▾ Breuer House II, view from living room into
    dining area.
▸ Breuer House II, living room.
▸▾ Breuer House II, the Breuer family eating together.

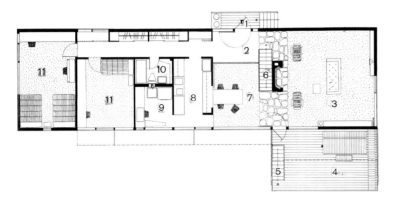

hallway, the complete spatial division of the two sections making the module-like composition of this "double-box house" clearly evident at first glance. In addition, juxtaposed sloping roofs pointing upwards in opposite directions often visually separate the wings and thus serve to reinforce the additive principle. The "binuclear plan" was employed by Breuer for a number of his most attractive villa designs, most prominently the Robinson House and Hooper House II. With their natural stone walls circumscribing the volumes, and exterior wall sections articulating the garden area, these two villas are indebted to Gane's Pavilion.

The description "double-box house" also applies to the "offset, two-storey houses", with a main level box unit upon which an upper container is set off to one side, as well as to the U-shaped houses. A variant of the "binuclear plan", the latter category includes the third house Breuer built for himself in the United States. In response to the blatant structural problems of his first house in New Canaan, the architect designed another a few years later – a bungalow featuring massive natural stone walls and no overhangs, which was completed in 1951.

Finally, there are the "multi-level houses", typically consisting of a double-storey box for the main section, around which annexe units are grouped, comparable to the verandah wings of the Harnischmacher House. Characteristic of these houses is the gallery-like opening of the bedroom to the high-ceilinged living room, derived from Breuer's Lincoln House. Such a solution demands that the occupants, for whom it is likely that a quiet refuge matters more than a special architectural "calling card", have a tolerant understanding of the spatial concept. It is therefore hardly surprising that only a few such "multi-level houses" were

Hooper House II, Baltimore County, Maryland, 1956–59, view from east.

▶ Hooper House II, view from living room
on to Lake Roland.
▼ Hooper House II, play room with fireplace.

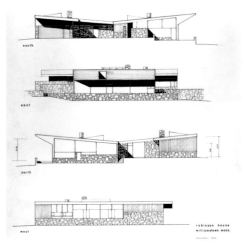

Robinson House, Williamstown, Massachusetts, 1946–48.

Robinson House, living area, view from south.

Robinson House, view from north-east.

Robinson House, initial design, elevation of southern, eastern, northern and western façades, December 1946.

▼ Robinson House, during construction.
▼▼ Robinson House, view from west.
▶ Robinson House, during construction.
▶▼ Robinson House, view from south.

Robinson House, pool in front of living area, present condition.

▼ Tompkins House, Hewlett Harbor, Long Island, New York, 1945–46; a classic example of Breuer's "offset, two-storey house" type.
▼▼ Tompkins House, side view.
▶ Breuer House III, New Canaan, Connecticut, 1951, view of entry front.

realised. With his other residential house types, on the other hand, Breuer dispensed with relatively complex spatial systems in favour of options for private retreat. The popularity enjoyed by the "binuclear plan" above all was likely to have been additionally driven by the complete separation of the bedrooms. This "advantage" in prudish post-war America apparently outweighed the fact that the full separation of the functional zones actually ends up dictating an abstract and, to a certain extent, even arbitrary programme for living.

Except in his most prominent commissions, Breuer seldom worked with garden architects. Although his houses fit in well with the landscape, their geometrically severe form stresses their character as man-made objects antithetically opposed to nature. Only in a few rare instances did Breuer let himself get carried away into using an "organic" formal language, seen in the sketches mentioned above in connection with the house in Lincoln. He wrote: "The formation of the land, the trees, the rocks – . . . all these will suggest something about the design of the building. ... The landscape may traverse the building, or the building may intercept the landscape. [But] I can not believe that the two should be mixed up, confused, joined by imitation or assimilation."[24]

Such words were aimed at Frank Lloyd Wright, but probably at Alvar Aalto as well.[25] Scholars have attempted to establish parallels between Aalto's architecture and Breuer's houses from the 1940s and '50s in regard to the juxtaposition of seemingly incompatible elements – one of Breuer's houses was even described as a "Surrealist collage".[26] The house in Lincoln certainly qualifies as a collage, with its reworking of earlier designs by Breuer along with observable citations from Le Corbusier's architecture and Schlemmer's paintings. It remains open to discussion, however, whether this also applies to Breuer's American

24 Marcel Breuer, Sun and Shadow: The Philosophy of an Architect, ed. Peter Blake (New York, 1955), p. 41.

25 In 1949, for instance, Aalto's famous Baker House had been completed on the MIT campus in Cambridge, Massachusetts. Breuer's words may well have been directly targeted at the student dormitory's undulating curved form, which allegedly makes reference to the adjacent Charles River. By this time, however, it is likely that Breuer had developed a personal grudge against Aalto that went beyond dissent over formal details. For in the second, enlarged edition of Space, Time and Architecture, Sigfried Giedion had dedicated an entire chapter to the Finnish architect, thus putting him on a par with Gropius, Le Corbusier and Mies van der Rohe. All his life, Breuer was denied a comparable "nobilisation". See Bruno Maurer, Arthur Rüegg, "Alvar Aalto and Switzerland", in

▾ Breuer House III, entry area.
▸ Breuer House III, garden side.
▾▾ Breuer House III, living room.

◄ Marcel Breuer and Eliot Noyes, Kniffin House,
New Canaan, Connecticut, 1947–48, another
example of a "multi-level house".
▼ Kniffin House.
▼▼ Kniffin House, living room.

▼ Kniffin House, living room with fireplace.
▸ Kniffin House, view into two-storey area.

▾ Model House in the Museum Garden of the Museum
  of Modern Art, New York, 1948–49, view from living
  room into open bedroom.
▸ McMullen Beach House, Mantoloking, New Jersey,
  1958–60, living room, also a "multi-level house".

◄ Alvar Aalto, Villa Mairea, Noormarkku, Finland, 1937–39, living room.

▶ Staehelin House, Feldmeilen, near Zürich, Switzerland, 1956–59, entry front.

post-war houses, in the sense of a surrealistic combination of traditional construction methods and industrially produced components. Together with the highly technical details and the large painted sections and expansive window surfaces of his houses, Breuer's formulation of the balloon frame and natural stone walls is always aimed towards overall abstraction in the architectural composition. The aim of linking tradition and modernism or nature and culture is clearly subordinated to a (syn)aesthetic play with surfaces and constructivist inventions. In this respect, Breuer's houses – and likewise his earlier Gane's Pavilion – are just as far removed from Aalto's famous collage, the Villa Mairea, as from the architecture of a "new regionalism".[27]

Late villas

It was in Switzerland of all places, where Le Corbusier's design for the Palace of the League of Nations had once been rejected, that the relationship of house and palace would turn around for Breuer decades later – owing to, of all things, a building he had designed for an institution of the United Nations. In 1952, Breuer had been appointed as one of three architects for the UNESCO Headquarters in Paris together with Pier Luigi Nervi and Bernard Zehrfuss; for Breuer the project meant worldwide renown and the breakthrough to further major commissions in Europe and America. Yet it also meant that a new circle of clients was now turning to Breuer, expecting the architect behind this important international organisation's headquarters to provide them with a prestigious building of their own – even when they had "only" commissioned him with the design for a villa. While Le Corbusier had

Winfried Nerdinger, ed., *Alvar Aalto. Toward a Human Modernism* (Munich / London / New York, 1999, pp. 113–41), p. 131.

26 See Edward Ford, "Alvar Aalto and Marcel Breuer: Light, Industrialization, and the Vernacular, 1928–1963", in Ford, *The Details of Modern Architecture, Volume 2, 1928 to 1988* (Cambridge, Massachusetts / London, 1996, pp. 117–63), pp. 149–57. In this essay, Ford uses the term "Surrealist collage" to describe Breuer's Wolfson House, a wood and natural stone structure that incorporates a gleaming silver metal trailer. The trailer was a request from the client, however, and not a special design intention on Breuer's part.

27 A grandiose synthesis of modern and historical as well as international and regional architectural motifs, combined with an ironic dialogue with the surrounding natural landscape, characterises Aalto's Villa Mairea,

advocated for his Geneva project in *Une Maison – Un Palais,* claiming it was planned like a house, certain of Breuer's clients, even if they did not explicitly express it, now wished for houses like "palaces". And while Le Corbusier in his 1928 plea had used his houses to explain the design principles and structural composition of his League of Nations project, Breuer's villas from the late 1950s onwards followed the UNESCO Headquarters in their construction method. Under the influence of Nervi, Breuer began to use exposed concrete in his designs, not only for "tension constructions" but also increasingly as a means of expressing an affectation for the monumental. Even in the private residences designed by the architect, there was at least a partial return of the "monumentality of masses".

This development is most notably exemplified by Breuer's three Swiss villa designs. In the first, the Staehelin House completed high above Lake Zurich in 1959, the use of board-marked exposed concrete is still limited to the ceilings and supporting piers. In addition to hiring Breuer as architect, the client had enlisted the artist Henry Moore, another of the creative figures involved in the UNESCO Headquarters project, to create original sculpture pieces for the luxurious residence. Thus the Feldmeilen site accommodated not only one of the pre-eminent modern villa constructions of the 1950s but an equally exquisite sculpture collection.

Breuer designed his second Swiss villa project for the actor Peter Ustinov. The planned focal point of the expansive "quadrinuclear house" near Vevey was the living pavilion with its striking concrete shell roof in the form of two hyperbolic paraboloids. The Ustinov House, however, never progressed beyond the planning phase.

dating from the same period as Breuer's Lincoln House. A comparable synthesis is not found in Breuer's houses, which neither integrate set pieces of exotic architecture nor tolerate grass-covered roofs or interpretations of the support structure as a metaphoric "forest of pillars". For Aalto's use of the collage motif in the Villa Mairea, see Richard Weston, "Between Nature and Culture: Reflections on the Villa Mairea", in Winfried Nerdinger, ed., *Alvar Aalto* (1999), pp. 61–76. In addition, the Villa Mairea features a number of details that seem explicitly primitivistic, such as the exterior fireplace built in natural stone. Breuer's natural stone designs, by contrast, are characterised by a geometrically determined form with clear-cut edges; he stressed that he wanted to avoid any impression of creating a "grotto" or a "romantic anachronism". If, like Aalto, Breuer did occasionally employ *Verfremdungen* (alienated or defamiliarised forms),

◄ Staehelin House, view from west.
◄▼ Staehelin House, view from south-west.
▼ Staehelin House, detail of south-west façade.
▼▼ Staehelin House, view from north-west.

▾ Staehelin House, view into courtyard.
▾▾ Staehelin House, court in front of children's room.

▾ Staehelin House, view from entry hall into living
   room and interior courtyard.
▾▾ Staehelin House, dining area.

▾ Ustinov House, near Vevey, Switzerland, perspective
view, December 1959 (unrealised).

The third of Breuer's Swiss villa projects was the zenith: the Koerfer House on Lake Maggiore, which took more than four years until its ultimate completion in 1967. Located on a steep slope, this quite costly house was designed as a concrete cube with a level above for the children's rooms. The client, Jacques Koerfer, was a passionate art collector and this, combined with the special site, is likely to have had a special appeal for Breuer. Back in the early 1930s, he was to redesign a house in Ascona for the Wuppertal banker Eduard von der Heydt – a project that, for unknown reasons, was never realised.[28] In 1928–29, von der Heydt had commissioned Emil Fahrenkamp, in his time one of the most prominent German architects, to construct an elegant resort hotel on Monte Verità, which was furnished with objects from von der Heydt's art collection.[29] Here a group of Bauhaus members, Breuer among them, had come together for afternoon tea on a number of occasions during visits to Ticino.[30] When Koerfer asked him to design a stately villa in Ascona-Moscia more than three decades later, Breuer must surely have recalled those earlier visits – along with the fact that he was then not in the circle of architects whom rich collectors would supply with nearly unlimited resources for the construction of their private "art palaces". The mighty Koerfer House thus came to symbolise Breuer's professional ascent – as well as the defiant self-confidence and will to make a complete artistic statement of an architect whose work was already being critically discussed by members of the next generation.

With the Koerfer House, Breuer put every effort into achieving perfection, even up to the multicoloured gravel admixture and careful bush-hammered finish of the exposed concrete walls. Yet with this unrestrained display of a consummate ideal, partly indulging in the aesthetic end in itself, one could scarcely speak of that "dignity from a decent bearing"

it was with a decidedly abstract formal language. This also distinguishes his houses from regionalistic architecture. With the balloon frame, for instance, Breuer typically utilises a vertically laid smooth exterior shell (here again in correlation with Aalto), as this is particularly effective in transmitting the impression of a uniform volume shell; if he had sought to establish a reference to traditional New England clapboard construction, he would instead have employed the laths in a horizontal and overlapping arrangement.

28 See Bruno Maurer, "Manifest des Neuen Regionalismus", in the volume of commentary issued with the reprint of Eduard Keller, ed., Ascona Bau-Buch (Zurich, 2001), pp. 4–36; original edition Zurich, 1934), p. 26. Breuer had designed the interior of Eduard von der Heydt's Berlin residence in 1929–30.

29 See Detlef Bell, "Eduard von der Heydt

◄ Marcel Breuer and Mario Jossa, Saier House,
Glanville, France, 1972–73, realisation of the design
concept of the unrealised Ustinov House.
◄▼ Saier House, view from north.
▼ Saier House, exterior view into living room.
▼▼ Saier House, fireplace.

▲▲ Previous page: Marcel Breuer and Herbert Beckhard,
Koerfer House, Moscia, Switzerland, 1963–67, west
side of roof terrace with view on to Lake Maggiore.
◄ Koerfer House, view from north-east.
▼ Koerfer House, view from east.

◄   Koerfer House, view from east.
◄▾   Koerfer House, living room with paintings by
     Léger and Mondrian on rear wall.
▾   Koerfer House, view on to roofed terrace in front
     of living room, ground floor, looking west.
▾▾   Koerfer House, vestibule.

earlier invoked by Le Corbusier.[31] Even Breuer himself seems to have ultimately come to this conclusion, as his last two houses – the relatively modest-seeming Gagarin House II and Stillman House III – exhibit a return to the design origins of his residential architecture and the formal vocabulary of his houses from the 1940s and '50s. In those earlier designs, economy and simplicity certainly did not always prove to be the defining factors either. Yet it is Breuer's American post-war houses, above all, that continue to captivate with their harmony of proportion and material and their clarity of spatial organisation. These, combined with their virtuosic structural details, move one to exclaim: "Mais ces maisons sont des palais!"

– Ein Leben hinter der Kunst", in Sabine Fehlemann, Rainer Stamm, eds., Die Von der Heydts. Bankiers, Christen, Mäzene (Wuppertal, 2001, pp. 46–71), pp. 64–66.

30 See Reginald Isaacs, Walter Gropius. Der Mensch und sein Werk, vol. 2 (Berlin, 1984), pp. 590 f.

31 Corresponding criticism was levied against the house in the professional press, namely in an article in the Swiss magazine Werk that made direct reference to Le Corbusier: "Breuer calls this building 'a collector's house'. One might therefore be permitted to draw a comparison with the Villa La Roche in Paris. The latter was certainly a much less perfect work, yet Le Corbusier held back to give emphasis to the works by Léger, Gris, Braque, Picasso – though to a few by Jeanneret himself as well." Werk 54, September 1967, pp. 556–60; p. 557; translation from German.

Marcel Breuer and Tician Papachristou, Stillman House III, Litchfield, Connecticut, 1972–73, view from north-east.

ENCOUNTERING AMERICA:

MARCEL BREUER AND THE DISCOURSES OF THE VERNACULAR FROM BUDAPEST TO BOSTON

ENCOUNTERING AMERICA: MARCEL BREUER AND THE DISCOURSES OF THE VERNACULAR FROM BUDAPEST TO BOSTON

BARRY BERGDOLL

Marcel Breuer had grand hopes of the reception that awaited him in the New World as he sailed from Southampton away from two years of professional frustration in England in late July 1937. As the ship approached the American coastline, on 2 August, he probably was not on the lookout for the grand modern house Richard Neutra was building on Fishers Island, an outpost of New England at the mouth of Long Island Sound.[1] There alone was ample proof of the extent to which American architecture did not really need to await those messiahs of the Bauhaus whose names are now recorded on a famous page of the Museum of Modern Art guest book of September 1937, a period when Walter Gropius was much present in New York planning the Museum's great "Bauhaus" exhibition, in which Breuer signed in just a few lines above Mies van der Rohe.[2] Breuer was no doubt more intent on the excitement of reaching New York and on the salesmanship he hoped to muster to sell the exhibition proposal he was carrying for the forthcoming New York World's Fair, an ambitious display treating, as he put it, "the Man of the Future". He and Herbert Bayer, who would soon follow him on the path of emigration to the US, had enlisted a friend at the Carnegie Institute's London office to translate it into English; and they had made appeals to their American acquaintances Alfred Barr at the Museum of Modern Art and the architect Wallace K. Harrison, well connected to the Rockefellers, to make appointments with figures who might help in bringing the scheme to reality – businessmen, they hoped, and perhaps editors at *Time* and *Fortune*. The planned display would entail several buildings and landscape.[3] It would make visible just how modernism had changed from its heroic days of the 1920s, in the face of the challenging circumstances of the current world order and in the hands of a younger generation. Their venture took a much wider lens, which included

1 See Dietrich Neumann, ed., Richard Neutra's Windschield House (Cambridge, Mass.: Harvard University Graduate School of Design and Harvard Art Museums, 2001), esp. pp. 34–65. On 11 March 1938, Richard and Dion Neutra wrote to Breuer after a meeting in Cambridge: "thank you once more for your friendliness. I very well understand your feeling of frustration during your years of involuntary being driven about in the world and I know that you are again on the right track, as good as one can have it in life!" (Breuer Papers, Syracuse University Library, Box 5, File 4, Correspondence).

2 Cammie McAtee, "Alien #5044325: Mies's first trip to America", in Phyllis Lambert, ed., Mies in America (New York: Harry N. Abrams, 2001), p. 132.

3 The prospectus, in German and English, is appended to a letter from Bayer to Breuer dated 24 April 1937 (Breuer Papers, Syracuse University Library, Box 15, File 11).

concerns with architecture and technology's relationship to nature and with a new notion of a characteristic form of vision that made modern man a fundamentally new subject. This was an implicit rejection of the narrow focus on individual buildings of MoMA's seminal 1932 International Style show, in which Breuer had been included with a single project, an apartment.

"The formation of a new conception of art and design for our present age has developed to such a degree that the time has come to examine its meaning and value and to give it a comprehensive representation," Breuer and Bayer proclaimed. "With a view towards demonstrating this new spirit ... people who work quite independently, in seemingly unconnected spheres of activity, have combined ... efforts ... Their work concerns architecture, technology, designs for house equipment, painting, sculpture, music, the stage, films, literature, science, philosophy, and education." They promised to assemble an array of European artists from Le Corbusier and André Breton in Paris to El Lissitzky in Moscow. Alongside the artists were intellectual and social leaders, men whom Breuer and Bayer considered expressed the changing spirit of the age: Albert Einstein, Sigmund Freud, James Joyce and Henry Ford. Ford was the only American on the list apart from Barr, but he embodied in himself the whole myth of American no-nonsense technological culture that had fired the imagination of a generation of artists and architects in the 1920s, many of whom had come together at the Bauhaus with its curriculum devoted to addressing the relationship of machine culture to daily life and to architectural form. Breuer and Bayer would also enlist the Bauhaus émigrés who had proceeded them to America: Albers and Schawinsky at Black Mountain College, and Gropius at Harvard's Graduate School of Design, where Breuer was himself going to take up a teaching appointment.

The decade since Breuer had left the Bauhaus in 1928 had been spent in fitful and generally abortive new starts. He launched an architectural practice in Berlin; after the stock market crash, nearly two years of wanderlust took him to Paris, Spain and Morocco; then, after Hitler's accession to power convinced him, as a non-religious Hungarian Jew, that he had to close his fledgling office in Berlin, he embarked on years of exile in which he sought work almost simultaneously in his native Budapest, in Switzerland and in England. During these peregrinations, Breuer formed two intense friendships that remained as fixed poles in his centreless world; the names of these men, mentors in a sense, figured prominently in the World's Fair project. They, in turn, would embark for America within a year of Breuer, and play important, if as yet unscripted, roles in promoting and interpreting his efforts to forge a modern architecture in the New World: Alexander Dorner and, more importantly, Sigfried Giedion.

"The World's Fair ... seems to us the perfect occasion to put on display before the American people the world of this new man. The metropolis of New York, a symbol of modernity, is especially suited for this display. We ask the new world to give us the opportunity to familiarize the American people ... with our efforts and achievements." In the end, this bid was answered with something far more modest and compromised, even fraught. Breuer's and Gropius's contribution to the New York World's Fair represents something of both the struggle and the transformation of their joint encounter with the reality of America rather than the European fantasy of "Americanismus". Two years after Breuer's arrival, he wondered in a letter if he should even bother to attend the inauguration of the display he had helped to design for the Pennsylvania pavilion in the Court of States on the fair grounds in Flushing Meadows. Far from having the liberty to give didactic form to their own images of new worlds, Breuer and Gropius had accepted an assigned theme, one that was historical rather than projective. They were to give architectural and spatial form to a didactic display of Pennsylvania's leading role in the establishment of American Democracy"; the display, moreover, was to be incorporated in another architect's work, a full-scale replica of Philadelphia's Independence Hall. Inside that cliché image of the American colonial past, the young Hungarian architect who had rushed in early August 1937 to photograph the Rockefeller Center as the embodiment of the American spirit in the twentieth century found himself, just a year later, crafting a startling display made of columns of steel, a suspended aluminium bridge and massive rustic walls of anthracite coal. The display tactic was adapted from one perfected by Lily Reich and Mies van der Rohe a few years earlier in Berlin, in which the subjects and support of the display were literally merged.[4] Breuer had worked side

4 Wallis Miller, "Mies and Exhibitions", in Terence Riley and Barry Bergdoll, eds., Mies in Berlin (New York: The Museum of Modern Art, 2001), pp. 338–49; "Mies van der Rohe und die Austellungen", Mies in Berlin, Ludwig Mies van der Rohe, Die Berliner Jahre 1907–1938 (Munich: Prestel Verlag, 2001), pp. 338–49.

by side with Mies and Reich at the Berlin Building Exposition of 1931, and surely knew their "mining" entry in the 1934 "German People – German Work" exhibition in Berlin, in which the displays were played off against great freestanding coal walls. But even as Gropius's and Breuer's great wall of anthracite (the very stuff of Pennsylvania) embodied Breuer's new-found interest in almost primitively rugged textures and tones within a broader material palette for modernism, the notion of collage was not emerging in his practice in the 1930s. That was more clearly evoked in the names of prominent surrealists and figures from psychology that figure on his wish list of intellectual collaborators for the failed exhibition on "the man of the future", an attraction to the surreal and the irrational as a counterpoint to the rationalism of the late 1920s that was clearly emerging in Breuer's work and friendships. A different, much more difficult, kind of disjuncture was coming to the fore, one that was hardly expected and that would require a subtle negotiation between Breuer's ideas of the vernacular and the American audience's concept of vernacularism, embodied in the perennial appeal of the American colonial revival in the twentieth century as well as in the strong regionalist tastes and discourses already at play in American culture in the 1930s.

"The USA generally attracts me," Breuer wrote in a declaration of independence to his short-lived English business partner F. R. S. Yorke, a month after his arrival in Boston, "I am sorry I could not fill this letter with only a good description of the beautiful bathing here, the Colonial style and the skyscrapers." Skyscrapers, along with factory buildings, had been the leitmotif, the veritable dream objects, of the European architectural avant-garde for over a generation; this sudden discovery of America's colonial past seems altogether new, even oddly patriotic, for this exile now thrice removed from his homeland. But the ground had been well prepared. Ise and Walter Gropius had written to their former protégé in London in April 1937 of the appeals of the New World: "It's really first-rate here! I know I'm betraying the English but we are both divinely happy here far from the land of clouds in a countryside of sun and a Roman blue sky. All around there is an unspoiled, untamed landscape, which has rarely been degraded by being transformed into an English "park landscape" and in which one doesn't always feel like a trespasser. And all around us fine, white-painted wooden houses in the colonial style which will enchant you as much as they have me. They are in simplicity, in functionality and unity entirely in keeping with our line of thinking, and the unassuming demeanor of these houses mirrors the incredible hospitality of this country, which probably comes directly from the time of the pioneers; even the spirit of the Indians is still around. The larger towns here were all founded in the beginning of the seventeenth century (Mayflower); all my childhood memories of stories of Indians ... have sprung to life again in me and I am seriously studying American history to get to know better the roots of this remarkable country."[5]

5 Letter from Ise Gropius (Gropius Papers, Harvard).

What is striking is not only the obvious sense in which Gropius looked at America through the exotic myths of his own childhood – which included stories of the Wild West, the wilderness, pioneers and, of course, cowboys, particularly derived from Karl May's popular children's books[6] – but the extent to which his argument is a transposition of an established discourse about the vernacular past in Germany which had been prevalent in his early years around 1910 as an architect in Berlin. In Behrens's office and in the vibrant discussions of the German Werkbund, for which Gropius penned his famous article extolling the Sachlichkeit of American factories and grain silos in 1913, Gropius imbibed and extended the calls of the Wilhelmine reform culture debates. Exemplified by the writings of Hermann Muthesius and Paul Mebes, notably his popular *Um 1800*, reform "Sachlichkeit" looked back to, as it was phrased in Mebes's subtitle, "Architecture and handicraft in the last century of its natural development", with the aim of setting in motion a new organic development of authentic culture within the realities of modern industrial society. To break through the disruption caused by the proliferation of imagery made possible by industry's new capacity to reproduce every detail, architecture and design must return to the unpretentious and direct expression of pre-1800 culture and instil this into the products of industrial modernity. The aim was to reconcile autochthonous culture with the new universalising forces of industrial production. Throughout, the search was for a higher unity through the reduction of seeming oppositions to analogies.

6 See Jean-Louis Cohen, "German Desires of America: Mies's Urban Visions", in Terence Riley and Barry Bergdoll, eds., Mies in Berlin (New York, 2001), p. 371; "Deutsche Erwartungen an Amerika: Mies van der Rohes Stadtvisionen", Mies in Berlin, Ludwig Mies van der Rohe, Die Berliner Jahre 1907–1938 (Munich, 2001), p. 371.

BARRY BERGDOLL

▸ Montage with designs by Breuer, published with the title "a bauhaus film, five years long" in the journal Bauhaus, vol. 1, 1926. Breuer commented on the development of his chairs between 1921 and 1925 as follows: "Things get better and better each year. In the end, you will be sitting on an elastic column of air."

Positions polarised in the 1920s between the industrial aesthetic of Gropius's Bauhaus – where Breuer himself made his rapid transition from craft to industrial serial objects, exemplified by a famous contrast of chairs that he prepared for a Bauhaus film in the late 1920s – and a more conservative, nostalgic interpretation of the return to the spirit of authenticity c. 1800. But by the 1930s, many of the major figures of the modern movement, in parallel with the worldwide economic crisis, began to seek a richer palette for modernism that might incorporate, rather than sublimate, a relationship with the rustic vernacular – indeed, with the notion that culture was a complex dialectic of tradition and innovation.[7] In the late 1920s, in his private notebooks, Mies had begun to record his doubts about technology as a driving force in culture. Le Corbusier had taken a position against the so-called Neue Sachlichkeit in the controversy over the Mundaneum in 1929, and by 1934 Breuer, younger by a generation and thus the first to be trained entirely after the First World War, was carving out a comparable intellectual position for his future work. Breuer was, in short, receptive to Gropius's enthusiasm for American colonial architecture as the New World's equivalent of "architecture and handicraft in the last century of its natural development".

7 Francesco Passanti, "The Vernacular, Modernism and Le Corbusier", Journal of the Society of Architectural Historians 56 (December 1997), pp. 438–51.

▸ Marcel Breuer and Alfred and Emil Roth, Doldertal
Houses, Zurich, Switzerland, 1932–36, view from the
south-east.

In 1934 Breuer made his mark for the first – and, arguably, the only – time in his life, through words as much as through design work. Under Giedion's sponsorship, he was working on designs for Zurich – the Doldertal apartments and the interiors of the shop Wohnbedarf, which were both completed by 1936. While they were under construction, Breuer gave a keynote speech to the Swiss Werkbund, entitled simply "Wo Stehen Wir?" (Where do we stand?), in which he launched a critique on an exclusive attachment to machine analogies and imagery for shaping an architecture attuned to the latest evolution of daily realities. After sketching the demands of the modern age in a period of diminished resources he turned to the issue of the vernacular: "At this point I should like to consider traditionalism for a moment... That the type of men who are described as modern architects have the sincerest admiration and love for genuine national art, for old peasant houses as for the masterpieces of the great epochs in art, is a point which needs to be stressed. On journeys what interests us most is to find districts where the daily activity of the population has remained untouched. Nothing is such a relief as to discover a creative craftsmanship which has been developed immemorially from father to son, and is free of the pretentious pomp and empty vanity of the architecture of the last century. Here is something from which we can learn, though not with a view to imitation. For us the attempt to build in a national tradition or an old-world style would be inadequate and insincere...

One can roundly damn the whole of our age; one can commiserate with, or dissociate oneself from, or hope to transform the men and women who have lost their mental equilibrium in the vortex of modern life, but I do not believe that to decorate homes with traditional gables and dormers helps them in the least. On the contrary, this only widens the

gulf between appearance and reality and removes them still further from that ideal equilibrium which is, or should be, the ultimate object of all thought and action."[8]

8 "Wo stehen Wir?" Marcel Breuer. 1921–1962, preface and legends by Cranston Jones, 1962, p. 260

He concluded his introductory remarks with a poignant call for a modern architecture that could rival the anonymous production of a region's vernacular without any literal imitation, and by new means based on the deliberate cultivation of contrasts and disjunction: "It may, perhaps, seem paradoxical to establish a parallel between certain aspects of vernacular architecture, or national art, and the Modern Movement. All the same, it is interesting to see that these two diametrically opposed tendencies have two characteristics in common: the impersonal character of their forms and a tendency to develop along typical rational lines that are unaffected by passing fashions." This phrase not only links Breuer's European work of the 1930s with his first American projects, but also makes a real link between the two critics who were to come to his aid as he adapted this intellectual position to make it rough and ready for the New World. These were Sigfried Giedion, the Swiss historian and propagandist for the modern movement, who vetted Breuer's text in Zurich and whose theories of the role of the anonymous in construction as well as the resolution of opposites is strongly echoed here, and the American Henry-Russell Hitchcock who selected this very passage as the headnote to a mimeographed text, "Marcel Breuer and the American Tradition", which he wrote for the exhibition of Breuer's work staged at the Harvard Architecture School during graduation in June 1938 following Breuer's first year of teaching in Cambridge.

Breuer had spent the years 1931–32 motoring in a Ford through Spain and Morocco looking at what he called "peasant architecture". Even though he sent Swiss and later English friends in these years to visit the rural landscapes of his native Hungary and to patronise his sister's shop of Hungarian folk and peasant art in Budapest's Vormarsty Square,[9] Breuer apprehended these "peasant arts" through a well established modernist discourse on the vernacular. This can be traced back at least to Josef Hoffman's articles of 1897 on the white-stuccoed cubic architecture of Capri, and the claim that all peasant arts are already Secessionist because of their innocence of academic culture.[10] It can be traced through the reform movements in German architecture, which celebrated the authentic national architecture of c. 1800 and are the direct background for Le Corbusier's discovery of the Balkans and Turkey in his trip to the Near East of 1911. Breuer was trained entirely in the spirit of the Bauhaus, which in essence he discovered during his elected exile from the culture of national romanticism that still dominated architectural discourse in Budapest around 1920. Politically conservative and artistically nostalgic, it still adhered to the folksy architecture of the charismatic Hungarian designer and teacher Karóly Kós and his circle whose influential sketching expeditions in Transylvania had taken place in the opening decades of the century.[11] Breuer had left all this for the modern; his "conversion" to the vernacular seems rather to have been catalysed by Le Corbusier, perhaps as early as the late 1920s, if the story he later told Peter Blake can be believed. According to Blake, when Breuer called on Le Corbusier in Paris in the late 1920s and explained that he had come from Pécs in southern Hungary, "Le Corbusier at once began to describe peasant buildings in that area as he recalled them from his travels, and picked up a pencil to illustrate his points as he went

9 Randall Evans, Breuer's and F. R. S. Yorke's draughtsman, recounted a trip from Salzburg to Budapest in August and September 1937: "In the morning we went to the Vörosmarty tér, where Breuer's sister has a shop specializing in Peasant work (that's where I got bags and cushion). She is a charming woman, speaks English pretty well ..." (Randall Evans diary pages, preserved at Breuer's and Yorke's house, Angmering, Sussex).

10 Josef Hoffmann, "Architektonisches von der Insel Capri", Der Architekt 3 (1897), p. 13. Transcribed in Eduard Sekler, Josef Hoffmann: The Architectural Work (Princeton: Princeton University Press, 1985), p. 479; Josef Hoffmann, das Architektonische Werk: Monographie und Werkverzeichnis, 1982.

11 On Karóly Kós (1883–1977), see Dora Wiebenson and József Sisa, eds., The Architecture of Historic Hungary (Cambridge,

▼ Farmhouses in the Central Balkans, illustration
from Peter Blake's book Marcel Breuer. Architect
and Designer (New York, 1949).

along."[12] A few years later, en route to bask in the sun and vernacularism of Spain and Morocco when commissions for apartment renovations had dried up in Berlin, Breuer stopped to see Le Corbusier's newly completed house for Hélène de Mandrot near Toulon on the French Mediterranean coast. The powerful collaging there of cleanly planed and lightweight walls of purist facture, opened up with huge panes of glass to the surrounding countryside, with load-bearing walls of rubble masonry left visible, as in local farm buildings, announced a new departure in Le Corbusier's work. Here, Le Corbusier extended his notion of a modern industrial vernacular to incorporate its rustic complement, a vernacular at once primeval and contemporary. "Ever since I saw Le Corbusier's Mandrot House," Breuer wrote to Ise Gropius, "my confidence has been unsettled ..." He admitted, however, that there were still problems to resolve: "the house leaks from every side, not only from above, but from the walls ... and the window panes are popping out. Poor Mandrot is in a state."[13] At this point Breuer found the villages of Spain, in which he lingered for much of the winter, and the landscapes of Morocco more satisfying.

Mass.: MIT Press, 1998), especially pp. 236–37.

12 Peter Blake, Marcel Breuer: Architect and Designer (New York: Architectural Record and the Museum of Modern Art, 1949), p. 7.

13 Letter from Breuer, November 1931 (Gropius Papers, Harvard).

Breuer's 1934 Zurich speech makes no reference to a specific country or national tradition. It was, in essence, a discourse prepared to travel, even if, as the frustration of exile grew, Breuer wondered if progress would ever be resumed. When the text appeared in English in the London *Architectural Review,* Breuer vented his frustrations privately to Gropius: "I received the *Architectural Review* with my article. In my current mood I would have called it "where do we remain standing?" or "what are you speaking about?" or "in which direction do you stand?" or "why do you speak standing?" or "Architecture, a groundless beauty", or "The Bride stood the entire night", or "build and scream, a new unity?" ... now my article has appeared in Hungarian, Italian *(Casa Bella)* and English, only not in German."[14]

In England, Breuer's architecture took a new turn. In an exhibition pavilion built to showcase the furniture designs of Crofton Gane's home furnishings company in Bristol, Breuer incorporated the stone of Cotswold farmhouses and country walls into a new framework for architecture. In 1937, on a skiing holiday in the Austrian Tyrol, he had a discussion with a ski instructor turned developer, Hans Falkner. As a consequence, he began work on a design for a hotel in which the alpine vernacular would become a modernist collage of bearing walls and light spanning trusses, a collage of materials and construction methods that had the potential to expand the vocabulary of modernism and also meet on its own territory the local conservative Heimatschutz, or heritage protection movement, which had emerged from the pre-war discourse on the native vernacular. Back in London, Breuer wrote to his client: "I haven't yet been able to do the perspective drawing; I will send this along later in case you should have any problems (Heimatschutz), which I can hardly imagine since in fact the building is much closer to the character of the landscape and the old farm

14 Letter from Breuer, April 1935 (Gropius Papers, Harvard).

◂ Le Corbusier and Pierre Jeanneret, Madame de
Mandrot's villa, Le Pradet, France, 1931.

▾ Marcel Breuer and F.R.S. Yorke, Gane's Pavilion,
Bristol, England, 1936, view from the south-west.

houses than, for instance, the Hotel Hochfirst or Jennewein [two recently build hotels in town]."[15] But in February 1938, with the Anschluss imminent, Falkner spent five days in jail for anti-German propaganda; on his release he emigrated to Quebec to start a new life. His project briefly reappeared there, it seems: in a letter of early 1941 to Edgar Kaufmann, Jr., Breuer tried to interest the son of the Pittsburgh department store magnate, who was by then selling Breuer's furniture in the store, to invest in a ski hotel in Canada, enclosing a photograph of the model left behind in Europe. "You will perhaps be interested in the consequent use of supporting stone walls and non-supporting window walls," Breuer suggested, to the proud owner of Frank Lloyd Wright's recently completed Fallingwater![16]

15 "Die Perspektive
habe ich noch nicht
machen können, ich
werde diese nach-
schicken, falls Du
tatsächlich Schwierig-
keiten (Heimatschutz)
haben solltest, was ich
mir kaum vorstellen
kann, da doch das Haus
tatsächlich dem Charakter
der Landschaft und
den alten Bauernhäuser
näher liegt, wie z.B.
Hotel Hochfirst oder
Jennewein." Letter from
Breuer to Hans Falkner,
29 October 1937
(Breuer Papers, Syracuse
University Library, Box
5, file 32).

16 Letter from Breuer
to Edgar Kaufmann,
31 January 1941
(Breuer Papers, Syracuse
University Library,
Box 6, file 2).

▾ Winter sports hotel, Obergurgl (unrealised),
  Tyrol, Austria, 1937, model.
▸ Winter sports hotel, Obergurgl, model.

Contemplating his new life from the Massachusetts shoreline in 1937, Breuer's task was now to translate "Where do we stand?" into American English. Henry-Russell Hitchcock was ready with an encouraging answer, proclaiming the arrival of a new architectural messiah for the most pressing problem facing American architecture: "the initiation of modern architecture demanded the work of extremists of both types; the relentless intellectual analysis of Gropius is as much, if not more, at the core of our ideas of modern architecture as the less verbally explicable creative synthesis of Le Corbusier. But the continuance of modern architecture, above all its healthy development in America, demands rather the appearance of the mixed types, of which Breuer may stand as an admirable example."[17] Hitchcock cited the Ganes Pavilion and the Ski Hotel as the first steps in that direction: "At the moment of the German conquest of Austria last spring a small mountain hotel ... was about to be built ... the project shows how Breuer, working from the special facilities of modern civilization, was ready to use rough stonework and timber construction with the ease and simplicity of a rural American carpenter-builder, and yet with all the technical imagination and aesthetic purity of the modern."[18]

17 Henry-Russell Hitchcock, "Marcel Breuer and the American Tradition in Architecture" unpublished typescript, 1938 (Harvard University Archives), p. 17.

18 Ibid, p. 16.

276

Hitchcock needed Breuer for his evolving stance as an engaged historian, as much as Breuer would be served by this powerful shaper of American taste. It is too often forgotten that a year after the 1932 show of modern architecture at the Museum of Modern Art, which was much criticised for slighting American architects, Hitchcock and Johnson staged an exhibition of Chicago commercial architecture of 1870 to 1920, the first in a series of projects in which Hitchcock set out to craft a genealogy for the native modernism of the present and future; now that Europe seemed under a dark political cloud, he was eager to show that modernism no longer needed to be imported but was in fact well rooted in native soil. By the mid-1930s, Hitchcock's role as a critical historian of modernism's American roots had taken on a regional focus, with exhibitions in Springfield and Worcester, Massachusetts, while he continued to track the movements of the European architects he admired as they went into emigration. In an exhibition at the Museum of Modern Art in 1937, he heralded "the sudden appearance of England" on the radar screen of modernism since the 1932 show in which England had virtually nothing to show. The chief progress made was in a whole new attitude to materials. Whereas steel and concrete still remained in conflict, as they did in America, the chief difference was that "light wooden construction, the chief traditional method in America, appears in England rather as an innovation ... and is unhampered by the association with traditional forms which makes it a brake upon modern development in America."[19] Continuing the comparison, he noted England's great advance on America and regretted that America has not yet had "the honor of harboring foreign refugees as important historically as Gropius and Mendelsohn, or as promising as Breuer."[20]

19 Henry-Russell Hitchcock, Modern Architecture in England (New York: The Museum of Modern Art, 1937), pp. 33–34.

20 Ibid, p. 39.

In mid-June 1938, Hitchcock sent Breuer the final draft of his text "Marcel Breuer and the American Tradition" for review. Breuer had only two amendments to make: one a turn of phrase he feared might give offence to Gropius, the other a desire to clarify his position on the vernacular: "on page three where you speak of my relation to some peasant architectures … I think one should not have the possibility of understanding this part of your article in the way that I am trying to find some exit out of the modern architecture by using a traditional one. You might express that by using traditional materials, together with new ones, transforming the spirit of tradition into a contemporary one, it guides to new forms and is a further development but not a reduction of the modern movement."[21] In the final version, Hitchcock incorporated Breuer's text, rendered of course in mellifluous English, and he returned it to Breuer with an invitation to Wesleyan for graduation weekend in which Frank Lloyd Wright was to receive an honorary degree, holding out the extra bonus of a visit to Fishers Island to see the Neutra house, just nearing completion.[22]

21 Letter from Breuer to Henry-Russell Hitchock, June 1938 (Breuer Papers, Syracuse University Library, Box 5, file 23).

22 As shown in recent research by Thomas Michie for a travelling exhibition on Neutra's Windschield House, Neutra had encouraged the Browns to consider ordering Breuer's Isokon line of laminated plywood furniture. In autumn 1939, Breuer had to disappoint another supporter, Alexander Dorner, by this time Director of the Rhode Island School of Design Museum in Providence, N.J.; he was unable to acquire from Germany a tubular steel desk or any other pieces for the collection of modernist furniture being formed there. See Dietrich Neumann, ed., Richard Neutra's Windschield House (Cambridge, Mass., 2001).

Breuer, Hitchcock noted, like European émigrés and visitors from Neutra to Mies, did not suffer from Le Corbusier's syndrome of "eyes which do not see": "With X-ray eyes foreign architects have seen through the stylisms of surface of American wooden and other small-scale construction as easily as from the first they saw through to the skeleton of our skyscrapers and factories. Since the particular ways of using such materials as wood or brick or metal to which we are habituated as 'traditional' were new to them, they have seen them, quite divorced from particular stylistic expression, as belonging among the raw ingredients with which a valid contemporary architecture could and should work as freely as with the new materials and methods with which modern architecture has been in America perhaps too exclusively associated."[23]

Gropius's house in Lincoln, in the design of which Breuer played a considerable role, was celebrated as a fulfilment of that programme, first privately by Lewis Mumford, who wrote in the guest book, "Hail to the most indigenous, the most regional example of the New England home, the New England of a New World,"[24] and then publicly in the photograph captions of the popular compilation *The Modern House in America* (1940) by Katherine Morrow Ford and James Ford. The Fords were among Gropius's and Breuer's earliest clients and neighbours; theirs was the third of three houses the two men designed in the Wood's End Lane compound on Mrs James Storrow's estate in Lincoln; they furnished it with their own traditional furniture almost in deliberate counterpoint to Gropius's collection of Breuer designs. Of Gropius's house they noted: "Design deliberately tries to fit into the order of white colonial houses in the vicinity without imitating them. The main type of construction, the exterior sheathing and the white paint indicate some of these connections."[25] Beneath the

23 Henry-Russell Hitchcock, "Marcel Breuer and the American Tradition in Architecture", 1938, op. cit., p. 2.

24 Cited by Reginald Isaacs, Gropius, An Illustrated Biography of the Creator of the Bauhaus (Boston: Little, Brown, and Company, 1991), p. 236;

25 Katherine Morrow Ford and James Ford, The Modern House in America (1940), p. 41.

▾ Marcel Breuer and Walter Gropius, Gropius House,
Lincoln, Massachusetts, 1937–38, view from the
north-west.
▾▾ Gropius House, view from north-west.
▸ Gropius House, view into the living room.

◄ Gropius House, view from the north-west.
▼ Gropius House, view from south.
▼▼ Gropius House, view from the drive (east).

wood cladding, however, the structure was much more complex than this polemical assimilation of the building with popular colonial revivalism would suggest. Nearly every detail was used in a novel way: the clapboards were laid vertically and flush, to express clearly their role as cladding over an interior frame and to maintain a geometric purity that might be cut into and penetrated to create a subtle composition of complementary volumes, interweaving spaces for outdoor living that extend into the landscape with those that penetrate the box. Gropius and Breuer had no compunction about creating a true collage of steel and wooden members throughout. The ad hoc nature of the framing, as noted in a perceptive analysis by Edward Ford, seems in the tradition of the Yankee solve-it-on-the-spot mentality, rather than the quest for a universal factory idiom that had predominated in the Dessau years.[26] In contrast, the use throughout the house of out-of-the-catalogue modern fixtures was part of a deliberate collation of what was rendered anonymous common heritage through a long American building tradition and what had achieved the same status through the speeded-up time-frame of industrial production.

26 Edward Ford, The Details of Modern Architecture (Cambridge, Mass.: MIT Press, 1990), p. 289.

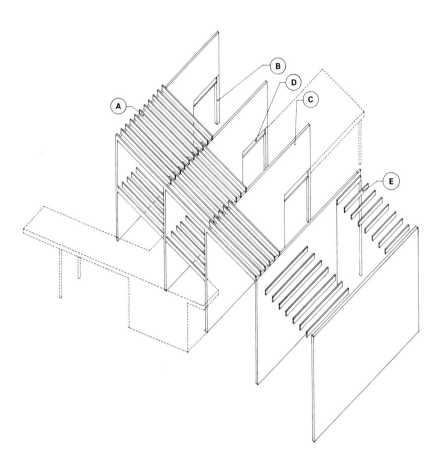

Whereas, for the most part, Gropius preferred to sublimate this collage, obscuring the differences between load-bearing brick walls and thin wooden cladding over fir or spruce wall and roof joists, and working largely within the geometric purity of the New England high style house, Breuer created a composition that celebrated the hybrid nature of this new Americanised modernism or modernised Americanism, and accepted the almost ad hoc way in which American houses were added to over time. In his house for a bachelor, he pulled functions apart: a great two-storey living room is dominated by a curved stone wall with a fireplace; in a double-height section, sleeping quarters are superimposed over a dining room, and both are visible from the living room. Of the three exterior walls of the living room, each is completely different in structural nature: one is made of local field stone, one of traditional wood frame construction, and the one facing the private landscape behind is composed of enormous planes of glass set back behind two thin but rustic wooden columns that carry the roof – almost as if the timber of the pioneering first settlers was being placed at the service of modernist invention.

◀ Marcel Breuer and Walter Gropius, Breuer House I, Lincoln, Massachusetts, 1938–39, view from the south.
▶ Marcel Breuer and Walter Gropius, Fischer House I, Wrightsville, Pennsylvania, 1938–39, view from the south-east.

Externally, Breuer's house was finished with redwood vertical siding, painted white in counterpoint to the stone wall and to the great open cage of brass mesh. In 1939, when Breuer put out bids for an addition to the house, he hoped to treat the new framed extension in red cedar laid vertically and treated only with oil sealant, but this proved beyond his budget and the addition in the end conformed with the white palette of the wood throughout.[27] The house, in short, seems to be the absolute embodiment of a passage in Breuer's 1934 Zurich speech: "We reject the traditional conception of 'style', first, because it gainsays sincere and appropriate design; and second, because the link between quite justifiable differences in appearance produces the sort of contrast we consider is characteristic of modern life. Contrasts such as house and garden, a man's working and home life, voids and solids, shining metal and soft materials, or even living organisms such as animals and plants can all be realised against the stark plain surface of a wall; also in the opposition of the discipline of standardisation to the freedom of experiment that leads to its development. Such contrasts have become a necessity of life. They are the guarantees of the reality of the basis we have chosen to adopt."[28]

Breuer's studies in contrasts brought the optical and material experiments of Bauhaus composition – redolent with the lessons of the "Vorkurs" of Johannes Itten he had enjoyed twenty years earlier – into the new palette of American architecture. His own house design evolved in dialogue with a house for two old friends from Bauhaus days, the sculptor Margit Fischer and her husband Edward Lee Fischer, an advertising man. Breuer enjoyed frequent visits to these friends who had arrived in New York shortly before he did, consulted with them on his plans for the World's Fair Project, and offered advice on their quest for a site to

27 Breuer Papers, Syracuse University Library, EXACT LOCATION?

28 "Wo Stehen Wir?" Marcel Breuer. 1921–1962, preface and legends by Cranston Jones, 1962, p. 262

build a house and studio near the artists' colony of New Hope, Pennsylvania. Over the winter of 1938–39 the Fischers followed Breuer's design of his own house in Lincoln with passionate interest, their reactions to its visual collage helping them to imagine some of the three-dimensional effects that could be achieved on the high wooded site they had purchased in Wrightsville, outside New Hope. While the Fischers toyed with the idea of a solid ground floor built of local stone from which a wood-framed second storey might emerge, Breuer was eager to develop his new interest in counterpoint: with stone walls projecting beyond and above an enclosed white-painted wooden skin; with lightweight elements cantilevered to create a tight and dynamic interweaving of light and heavy; with interior enclosure and exterior terraces, and with texture. Breuer rejected a local quarry that might have supplied a smoother, darker stone in favour of a fieldstone that recalled both the New England walls and the Pennsylvania barns he had admired on outings with the Fischers. The Fischers asked him to consider the newly published designs for Frank Lloyd Wright's Jacobs House, but apart from a shared instinct to curve the great stone fireplace wall, Breuer seems not to have responded to the new geometries emerging in Wright's explorations of masonry primitivism. The Fischers themselves built models from Breuer's sketches to study the collage effects of materials and forms, but after they visited Breuer's completed house shortly after New Year in 1939, they agreed to give their friend a freer hand: "Now that I've seen your house, I am even more convinced that you are, along with Le Corbusier, perhaps the only one who can overcome the machine-for-living syndrome and who is capable of expressing the spiritualness of the form, the new form. What you have sought to bring forth is spirirt and art and thus terribly important in and of itself ..."[29]

29 "Nachdem ich nun Dein Haus gesehen habe, bin ich noch mehr der Ueberzeugung, dass Du neben Corbusier vielleicht der Einzige bist, der das Wohnmaschinenhafte ueberwunden hat und faehig ist die Geistigkeit der Form, der neunen Form, auszudruecken. Es ist Geist und ist Kunst was Du hinzustellen versuchst und deshalb ist es so wichtig an und fuer sich ..." Margit Fischer to Breuer, January 1939 (Breuer Papers, Syracuse University Library, Box 16).

Breuer rarely theorised during his years of teaching and building in Cambridge; by this time, his creative reinterpretation of American tradition had found a new spokesman and historian in Sigfried Giedion whom Gropius had successfully suggested as the next Charles Eliot Norton Lecturer at Harvard. His lectures, published in 1941 as *Space, Time and Architecture: The Growth of a New Tradition,* included a lengthy exposition of the history of American architecture told in relationship to the growth of indigenous structural techniques perfected over time rather than, as more frequently in accounts of American architecture, as a narrative of restless stylistic change in a hopeless race to catch up with European taste. Giedion began with an observation that might have pleased any members of old New England society in the Harvard audience when he claimed: "The colonial and republican periods were of great importance to American development; they provided a solid foundation for future advance." But he quickly turned to a celebration of the American balloon frame of the Conastoga wagon used in the conquest of the West, which he saw as equally important: "Its invention practically converted building in wood from a complicated craft, practiced by skilled labor, into an industry."[30] Although he celebrated the balloon frame primarily as a veritable anonymous product which almost had the status that a Thonet chair had for Adolf Loos or Le Corbusier (in fact he compared it, in its lightness and elegance, with an American Windsor chair), Giedion devoted a great deal of energy to tracking down the biography and even the descendants of the balloon frame's inventor, George W. Snow, whom he proudly declared to be a New Englander born in New Hampshire in 1797 of a family who came over on the *Mayflower*. "George Snow's name is nearly unknown. There is no portrait of him in any of the local histories, but one has

30 Sigfried Giedion, Space, Time and Architecture: The Growth of a New Tradition (Cambridge, Mass.: MIT Press, 1941), p. 233.

obtained from a family album a portrait which reveals a face at once full of Puritan energy and of human sensibility."[31]

31 Ibid, p. 236.
32 Ibid, p. 239.

      Breuer's house was still under construction when these lectures were given, although a later observer cannot help but feel the dialogue when, on the same page, Giedion celebrates the two principle materials of Breuer's American palette, noting that "the wooden wall has been governed by eighteenth-century American traditions ... Clapboards had been used in England, but only for unpretentious farmhouses. In America they dominated the whole field of wooden building ... from the rudest hut to the finest mansions, churches, and town halls. Their use automatically tends toward balanced and simple treatments of the wall ... and they discourage the use of applied ornament." And a few lines later he notes: "Stone walls were treated with the same simplicity in stones where stone was used as a building material. Excellent workmanship was displayed in New England states ... in the houses of the Shakers ... and in the granite warehouses along the Boston wharves and in the commercial buildings of Boston of the fifties and sixties. These ... display typical plain surfaces and economy of detail."[32] During the summer of 1938 Giedion conducted a Harvard seminar to research Boston office buildings between 1830 and 1860. By the time Breuer was contemplating how to expand his house, Giedion had supplied the seeds of a new thinking about domestic planning. This was to become, after 1945, one of the principle preoccupations of Breuer's influential housedesigns: an informal opening to the exterior, combined with asymmetrical binuclear planning. This, too, was an innovation based in tradition. "The American practice of adding new units to the original one can be seen in those New England houses which survive from the seventeenth century," Giedion explained, while projecting slides of the

Hancock House in Lexington, the Jackson House in Portsmouth, N.H., and the Whipple House in Ipswich. "The flexible and informal ground plan which was, on the whole, standard in America, grew up without any names attached to it. Like tools and patent furniture, it remained strictly anonymous. It is the outgrowth both of the urge for comfort in the dwelling and the American tendency to tackle problems directly."[33] In contrast to the imagery of the Colonial revival of the 1920s and 1930s, Giedion sought out earlier, more primordial examples of American indigenous architecture, preferring the truly vernacular to the high style of New England's towns which served as the model for so many suburban houses of the period.

33 Ibid, p. 244.

▾ Richard Neutra, Windshield House, Fisher's Island,
New York, 1936–38.
▸ Marcel Breuer and Walter Gropius, Hagerty House,
Cohasset, Massachusetts, 1937–38, view from the
south-west.

In the first edition of *Space, Time and Architecture,* praise was largely directed at 34 Ibid, p. 236. Richard Neutra (in later editions Gropius's house was also brought in): "The simple and efficient construction is thoroughly adapted to the requirements of contemporary architects. Many of Richard Neutra's houses in Texas and Southern California reveal the elegance and lightness which are innate qualities of the balloon-frame skeleton."[34] Discreetly, he did not mention Neutra's largest commission, John Nicholas Brown's weekend house Windschield, which had blown down in the great hurricane of summer 1938 just before the autumn term began at Harvard. That hurricane, it might be noted, skirted just far enough away from the Massachusetts coast to spare Breuer's and Gropius's Hagerty House, which was still under construction on the shoreline at Cohasset. There, the collage of load-bearing stone walls and light, modernised balloon frame construction made of a mixture of wooden and steel elements, was as much to maximize the open planning of the great interior which commands a panoramic view of the sea as to lift the house up on steel columns to allow a visual connection from road to beach and to let high storm tides pass under the house. The unpretentious lally column, those utilitarian steel pipes so often used – but so rarely exposed – to solve the problem of opening up the wood frame house, for instance to the arrival of the car, was here celebrated as a fragment of American pragmatic construction readily available on the market, a kind of ready-made.

The reception of this house is indicative of the way that the American discourse on modernism and Breuer's and Gropius's definition of a house style evolved in tandem. Hitchcock contrasted the Hagerty House with its immediate neighbours on its tight ocean-front lot, which were Mediterranean and English Tudor in style: "Neither has the same close analogy to the best earlier examples of American cottage architecture in plan and in expression as the new house now in construction. For both are intentionally exotic in design," – he might as well have said foreign – "ill-adapted to the magnificent site ... whereas the Gropius-Breuer house has in its forms the 'impersonal character' and is developed along 'the typical rational lines' which are to be found on the one hand in the vernacular of the colonial farmhouse and again later in the best seaside cottage architecture of the nineteenth century."[35] More telling is the handling of the house in the April 1940 issue of *Architectural Forum*, which constructed a set of contrasts worthy of Pugin. Under the title "The House Divided", the editors juxtaposed the Hagerty House with the newly completed grand Colonial Revival Thorpe House in Sudbury by the architectural firm of Derby, Barnes & Champney: "These house are the extreme components of this trend, utterly contradictory in their basic approach: symmetry versus the free plan, and design from a preconceived exterior against design for a special living problem in a particular location. One opens to the out of doors; the other shuts itself in ...

35 Henry-Russell Hitchcock, "Marcel Breuer and the American Tradition in Atchitecture" (1938), pp. 2–3.

The question here, however, is not one of good or bad but rather of contrast: here is the composite symbol of an architecture in transition – the house divided."[36] Breuer's first independent commission in the United States came through Richard Neutra, who recommended him for a project for a second house in Palm Springs for the wealthy Margolius family of Chicago. Little noted by students of Breuer's work, with the exception of a perceptive article by Isabelle Hyman,[37] the Margolius commission raises the question of regionalism, for here Breuer not only moved from New England to the Southwest, but from a discourse framed by the Colonial to one marked by the Mission and Spanish Colonial styles, which had been gaining adherants and popularity consistently for nearly three decades.[38] Neutra had been happy to walk away from this commission; he was not interested in complying with the requirements of the subdivision of Las Palmas Estates of Palm Springs for a "modern Spanish exterior" in the spirit of the Spanish Colonial Regional style. This had gained a legal status when Santa Barbara, California, had adopted a municipal ordinance requiring it in the mid-1920s. By the 1930s more and more cities in the region were adopting such stylistic guidelines.

Breuer wrote to Margolius: "I only hope that 'Spanish exterior' isn't taken too seriously by you ... I think a one-story modern house with good relations to the garden, with a possible patio, would look quite naturally Spanish even if it were not designed in the Spanish style."[39] The planning board clearly agreed, since they approved the house in December 1938, but by then it had become clear that the client had decided to divorce his wife even before his architect.

36 "The House Divided", Architectural Forum 72 (April 1940, pp. 295–303), p. 295.

37 Isabelle Hyman, "A Marcel Breuer House Project of 1938–1939", Syracuse University Library Associates Courier, vol. 27 no. 1 (Spring 1992), pp. 55–84; see also I. Hyman, Marcel Breuer, Architect; The Career and the Buildings (New York: Harry N. Abrams, Inc., 2001), pp. 327–28.

38 David Gebhard, "The Spanish Colonial Revival in Southern California (1895–1930), Journal of the Society of Architectural Historians 26 (1967), pp. 131–47.

39 Letter from Breuer to H. Margolius, 11 August 1938 (Breuer Papers, Syracuse University Library, cited by Isabelle Hyman in "A Marcel Breuer House project", p. 58).

▾ Marcel Breuer and Walter Gropius, Chamberlain
Cottage, Wayland, Massachusetts, 1940–41, living
room with hearth.
▸ Chamberlain Cottage, view from the west.

Breuer's great breakthrough to a style at once independent of Gropius and of any literal relationship to his newly adopted New England came with a commission for a small weekend cottage for the Chamberlains at Wayland, Massachusetts, in a large rustic site on the Sudbury River deep in extraordinary meadow lands. In keeping with the notion imbued in him by his Bauhaus training and renewed by contact with Giedion, Breuer conceived of the fundamental issue as the creation of an envelope for a new kind of open space, a space at once free not only of walls but even of the ground. This idea was no doubt encouraged by the fact that the river was known to rise greatly above its normal banks. To some extent, he was continuing a lightweight aesthetic pioneered in his very first free-standing commission, the Harnischmacher House in Wiesbaden of 1932, but he realised it now not in steel frame but in the language of Yankee ingenuity, the studded ballon frame. But this was not any traditional balloon frame: keeping the balloon, Breuer revolutionised the frame. Exploiting the qualities of American plywood, which fascinated him, to create a whole new approach to structure, Breuer replaced the clad studs of the American frame with a triple ply system of tongue and groove boarding laid in different orientations so that the finished walls became stiff slabs. Thus he was able to create a great volume that could cantilever out a full eight feet without the addition of any heavy beams. Likewise, the rigidity of the wall made it possible to punch large windows without thickening the lintels for the openings. The result was at once a revolutionising of American timber construction and, as photographed by Ezra Stoller, an icon of American life in nature.

▼ Chamberlain Cottage, ground plan.
▸ Chamberlain Cottage, view of the glazed veranda.

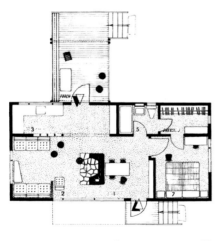

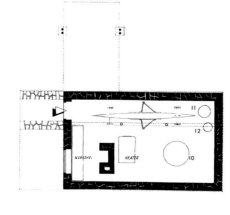

By the middle of the decade, this image had travelled even further than Breuer had. Elizabeth Mock included it not only in the "Built in USA 1932–1945" exhibition which toured the country immediately after the Second World War but, along with the Hagerty House, in the show "New Architecture in the United States", prepared for the office of War Information, which began its tour in Cairo.

▾ Yankee Portables (unrealised), 1942, presentation
drawing and building plans.
▸ Yankee Portables, ground plan and perspective.

America's entry into the war allowed Breuer to turn his attention to his commitment to pre-fabrication and the use of industry as a partner in the quest for a modern vernacular. In 1942, he perfected a system of frame construction that could not only be produced on the assembly line but was forever de-mountable and transportable, and could even be poised lightly on a single point on the ground. This flexibity was inspired by the dwellings of the American pioneers whom he, Gropius and Giedion idolised. He baptised this all-wood house the "Yankee portable". It was almost a merging of Giedion's two icons: the balloon frame and the Conestoga wagon. The name was a perfect coinage for this Americanised exile; it might even be argued that it was the first adequate translation into English of the complex concept of Sachlichkeit, with its notion of vernacular that was anything but regional. To a certain extent, it was the germ of his own experimental houses begun in 1947 in New Canaan, Connecticut, and in 1948 at Wellfleet on Cape Cod. Taking up the butterfly roof of his 1945 project for Veterans' Houses (a project that lost out to Levittown), Breuer's new American vernacular was promoted in 1949 by the Museum of Modern Art in the famous "House in the Garden". For a moment, at least, it found takers: copies abound, from Breuer's own (two near Princeton, New Jersey) to the work of Gropius's students and associates, notably within the Moon Hill Development in Belmont, Massachusetts.

◀ Edgar Stillman Cottage, plan.
▼ Edgar Stillman Cottage, Cape Cod, Wellfleet,
Massachusetts, 1953–54, side view.

▼ Cape Cod Cottages, Wellfleet, Massachusetts,
  ground plan.
▼▼ Breuer Cottage, living room, in 1970.

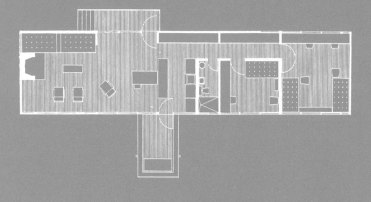

302

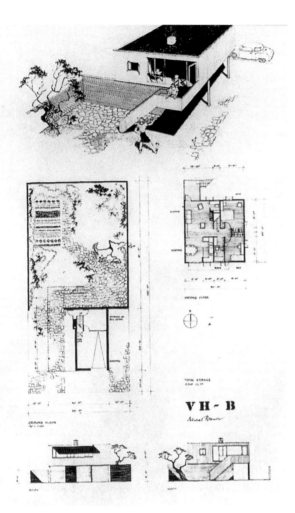

VH - B

Marcel Breuer

◄ Veteran's House B (unrealised), 1945,
design drawing.
▼ House in Pocantino near New York, originally in the
Museum of Modern Art Garden, New York.

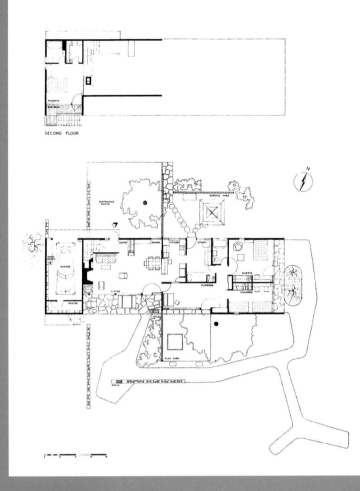

SECOND FLOOR

▾ Breuer House II, New Canaan, Connecticut, 1947–48,
view from the south-east, after construction
of a retaining wall under the projecting balcony.

By 1951, as Berlin mounted a show of new American architecture, few doubted the role the Germans had played in crafting the modern vernacular which, along with the "Pax Americana", was to become an export item. On the cover of the exhibition catalogue *Amerikanische Architektur seit 1947,* the former Bauhaus directors and masters appear near the top of the roster. By the mid -1960s, so successful were Gropius, Breuer and Mies van der Rohe in creating a new American vernacular in every landscape from the suburban house to the office that Breuer's great space truss timber house in New Canaan, draped with an American flag, along with Philip Johnson's nearby Glass House, had both made their way into the *Annual of the New Canaan Historical Society.*

That was in 1967. The culmination of a forty-year investigation of the American vernacular by these émigré Europeans, it might also be said to have marked the ultimate relegation of Breuer's work to history. One year earlier, Robert Venturi had published *Complexity and Contradiction in Architecture* – a critique of the sterility and supposed repetitiveness of modernism, which promoted, ironically enough, a re-engagement with the vernacular and with popular taste as one of many routes to a re-engagement with history and complexity. Remarkably today, as the notion of regionalism continues to sell houses of ever greater dimensions and pretensions in the ongoing subdivision of the American landscape, the nostalgia lifestyle industry in the hipper interior magazines has rediscovered modernism, and notably the houses of Marcel Breuer, even as one by one they are being felled to make room for starter mansions.

ECHOES

modern life style

Breuer's Houses

Harvey Probber's Modulars
Modernism with a French Accent
Paul Rudolph and Toshiko Mori

$5.95US $8.95CAN
www.deco-echoes.com

7 25274 84175 2   14>

WORKING WITH MARCEL BREUER

WORKING WITH MARCEL BREUER

ROBERT F. GATJE

Marcel Breuer had many collaborator-partners during his long and productive professional life, including his Bauhaus student Gustav Hassenpflug, the Swiss cousins Roth, the Londoner F. R. S. Yorke, and – most notably – his great friend and mentor, Walter Gropius. I write as one of the four young partners he took on in the late 1950s and who stayed with him until his retirement in 1976.

When looking for a new job in 1953 after my return to New York from a year of study abroad, I was thunderstruck to learn that this "god" had left Gropius behind in Cambridge, Massachusetts, and was running a small practice in my own home town. I should have felt intimidated about approaching what older and wiser hands considered *the* office to work in at that time in New York. But I was young and cocky and what did I have to lose?

Breuer, his wife Connie and son Tom were living in Paris at the time in the midst of work on UNESCO, the first big commission of his life and, he would later say, his most productive collaboration with the great Italian structural engineer Pier Luigi Nervi. Breuer had sent word to his office manager that the New York office could use more help on the second biggest commission of his life, St John's Abbey in Collegeville, Minnesota. Hamilton (Ham) Smith, with a recommendation from Eero Saarinen, had joined the staff and begun work on the project a month or so before. I presented my résumé "cold" with no recommendation from anyone. When I called back a week later, my name was remembered, an interview was scheduled, and what followed was the rest of my professional life.

I suppose I was just a bit scared by the prospect of a job interview with Marcel Breuer but he had a way of putting everyone at ease on first meeting. He asked me all about my European travels while he idly flipped through my portfolio and brought the interview to a close with a statement and a question: "I'm told that you would like to work here. *Is it?*" (This last bit of verbal punctuation, uttered in a soft Hungarian accent, was one of his favourites and was translated from either "N'est ce pas?" or "Nicht wahr?") At any rate, I hastened to assure him that he had correctly understood my intention, and I started work the next Monday morning at 113 East 37th Street.

The terraced house that served as his office was, and still is, a very ordinary white "brownstone" on a very ordinary Manhattan side street. The main floor at the head of a tall stoop had a reception area where our office manager hammered away on her typewriter and greeted visitors over the half-glasses that always dangled on a runaway ribbon across her ample frame. The front parlour was a drafting room dominated by some of the best designers of the day. They ranged from the very outspoken Belva Jane (BJ) Barnes to the soft-spoken William (Bill) Landsberg, who was called "chief draftsman" in those days. BJ had known Breuer for years and had worked in the UNESCO office in Paris. Bill was his student from Harvard who had worked for the Gropius/Breuer partnership in Cambridge and, on and off, had been in Breuer's offices ever since – sometimes as the only draftsman. Herbert (Herb) Beckhard had signed on the year before as an unpaid "volunteer" and explained: "I would have had to pay for this education at graduate school ..."

The rear parlour, overlooking a dark and dingy courtyard, was Breuer's office and conference room. We all passed by or through it many times a day since the storage corridor alongside it led to the only bathroom on the floor. His desk was a slab of granite on a swaying stainless steel base and featured a beautiful model of his Caesar Cottage and a multi-lensed piece of Plexiglas that mimicked an old invention of his. Upstairs there was more drafting space and, above that, a pied-à-terre since his home in Connecticut was being occupied by others during his family's stay in Paris. The dark wood panelling had been covered in white "pegboard" and the "ceiling" was an open gridwork of wooden beams that bracketed a staggered pattern of fluorescent light boxes. The atmosphere was that of an extended family dwelling, dominated by its friendly father figure whenever he was in residence.

There were about seven staff when I joined them and the number gradually grew as the practice expanded. People came and went: sometimes looking for a different experience or to set up their own practice; sometimes to pursue graduate studies; they were rarely fired.

The projects in the office at that time included a department store in Rotterdam, two Connecticut schools and a couple of small houses. I was put to work with Ham Smith on the master plan for St John's Abbey – the largest Benedictine abbey in the world, and a project that was to occupy Ham, on and off, for about fifteen years. Our work together was remarkable in several respects. We learned how Breuer liked to work and participated in the creation of a world-renowned architectural monument.

The Abbey had given Breuer a very detailed programme for the building areas that would be required to house its expanding activities. It was in this respect, and others, an ideal client. Breuer was an inventor and problem-solver and he liked nothing better than to see a client's programmatic needs laid out in boxes sized to scale with links to illustrate relationships. We developed and refined these diagrams for several months, sending them by special delivery air mail each Friday night to Breuer in Paris and receiving his written commentary on them within the week. A computer could have massaged these diagrams in a fraction of the time, and e-mail would have facilitated a virtual conversation at our drafting boards, but this was 1953 and I'm not sure the product didn't gain in quality from the time we "lost" in reflection.

After all the pushing and pulling, the outline of the Church, which lay at the heart of the plan for demolition and expansion, evolved from a longish rectangle to a theatrical trapezoid more suited to a central altar surrounded by monks facing the congregation. Although his commission had asked only for a master plan, Breuer was enough of a salesman to realise that giving his client a conceptual sense of its eventual appearance was the best way to gain approval of his proposals. So, while I worked on descriptive diagrams, Ham sketched up Breuer's ideas for the Church. The plan made functional sense, but anyone looking at his later work will recognise the trapezoid as a favourite shape. Isabelle Hyman, Breuer's biographer, was the first to record his admiration of "battered", or inward-leaning, walls in the work of the ancient Egyptians. (Both façades of his great parish church in Muskegon, the north façade of St John's itself and the windows of the Whitney Museum are all trapezoids!)

Spanning the space with thin folds of concrete came from his day-to-day relationship with Nervi on the UNESCO Conference Hall. Details of the great cantilevered balcony and the dark wood pews all followed his personal vocabulary of connecting straight lines with tight curves. We all learned to speak the language, and were comfortable with it. Those that didn't or couldn't weren't long in the office. Of course, Breuer loved to surprise us with quirky gestures that reminded him of the "accidents" that enrich indigenous architecture. I once blurted out: "You can't do *that!*" After a pause and a smile he assured me that he could.

The first four years in that comfortable terrace house seemed so natural at the time that it is only with fifty years of hindsight that I can recognise their unique and extraordinary quality. Here we were, a bunch of inexperienced kids – I was 26 at the time – entrusted with a share of the responsibility for an enormous undertaking, entering a relationship with a great man that we could only think of as a second father (my own had died during my first year at college.) We never joked about architecture, but we joked about everything else. Breuer encouraged the raucous informality that reminded him of his days on the Harvard faculty and he insisted upon being called by his nickname Lajkó (short for his middle name Lajos, or Louis in Hungarian). When he was in town, we always lunched together in the neighbourhood. He was a great movie buff, and told stories ranging back to his student days at the Bauhaus where Klee and Kandinsky painted, and Josef Albers taught him how to use a broom. BJ kept us up to date about all the architectural gossip in the city. Joe Neski mastered and imitated the cadence of Lajkó's indescribable accent. When Breuer and his family returned from Paris to their great stone home in New Canaan, we relaxed with the boss and some of his older friends on Sunday afternoons in the country.

In the drafting room, Breuer followed a rigid hierarchy of his own invention. He might sit at a draftsman's table unannounced, or by invitation, but always in the presence of the "job captain" whom he held responsible for the development of the project. If he felt the need to make any serious criticism of the project's progress, he would ask the job captain to step into his office; he would never embarrass him in front of his team members. Lajkó sitting at someone's table was an event that usually drew a small audience that he did not discourage. His suggestions were carefully made with a soft black pencil on a sheet of yellow tracing paper, carefully stretched over our drawing – he would not dream of marking our work directly. When he had to revise his line work he was equally fastidious in brushing the eraser crumbs out of the way. He always expected to see his proposals drawn up by the time of his next visit, and the only time I remember him angry was when someone neglected to do so. After that we were encouraged to elaborate or suggest alternatives which were frequently incorporated into the final project. He admired good drafting and considered his own hand rather clumsy. "I could never have gotten a job in this office ..."

The "language" we all spoke at that time was "modern architecture" – a cumulative mélange of what we admired in the work of Wright, Mies and le Corbusier. Breuer never acknowledged in my hearing any such influence on his own work, but Isabelle Hyman tells me that much later in retirement he spoke to an old friend about adapting the lessons learned from older purists to serve more human needs.

◄ Ham's wife Caroline Smith, with Lajkó and Rufus Stillman, one of Breuer's best friends and clients, in Breuer's garden in New Canaan, Connecticut, around 1956.

When Breuer realised that his practice was growing beyond what could be housed on 37th Street, he leased the third floor of a small office building at the corner of 57th Street and 3rd Avenue, next to the Sutton movie theatre.

While we prepared for the move, he made an even more dramatic decision – designed to hold together his design team at a time when he heard all his contemporaries complaining about losing their best people as they moved on to their own private practices. In return for a promise to remain in the firm, he offered five of us full partnerships at the end of ten years, before which we were to be called Associates. He told me: "Bob, I don't think we'll make a lot of money, but it *will* be fun ..."

Ham, Herb, Murray Emslie (who had replaced Bill Landsberg as chief draftsman) and I accepted the offer and, except for Murray (who left to join Richard Meier ten years later and was replaced by Tician Papachristou), we stayed together until Breuer's retirement in 1976. Joe Neski preferred to leave for private practice (and BJ wasn't even asked, to her furious disappointment). Lajkó was 54 years old. He had had many years as a beloved teacher at Harvard and the Bauhaus and surely recognised the role of his great mentor, Walter Gropius, in his own life. He chose as partners men who were 25 years his junior.

The ten years we spent on 57th Street were quite different from those in the terrace house but equally remarkable. The staff stabilised at about thirty and included colourful, talented people from all over the world. Breuer commuted regularly from New Canaan when he wasn't flying in service of a truly international practice. (His name has always been better known in Europe than in America.) Soccer was played at lunchtime with a ball of yellow tracing paper; funny presents were offered to the boss for his birthday, and long lists in magic marker on yellow tracing paper of "famous people you didn't know were architects" were hung on the wall – all vivid memories of the things that punctuated the serious, efficient design work that went on all day and into the night.

One famous house client of the era was Peter Ustinov, and I looked forward to making his acquaintance as I worked on our plans for a dramatic house overlooking Lake Geneva. No such luck: Breuer kept him and Mrs Ustinov completely to himself. The main pavilion of the house was sheltered by two hyperbolic paraboloid shells of thin concrete. But Ustinov didn't build it. Neither did Dr José Soriano, to whom we tried to re-sell the idea ten years later. Finally, Louis Saier built the house on a hillside above Deauville in 1973, to great critical acclaim. The warped concrete shell had been introduced to Breuer by his student and friend Eduardo Catalano as a way to span space with great economy of material. It was characteristic of Lajkó's sculptural sense that he chose to use it frequently because it could also be beautiful. He even went so far as to use it for the walls of the Muskegon Church where it made no economic sense at all.

Breuer returned from France one day in 1960 with some scribbled sketches on the back of an Air France envelope following his meeting with IBM at a rugged hillside site an hour north of Nice. My drawings, in development of his inventive ideas, included widely spaced supporting columns shaped like trees that straddled the tilted landscape in varying heights. A deep façade of folded concrete created tubes for the passage of laboratory utilities and shaded the windows from a very bright sun. Its sweeping plan in the shape of a double "Y" had first appeared in England in a 1936 model "City of the Future". The research centre for IBM France at La Gaude that resulted was his favourite creation. I was extremely proud to work on it. It has been quadrupled in size and almost lost in a pine forest since, and the French government has classified it as a "Monument of Modern Architecture".

Later the same year, I was talking to Lajkó in his office when he paused to take a phone call from an old New Canaan friend who had just returned to Paris. He explained later that it was an offer to act as chief architect for a new ski town in the French Alps. When the commission came in, Herb was assigned to be partner-in-charge and worked on the master plan for a year with Paul Koralek, before Paul left to return to London and later fame.

Without Paul's knowledge of French, Herb had second thoughts about his assignment to Flaine. Knowing of my interest in the project and my one year of college French, he asked Breuer if he could be reassigned to a much more realistic commission that had just come in from New Jersey. Lajkó, in principle, opposed "switching horses" but agreed to a very American toss of the coin during an Associates luncheon. Herb won, chose the New Jersey project, and I began work on Flaine that was to dominate my personal and professional life for twenty years.

During three years in New York we developed the components of an entire town based upon a revolutionary system of prefabricated concrete construction. The master plan evolved through at least ten variations as Lajkó responded to the terrain, changes in the real estate market, and experience of crowd control. His three-dimensional instinct had shaped the original composition of tall and low buildings at a time when their eventual use was far from clear. His choice of the one plateau in the midst of the tall northern cliffs as the "Forum" or town square reflected his happy experience with villages elsewhere.

As the function of each building was eventually determined, it was clad in a different, appropriate combination of precast concrete parts tied together with a restricted palette of rubble stone and natural wood. Flaine today is one of a kind – its uncharacteristic tall buildings make walks to the ski-lifts shorter and the absence of cars improve safety for small children. If Breuer had a vision of its eventual shape and texture at the outset, he kept it to himself: he let it evolve over twenty years of collaboration with our understanding client, a rigorous government, and thousands of happy skiers.

◄◄ Breuer with Frédéric Berlottier, chief project engineer, discussing the original masterplan for Flaine. A modest man of inexhaustible inventiveness, he took a huge risk by sacrificing the professional security offered by the French bureaucracy and devoting the remainder of his career to the pursuit of Eric Boissonnas's dream. On the occasion of his retirement in the early 1980s, a major ski trail was named "Le Fred" in his honour.

◄ This is how the future town centre of Flaine looked when I saw it for the first time in 1961. A two-storey sheltering hut for touring skiers, called "Fédération", defined the plateau upon which the forum would later be erected.

▼ A working lunch in the construction canteen. Sylvie Boissonnas, who invested her fortune in Flaine, is visible in the left foreground, with Breuer and Gatje seated behind the man with whom she is speaking. This remarkable and elegant lady brought her impeccable taste to bear with the greatest effectiveness, taking part in all decisions involving design and graphics for the entire skiing locale.

◂ Flaine, France, 1961–76, apartment buildings.
▸ Flaine, façade detail.

As construction began, our client and later great friend Eric Boissonnas asked that we set up an office in Paris. After madly studying French at Berlitz for three months at night, I moved my family and two associates (Allen Cunningham and Guillermo Carreras) to live and work in Paris in January 1964.

I lived in Paris for almost three years, returning just in time for the opening of the Whitney Museum in September 1966. Those years were wonderful in hindsight, but somewhat terrifying at the time. Flaine got caught in a political/financial crisis that shut construction down for most of the time I was there. Our staff dropped from fifteen to five and I was constantly defending the economics of our French venture to restless partners in New York. Nevertheless, the office got to build a number of successful projects in England and southern France, my family grew to include a second daughter, and we travelled all over Europe.

◀ Flaine, the hotel "Les Gradins Gris".
◀◀ To begin with, I was very sceptical when Lajkó
suggested cantilevering the Grand Hotel "Le Flaine"
out over the valley in order to gain space on the
plateau behind. But this daring scene soon became
the most frequently reproduced image of Flaine.
When the hotel opened in 1969, building engineer
Yves Teyssier joked about painting a dotted line on
the floor of the main lounge, accompanied by a
caption saying: "From this point on, you're in
Marcel Breuer's hands."

When Lajkó came to Paris he looked up old friends and had an active social calendar, but he did spend a lot of time in our small office and we had much more chance to get to know him than in New York. He loved the unprepossessing space we had finally found; its walls and floor were way out of plumb and you could hear an accordionist below when we threw open the windows in spring. During his visits we would order from our favourite restaurant down the street and have lunch on several drafting tables.

Both before and after our stay in Paris, I frequently travelled with Breuer and long conversations over innumerable dinners vastly enriched my life, professionally and personally. When I left the Paris office, I turned its day-to-day management over to Mario Jossa, a Roman-born American from the New York office, who eventually became our fifth partner and still lives in Paris.

I returned to an office in New York that was quite different from the one I had left. We were lodged in a banal Madison Avenue building with a staff that approached fifty. Lajkó missed the collegiality of our more modest digs and, for a while, he rented a part of a lower floor where subsidised sandwiches were prepared by a nice lady in what we called "Alice's restaurant". This encouraged the staff to know each other better but he rarely found time to drop in.

- ▸ Just before the opening, Sylvie Boissonnas acquired the rights to a unique typeface created by the great French graphic designer Adolphe Cassandre. It was used for all signage throughout the vacation resort.
- ▾ In the early 1970s, Flaine was an internationally recognised and beloved destination for ski tourists. Breuer and French ski champion Emile Allais (in the black turtleneck) who planned all of the trails both became the objects of considerable admiration.

▸ Each morning, a crowd gathers at the base of the hotel to await the opening of the ski school.

▾ On the final run down from the Grandes Platières, skiers enjoy a direct view of the forum. To the left, on the valley floor, we see the fringes of a group of low-lying apartment buildings for international ski clubs. These buildings, which rise from the crest of the cliffs, are linked to the rest of the area by a cable railway.

The last ten years of Marcel Breuer and Associates were characterised by an increasingly institutional clientele who, unlike his old house clients, didn't insist on Breuer's presence at every meeting. He left more and more of the day-to-day design in our hands, knowing that we would always refer the difficult decisions to him.

Despite the publicity that surrounded the first-ever show of the work of a living architect at the Metropolitan Museum of Art, 1973 was a slow year in the architecture business. A phone call from a friend of mine at the World Bank led to an invitation to Breuer to visit Kabul, Afghanistan, to make a survey of its tourist industry and to design several hotels in truly exotic locations. At 71 Lajkó was troubled by back pains and insomnia and no longer enjoyed travel the way I did. Nevertheless he agreed to make the trip at the urging of his partners in recognition of the prestige of the World Bank as a potential client. I met him in Paris after his return from Flaine and he was really tired; 36 hours later he was in the US Embassy infirmary at Kabul after a major heart attack. His three weeks of mandatory recuperation gave me an unforgettable experience in surveying the tourist potential of the country. Breuer was spoiled by admiring nurses who had never had such an important patient before, and by Peace Corps architects who had never played chess with Marcel Breuer before. He told me later that it was the best hospital stay he'd ever had, but I think he was just trying to make me feel better for having urged the trip.

After a summer of rest on Cape Cod, he returned to the office on a half-time schedule that inevitably became a full day. Four years later I was visiting our office in Tehran (which consisted of Tician's apartment, a telex machine and a driver) when Lajkó called to announce his doctor-enforced retirement at the end of the month.

▶ Breuer, Claes Eriksson and Gatje discussing the model for a new hotel in Flaine. The hotel was erected above the cliffs from materials tried out earlier in the forum below. In recognition of the detailed design Claes and I had developed in collaboration, Breuer referred to it as "your hotel", adding that he considered it to be one of the best buildings in Flaine.

▼ Breuer and his partners in the late 1960s (left to right): Gatje, Papachristou, Breuer, Beckhard and Smith in the conference room.

He lived for five more years and we made frequent visits to his apartment on 61st Street. The last vestiges of office discipline and awe melted during these times of reminiscence and review of current projects. I was finally able to put a hand on his shoulder and express the affection we all felt for this marvellous man.

Bob Gatje grew up in Brooklyn, New York, and attended college at Deep Springs, Cornell, and the Architectural Association School of Architecture in London. He has been active in the affairs of the American Institute of Architects. After the disbanding of Marcel Breuer Associates, he worked with Richard Meier for eight years and, in retirement, wrote "Marcel Breuer, A Memoir". He is working on a new book, "25 Great Public Squares and 10 Others".

◄ The new hotel, erected on the crest of the cliffs in Flaine, is today known as "Le Hôtel Résidence". It contains owner-occupied apartments as well the Boissonnas family's penthouse.

▼ The partners after Lajkó's retirement: Ham Smith, Mario Jossa, Herb Beckhard, Tician Papachristou and Bob Gatje, shown here behind their friend and mentor in 1976.

THE PARIS UNESCO COMPLEX

THE PARIS UNESCO COMPLEX

GABRIELE DIANA GRAWE

We are delighted with the way our building ... has become so much a part of Paris.
(Marcel Breuer, 1959)

Descriptive accounts of the UNESCO architectural ensemble in Paris have seldom refrained from delivering negative verdicts. Criticism has not been restricted to the architectural syntax of the forms alone – which, despite many individually impressive solutions, have generally been found wanting as a unity. Discussion has also focused on the cooperation between artists and architects, compelled, in the course of their close collaboration, to accept an excessive number of compromises.[1] The research tends to repeat Lewis Mumford's devastating pronouncements: he condemned the UNESCO headquarters in Paris shortly after its completion in 1958 as a museum for the antiquities of modern art and architecture.[2] Paradoxically, by contrast, and despite attempts to introduce the UNESCO buildings to the public during construction in the context of their advanced technologies, the reaction of the French press testifies to the apprehensiveness aroused by the international character of the complex, located in the historic centre of Paris.[3]

Symptomatic of the unease provoked by the UNESCO headquarters in France up to the present day is its consistent marginalisation within – even total omission from – the literature on twentieth-century Parisian architectural history.[4] This cannot be attributed exclusively to the fact that the UNESCO buildings confront contemporary viewers with a set of ideals that today appear both politically and aesthetically obsolete.[5] It is also due to the circumstance that up to the present, Breuer's larger buildings have yet to be assigned any system of classification or definition, for his architectural oeuvre – especially the public

1 Christian Beutler, Paris und Versailles (Stuttgart: Philipp Reclam jun., 1970; Reclams Kunstführer Frankreich, vol. 1), p. 381.

2 Lewis Mumford, "Unesco House: Out, Damned Cliché!" and "Unesco House: The Hidden Treasure", in The Highway and the City (New York, 1964), pp. 67–78, 79–87.

3 See Regis Demeulenaere, L'UNESCO dans le journal Le Monde 1954–1962 (dissertation, Paris: Université Paris-Nord, 1991), especially chapter 1, III: "La construction du palais: un monument d'imprévoyance", pp. 78–90; J. L. Lalande, "Le siège de l'UNESCO à Paris", in L'architecture d'aujourd'hui 58 (February 1955), pp. 26–31; "Le siège permanente de L'UNESCO à Paris", in L'architecture d'aujourd'hui 44 (September 1952), pp. 89–94; "Le nouveau siège de l'UNESCO à Paris, Place Fontenoy", in L'architecture d'aujourd'hui 7 (April/May 1953),

buildings devoted to recreation, administration and industry – has only recently become a topic of comprehensive scholarly investigation.[6]

Today, there remains little doubt about the extraordinary significance of the Paris UNESCO commission for Marcel Breuer's career; the ensemble marked a turning point within his architectural practice. For while he had been in demand previously as a designer of single-family homes and villas, this highly prestigious project earned him an international reputation and led to the award of additional major commissions. Furthermore, the UNESCO project succeeded in reconnecting Breuer to Europe in the aftermath of his emigration to the United States in 1937. It also contributed to his receiving notable subsequent commissions in France, Switzerland and the Netherlands, enabling him to establish a branch of his New York office – Marcel Breuer and Associates – in Paris in 1964. After World War II, Breuer reimported the most outstanding architectural features of his European works back to America, where they lent a fresh impetus to projects then simultaneously under way. In the 1950s, Breuer concentrated principally on his two most important – and moreover stylistically related – buildings, St John's Abbey and the UNESCO complex. The mutual influence exercised by the two projects is indicated by, among other features, the concrete construction of the abbey church, based on the elongated folds of the walls of the UNESCO building.[7]

pp. 77–81, and Géo Vacher, "Béton et verre pour l'UNESCO ... et pour l'avenir", in Batir 8 (December 1958), pp. 18–34.

4 See François Loyer, Histoire de l'architecture française: de la Révolution à nos jours (Histoire de l'architecture française), and Éric Lapierre, Identification d'une ville: architectures de Paris, exhibition catalogue (Paris: Pavillon de l'Arsenal, 2002).

5 See Christopher Pearson, "Hepworth, Moore and the United Nations: modern art and the ideology of post-war internationalism", in The Sculpture Journal 6 (2001), pp. 89–99.

6 See especially Joachim Driller, Marcel Breuer. Die Wohnhäuser 1923–1973 (Stuttgart, 1998) and Isabelle Hyman, Marcel Breuer, Architect: The Career and the Buildings (New York, 2001).

7 On the Paris office, see Robert F. Gatje, Marcel Breuer: A Memoir (New York, 2000), pp. 137–67. In

Given the plurality of participating architects and the regimentation imposed by the democratic committee organisation of the commissioning body and its advisors, the UNESCO complex can scarcely be characterised as an expression of Breuer's individual style. This also explains why the building has been stigmatised as aesthetically unsatisfactory. It would appear all the more important, therefore, to begin by emphasising three circumstances in particular. First, it was precisely the special working conditions and division of labour among the trio of architects – Breuer, Pier Luigi Nervi and Bernhard Zehrfuss – that endowed the complex with its exceptional architectural status. The turbulent post-war period, marked by economic difficulties and crisis-prone French colonial politics; the contested ground lying between UNESCO as client and an international committee of experts, consisting of five architects from CIAM (Congrès internationaux d'architecture moderne), and the French capital itself, so rich in tradition, yet still unreceptive to modernist architecture – all of these factors combined to shape the intricate context of Breuer's first large-scale architectural project. Not least, any evaluation of the artistic quality of the UNESCO complex must consider the compatibility – or irreconcileability – of certain political as well as architectural ideologies.

Secondly, notwithstanding the recognition accorded the engineering contribution made by Nervi's Parisian office, the form and design of the complex still has its origins with Breuer himself. Within the division of labour uniting the three architects, Breuer hence assumed responsibility mainly for the design of the façades and outside areas. During this preliminary work, he was able, for the first time, to replace a steel skeleton structure with concrete for constructive purposes. Concerning this decision, Breuer wrote in 1959: "the

her monograph, Isabelle Hyman observes that it was not Breuer's European works alone of the mid-1950s that were crucial for his American projects from the perspectives of both form and of constructive technology, but also his encounter with Europe itself. In 1956, for example, under the sustained impression of the Eiffel Tower, which was visible from the UNESCO construction site, Breuer altered his original design for the campanile at St John's Abbey, replacing the closed triangles at its base with upward arching curves. See Marcel Breuer, Architect (New York, 2001) p. 140.

construction of the UNESCO project was developed, in its principal features, simultaneously with the ground plan. Although each of us had a precisely defined personal task area, there was a constant, intensive exchange of ideas and concepts between the three of us; this was an entirely natural, friendly and down-to-earth process."[8] Nervi acted as a catalyst between Breuer and Zehrfuss and thus made an essential contribution to the collective work of the team – just as he did in his function as building engineer.[9] The numerous parallels that came to light between the works of Nervi and Breuer, moreover, inspired Breuer during the work to engage in an intensive exploration of concrete construction, and led to his success in recovering the sculptural qualities in architecture that would be so closely associated with his buildings in subsequent decades. Nervi's ideas concerning an architecture of structure exercised a strong and persistent influence on Breuer's later works.

Thirdly, the susceptibility to modelling and shaping and the technical potentialities of concrete enabled Breuer to transplant the individual architectural means he had developed for residential buildings on to this larger-scale undertaking. Of special relevance in this connection is Breuer's architectural philosophy, based on principles of contrast, which finds its expression in the interplay of glass, stone and concrete surfaces on the façades of the UNESCO headquarters, as well as in the effective formal and proportional polarity between individual buildings, especially the two main ones. The dominating curvatures of the Secretariat stand out from the sharp corners of the trapezoid-shaped Conference Building: while the curved wings of the Secretariat awaken an impression of widely outspread arms, the Conference Building has the effect of an inward-turning, self-contained architectural volume.

8 Cranston Jones, introduction and captions, Marcel Breuer: Buildings and Projects 192–1962 (New York, 1962), p. 253.

9 Ernesto N. Rogers, "Il dramma del palazzo dell'UNESCO", in Casabella (April 1959), p. 4; and Pier Luigi Nervi, Ernesto N. Rogers and Jürgen Joedicke, P. L. Nervi (Stuttgart, 1957), p. xii.

The central administration of UNESCO, sited in the 7th arrondissement of Paris, consists of four buildings. The largest of these, lying near the Ecole Militaire, is the Y-shaped Secretariat (Bâtiment I). A lower, slightly curved block connects the main volume of the Secretariat to the trapezoidal Conference Building (Bâtiment II), whose eastern and western façades consist of fluted concrete. At the north-eastern corner of the site sits an annexe (Bâtiment III), the four-storey building housing the permanent delegates. Today, these three structures have been supplemented and adversely affected by a later expansion by Bernhard Zehrfuss. His patio complex (Bâtiment IV), completed in 1965, lies deeper, in the garden between the Conference Building and the Avenue de Lowendal that closes the site to the north-west.

The issuing of a construction permit in early October 1954 by the UNESCO headquarters committee was preceded by a culturally volatile tug-of-war lasting several years, which revolved around finding a suitable type of architecture and building site, as well as around the selection of architects and their advisors. This intricate prehistory – so intimately bound up with conflicts of interest between the client, the participating architects and the French authorities – played a significant role in determining the outcome of the UNESCO project. This summary of the planning process, so difficult to reconstruct in retrospect, is necessarily restricted to indicating its influence on the architectural shape of the present day UNESCO ensemble.[10] This topic is of interest not only because it brings to light the restrictions confronting Breuer, Nervi and Zehrfuss in the course of the project, but even more because it underlines the creativity displayed by all three architects, which went far beyond the proverbial ability to convert necessity into a virtue.

10 In her Breuer monograph, Isabelle Hyman has recourse, in connection with the UNESCO complex, mainly to archival materials in the Marcel Breuer Papers (Department of Special Collections, Syracuse University Library, Syracuse, New York) and the Archives of American Art (Smithsonian Institution, Washington, D.C.). To date, the documents available for study in the Paris UNESCO Archive pertaining to the planning process have been systematically reviewed and evaluated only by Carl Tillessen in 1992, in the context of research for his MA dissertation at the University of Hamburg. Apart from this source material on the planning history of the UNESCO complex, there are in addition, to date only partially published, sketches and correspondence in the Bauhaus Archive, Berlin (correspondence between Walter Gropius and Marcel Breuer), as well as in the Fondation Le Corbusier, Paris (UNESCO Dossier).

UNESCO was founded in London in 1945 as the United Nations special organisation for education, science and culture. Its tasks are primarily the promotion of international collaborative efforts in the spheres of education, science and information, and the promotion of universal access to learning and culture. Its highest organ is the General Assembly; the Executive Board, selected from the General Assembly, is responsible for implementing its working programme.

The requirements set by UNESCO for the aesthetic profile of its headquarters in Paris were not inconsiderable, and pertained primarily to artistic aspects. Moreover, the architecture of the permanent residence of UNESCO in Paris was expected to reflect the values of culture, democracy and internationality represented by the organisation: "it must express by its design the spirit of UNESCO and symbolize its purpose and ideals... . The building as a whole must be created as an integrated work of art in which plan, structure, technical equipment and every expressive element of the building are synthesized into a symbol and expression of UNESCO."[11] In order to approach this goal, the ideal of an interaction of all the arts was required: "the building, as a whole, by its form, colour, light and space shall be a synthesis of all arts."[12] In keeping with this notion of a synthesis of architecture, painting and sculpture, all decisions – from the award of commissions to the contents of the building contract and its authorisation, all the way through to the final execution – were made not individually, but rather by working groups, consisting of the General Conference in the form of the plenary assembly, the Headquarters Committee, the architectural team, the Advisory Committee, and the Arts Advisory Committee.[13]

11 UNESCO Archives, Paris, 7C/ADM/32(I) Annexe II, p. 3. All of the aesthetic and formal givens set by UNESCO for the complex were explicitly formulated: see UNESCO Archives, Paris, CPG/HQ/5, Annexe, pp. 6–9. Carl Tillessen observes in this context that the client "formulated an extremely precise building program" ("Das Hauptquartier der UNESCO in Paris von Marcel Breuer, Pier Luigi Nervi und Bernhard Zehrfuss", MA dissertation, University of Hamburg, vol. 2, 1992, p. 8). Still, it must be added that UNESCO initially underestimated its own space requirements, so that belated communication of additional space requirements entailed the planning of an extension building (Bâtiment III), which followed the already presented and authorised designs for the Secretariat and Conference Buildings.

12 UNESCO Archives, Paris, 7C/ADM/32 (I), Annexe II, p. 3 [Chapter II – The Artistic character of the UNESCO headquarters].

In July 1951, during the sixth session of the General Conference in Paris, UNESCO decided that the director-general, in consultation with the headquarters committee, should assemble a committee of architects; CIAM was accorded advisory status. The committee, composed of five architects from various countries with international reputations, was contracted not actually to advise the executive architects, but instead to determine whether the proposed designs corresponded to the wishes of the client.[14] Walter Gropius (USA) was appointed to chair this committee; the other members of the advisory team were Le Corbusier (France), Lucio Costa (Brazil), Sven Markelius (Sweden) and Ernesto Rogers (Italy). The French government granted a 99-year lease on a three-hectare site at the Place de Fontenoy, where the UNESCO building sits today, in exchange for a symbolic rent of 1,000 francs per year. The first designs date from 1951, and were prepared by the architects who were initially appointed: Eugène Beaudoin (France) and his advisors Howard Robertson (England) and Eero Saarinen (USA). In particular because of the building regulations imposed by the French authorities, which uncompromisingly prescribed a symmetrical arrangement on the Place de Fontenoy, and because of Le Corbusier's incessant criticisms and refusal to accept any modifications in the plans, the advisory committee eventually rejected all proposals from Beaudin, Robertson and Saarinen. This pair of factors, which contributed substantially to the rejection of the initial designs, had a decisive impact on the continuing planning process. Breuer's role in the project, in particular, came to the fore at this point. He received the critique of the preliminary designs, as well as the official instructions, as sources of inspiration, opposing his ideas to those of Le Corbusier, who regarded him as a quarrelsome adversary.[15]

13 See Rogers 1959, p. 2, and UNESCO, ed., Le Courrier de l'UNESCO, Nr. 11 (November 1958), p. 3.

14 UNESCO Archives, Paris, 7C/ADM/32(I), Annexe I, pp. 1–4; 7C/ADM/32(I), Annexe II, pp. 1–9; CPG/HQ/1, pp. 1–7; Tillessen 1992, p. 13.

15 As Le Corbusier's sketches and persistent protests certify, he was convinced that the task of designing the UNESCO building in Paris should have decolved to him alone. In fact, the UNESCO director-general had already selected Le Corbusier as provisional architect in October 1951. But objections from A. Jacobs, the US State Department representative – based on the fact that the architect had been reproached with irregularities in the course of the UNO project in New York – blocked his nomination. Disappointed by this rejection, Le Corbusier none the less attempted to implement his ideas through the UNESCO

◂ The architects' committee for the UNESCO buildings lunching in a Paris restaurant. Breuer is in the right foreground, with Gropius across from him (with bow tie); behind Breuer is Le Corbusier (with black eyeglasses).

Once the first, provisional designs had been rejected, the French government was faced with the task of finding a new building site in Paris. Moreover, a new architectural team had to be assembled. A decisive role was played in its formation by Walter Gropius's professional experience. The fact that the UNESCO project did not founder completely on the reefs of perpetual controversy was due to his skills in diplomacy. Gropius kept Le Corbusier's continual protests from the commissioning body and the French authorities, and saw to it that the intrusions of the advisory panel into the work of the executive architects were kept to a minimum. In a letter of 4 July 1953 addressed to Dr John W. Taylor, the incumbent director-general of UNESCO, Gropius wrote: "I have succeeded in bringing the 'Five' and the 'Three' to friendly agreement for the further work on the building."[16] Gropius's decision to include Breuer in the architectural team once the initial plans met with failure seems to have been quite deliberate. The prehistory of the planning process of the UNESCO building offers grounds to doubt the veracity of the account given by Robert F. Gatje of the apparently fortuitous events that resulted in the selection of Breuer for the group known as "the three".[17] Gropius's decision to entrust Breuer with the design of the UNESCO building was based much more on his knowledge of his former collaborator's capacity for teamwork. At that moment, Gropius was almost uniquely qualified to assess Breuer's creativity and his gifts as a designer in the context of a collaborative partnership; viewed in this light, it is less astonishing that he would choose Breuer without (at least according to the current state of source research) having consulted the remaining quartet of advising architects.

General Conference and the headquarters committee, in opposition to agreements by the members of his own committees and existing arrangements with the executing architects. See Barbara E. Shapiro, "'Tout ça est foutaise, foutaise et demi!': Le Corbusier and UNESCO", in RACAR, XVI, 2 (1989), pp. 171–79, 298–307; UNESCO Archives, Paris, 1 HQ/SR.1; 13 HQ/4; 18 HQ/2 Addendum 1; CPG/HQ/2, pp. 4–5 and Tillessen 1992, pp. 11 ff., 43 ff., 48, 76 f., 106–11, 199. On the relations between Breuer and Le Corbusier, see also Gatje (New York, 2000), p. 35; and Gabriele Diana Grawe, Call for Action. Mitglieder des Bauhauses in Nordamerika (Weimar, 2002), p. 109.

16 UNESCO Archives, Paris, 12 HQ/3. See also Shapiro 1989, p. 177 and Fondation Le Corbusier, documents nos. I3-(4) 132 and I3-(4) 141.

17 Gatje 2000, p. 35: "In early 1952 the advisers met in Paris to

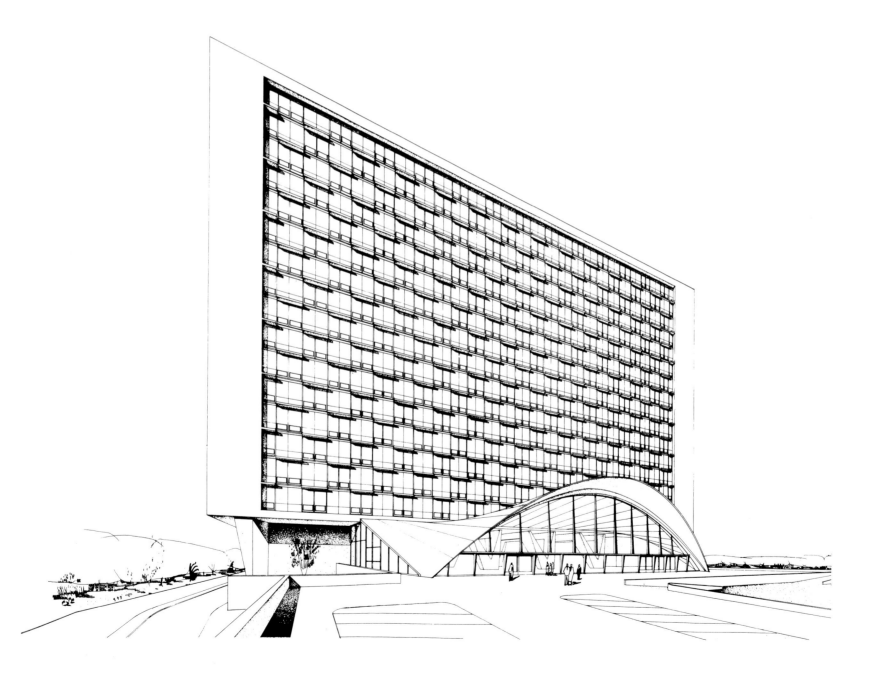

GABRIELE DIANA GRAWE

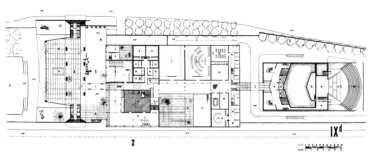

◄◄ UNESCO preliminary project, perspective view
of the Secretariat.
◄ UNESCO preliminary project, Secretariat, photo
of model.
▼ UNESCO preliminary project, design of the location
at Porte Maillot, 1952, ground plan.

In 1952, the contracts between UNESCO and the three architects were signed. In the same year, the French government made available a new building site on Porte Maillot. With their preliminary plans, Breuer, then working in New York City, Nervi in Rome and Zehrfuss, who headed an office in Paris, were especially concerned to evaluate the location in relation to the capital's significant existing historical monuments. The northern end of the property, located in the west of Paris, meets the grand axis of the metropolis leading from the Louvre and the Tuileries, the Concorde, the Champs Élysées, and the Etoile all the way to Porte Maillot.[18]

Both the forms chosen by the architects for the buildings, which were oriented to the UN complex in New York City, as well as their distribution within the site, were elemental in character. Three blocks stood in a row, rotated so that their outlines were either parallel to the main axis of Paris or at right angles to it. This proposal for three buildings – a 17-storey Secretariat, a two-storey Conference Building and an auditorium with open-air amphitheatre – also met with opposition.[19] The project failed, finally, for financial reasons, since the French Government was unable to acquire the site at Porte Maillot for UNESCO; instead, they requested a new design and suggested a return to the original site near the Ecole Militaire.[20]

With their new conception, Breuer, Nervi and Zehrfuss referred playfully to the building codes that had regimented the interim designs by Beaudoin, Robertson and Saarinen for the site at the Place de Fontenoy. Originally, the French authorities had insisted that the building should follow the perimetre of the site along the Avenue de Lowendal and the Place de Fontenoy. Already existing at the Place de Fontenoy were a pair of buildings, erected shortly before World War II and housing the Ministries of Labour and of Transport and

view Beaudoin's preliminary designs, and by the end of the afternoon had come to two conclusions: they didn't like his design, and they couldn't imagine that they would be satisfied by anything that he might come up with. Someone suggested a drink, and apparently minus Corb [Le Corbusier] they were all lined up at little café tables under the awning of the Deux Magots when Breuer came walking down the Boulevard St Germain. Gropius shouted, 'Lajkó, what the hell are you doing here?' Breuer joined them and talked about his sluggish practice and his plans to continue on to Rome the next day. After he left, the group discussed its problem further, and a consensus developed in favour of awarding the commission to an international trio (to ease the slap at Beaudoin). Envisioned were Breuer as design architect, the well-known Italian Pier Luigi Nervi as structural engineer, and Bernhard Zehrfuss of Paris as the project administrator."

343

◄ Secretariat Building.
▶ Fire stairs below the west wing of the Secretariat.

Maritime Affairs, whose curved main façades composed one half of the semi-circle of the historical layout, originally the work of Jacques-Anges Gabriel in the eighteenth century. The second half of the semi-circle was to have been formed by the main façade of the UNESCO building. In any event, in November 1952, the advisors succeeded in having all building codes suspended. Remaining in force, however, was the requirement that any buildings to be erected on the Place de Fontenoy should be conceived so as to avoid surpassing in height the Ecole Militaire (designed by Gabriel) as seen from the banks of the Seine. Hence the heights of the buildings were limited to five or six normal storeys.[21] Today's UNESCO Secretariat does follow the rounded shape of the Place de Fontenoy, albeit not exactly; it diverges slightly from the semi-circle. And the trapezoid of the Conference Building has not been adapted to the southern corner of the site, demarcated by Avenue Segur and Avenue de Suffren, but rather rotated, so that the acute angle of its façade diverges away from the adjacent street alignment. References to the site boundaries have been avoided, and the buildings are arranged asymmetrically, although this is not evident at first glance.

Moreover, with their new designs the architects responded to criticisms of their initial proposal. One of the fundamental differences between the project for Porte Maillot and the one for Place de Fontenoy is the division of the building programme. No longer determined by any obvious functionalism, these buildings now represent a contrasting variety of forms, whose function and significance is endowed in each case with a characteristic expressiveness.[22]

18 UNESCO Archives, Paris, 7C/ADM/32 (II), Add. I.

19 On such criticisms, see Hyman 2001, p. 234. A New York Times article appearing in Paris on 1 November 1952, for example, stated that the municipal authorities "have refused plans by the United Nations for the erection of a 17-storey skyscraper in the form of a sandwich, because it would have impaired views of the Arc de Triomphe." The planned structure is said to have "looked like the Notre Dame composed of radiators."

20 UNESCO Archives, Paris, 7C/HQ/SR.1 (prov.), p. 2: "For financial reasons, the French Government was no longer able to put the site between the Porte Dauphine and the Porte Maillot at the disposal of Unesco." Presumably, however, the refusal of the building site was not based exclusively on financial grounds, since the protocol also mentions doubts concerning the project

Originally, the main entrance of the Secretariat was positioned not on the Place de Fontenoy, but instead on the Avenue de Suffren. Correspondingly, the Y-form of the Secretariat Building is oriented not toward the Place de Fontenoy, but rather welcomes visitors to the east, along its longest façade, measuring 148 metres, and having an angle of 134 degrees. Each of the remaining two façades form an angle of 113 degrees; they measure 136 and 124 metres in length respectively. The entire building reaches a height of 28.75 metres. The seven storeys rise above 72 pillars in all, each seven metres in height. At the building's centre, the supports were originally enclosed by a glass wall, composing the public entrance hall. Today, numerous fittings interfere with this effect of transparency. The entrance hall is continued in the southern wing of the building. Passing between freestanding exhibition walls, visitors reach the walkway connecting Secretariat and Conference buildings. Outside the closed ground floor stand two pairs of pillars, at the end of the north-west wing, while beyond the library are four pairs of pillars. Via these freestanding pilotis at the ends of the wings, the fire stairs on the ground floor are exposed. These wind around a core of concrete triangles, into which they are inserted on one side. An additional set of fire stairs, in the form of a spiral staircase, stands completely outside the building in front of the eastern façade.

The form of the pillars of the Secretariat Building is the result of static considerations. They rise above an oval cross-section at their bases and terminate in fan-shaped faceted triangles, composing a corridor in the ground floor. Upon each pillar rests a vertical support, which becomes thinner above, in keeping with the decreasing thrusts; each is 1.4 metres thick below and only 0.4 metres in thickness above. The lengthwise intervals between supports are

expressed by the responsible authorities. UNESCO Archives, Paris, 7C/HQ/SR.2, pp. 2–6.

21 Shapiro 1989, p. 174; UNESCO Archives, Paris, 6C/HQ/SR.1; 7C/HQ/SR.2 (prov.), p. 3 ff.; 7C/HQ/SR.3 (prov.) p. 8 and Tillessen 1992, pp. 18, 80.

22 Tillessen 1992, p. 89.

six metres. As with the vertical space frame, the force of the floor plates also diminishes towards the exterior. For this reason, the office ceilings have seams. Room heights, measuring 2.64 metres in the central corridor, rise to 2.94 metres at the windows.[23] The offices, 800 altogether, are divided among the middle five storeys. Until today, only the first and seventh storeys of the Secretariat have not been subdivided into offices. In the first storey, the wings of the building are organised as open-plan offices where translations, publications and documentation for UNESCO are produced. The seventh storey accommodates communal facilities for UNESCO employees.

The entire skeleton is located within the interior of the building; no façade element has a load-bearing function. The end walls of the Y are closed and the curved façade is glazed continuously between the second and sixth storeys with 1,068 windows. Corresponding to their orientation to various points of the compass, the façades of the Secretariat have been subdivided into four differing sun protection zones. To the north, towards the Place de Fontenoy, no sun protection was installed. The windows are surrounded by a smooth travertine façade. The façade facing the delegation building, however, is divided into two sections. In addition to the 80 cm-deep vertical "brise-soleils" and the 80 cm-deep horizontal concrete grilles, the zone facing north is outfitted with perpendicular, angled panels of solar glass. The main façade, which looks out south-west on to the plaza, is covered across its entire surface with vertical cantilevered slabs of travertine and horizontal gridded concrete latticework, upon which metal brackets are mounted to carry panels of solar glass.[24]

23 UNESCO Archives, Paris, 8 HQ/SR.2, p. 4; Paolo Desideri, Pier Luigi Nervi Jr and Giuseppe Postano, Pier Luigi Nervi (Zürich, 1982), p. 60 and UNESCO, ed., Le Courrier de l'UNESCO [special publication], 11 (November 1958), pp. 4, 6.

24 See Tillissen 1992, p. 98 ff.: this solution for sun protection was undoubtedly a concession to proposals from Le Corbusier, who demonstrably asserted his right to have a say in connection with the sun protection devices.

▼ View from the Secretariat on to the Conference
Building. Near the upper border of the picture are
the solar glass plates used as sun protection.
▼▼ "Brise-soleils" on the Secretariat building.

GABRIELE DIANA GRAWE

In constructive terms, the freestanding Delegates' Building – a skeleton structure resting on pillars – is brought into line with the Secretariat. Here, in any event, the pillars are upright. With a height of 16 metres, four storeys and 120 offices, it mediates in terms of scale between the main buildings while remaining independent of them, while a connecting corridor, enclosing the so-called "Salle des Pas Perdus", links the Secretariat with the trapezoid-shaped Conference Building.

The Conference Building is spanned by a continuous space frame and covered by a copper butterfly roof. The façade is of fluted or pleated exposed concrete running vertically across the building. The folding along the end walls increases gradually from the base upwards toward the gables. A reinforced concrete panel strengthens the ceilings of this building, whose non load-bearing walls to the north-east and south-west are dissolved by plastically animated windows. The central pillars in the conference hall carry the weight of the ceiling girders; its cross-section is rectangular above, becoming rounded below.

A number of changes in the execution of the building in relation to the plans impair the intended effect of the architectonic ensemble. In the summer of 1958, a few months before the opening of the new headquarters, temperatures of up to 41 degrees Celsius were recorded in the offices of the Secretariat Building. In this context, Hyman refers to the fact that prior to the erection of the UNESCO building Breuer had designed only smaller buildings and facilities in Europe and America, and consequently had no experience with climate control systems – which, in any case, were not at this time regarded as indispensable. This leap to meet the demands represented by his first large-scale project, with its multitude of working

▾ Secretariat Building, the foreground showing
the patio courtyard of the expansion planned
by Zehrfuss in the 1960s.

individuals, was made without transition. The heat problem was documented in a nine-page "Report on protection against heat in the offices of the UNESCO building", published in March 1959. Breuer held that the materials employed were responsible for the problem – thin, mobile steel or composite walls and light, hollow, linoleum-covered floor panelling.[25] Hence the building was fitted in early 1959 with window shades for its first summer season. Later, both of the lower panes of glazing were painted within, and a few rooms were fitted with curtains.[26]

The architects had to yield to demands made by the authorities, prompted by security concerns, that the entire premises should be fenced in.[27] The site was enclosed within a wall of undressed stone, itself later extended upwards via a fence. Alongside these measures, the construction of Zehrfuss's patio complex ensured that the openness of the original composition was completely rescinded. The erection of the patio complex rendered the western garden frontage inaccessible, and the main entrance of the Secretariat, with Nervi's imposing central portal, could now be attained only via a path between patio and Conference Building. The entrance to the Secretariat, lying towards the garden, and the garden layout itself were thus diminished both aesthetically and functionally. The entrance on the Place de Fontenoy soon assumed the function of a main entrance.

It has already been mentioned that the incorporation of paintings and sculptures within the architectural composition played a pivotal conceptual role in the UNESCO project. That decor and furnishings played a comparable role has hardly been observed to date. The three architects were primarily preoccupied with the furnishings of the entrance hall, the Salle des Pas Perdus, the delegation foyer, the assembly hall, the grand commission

25 Hyman 2001, p. 235 ff.

26 UNESCO Archives, Paris, 28/HQ/ SR.3, p. 11.

27 UNESCO Archives, Paris, 10/HQ/4, p. 3: "Returning to the question of enclosing the site with a fence, Mr Eyraud believed that the Service of the Paris Police Headquarters would insist upon such enclosure, as a security measure."

hall, the hallways and the seventh storey. Following the finalisation of the contract on 4 December 1953, Breuer, Nervi and Zehrfuss became responsible for the decoration and furnishings of the assembly rooms, hallways and offices of the director-general. Yet they succeeded in evading this obligation by proposing to the arts advisory committee that the task be left to the UNESCO member states.[28] The latter, having declared themselves prepared to assume responsibility for the decor in one area of the building, were authorised by the headquarters committee to commission architects independently for its execution.[29]

While the special relationship between the plastic arts, interior furnishings and architecture already had an extensive history within modernist practice, in the case of the UNESCO project, a distinct disconnection becomes evident, expressed as a simple juxtaposition of architecture and artistic appendices. At that time, this strategy was in the process of establishing itself as the standard one for large public facilities. There can be no question here of a synthesis of genres, but instead – as Christopher Pearson has persuasively argued – of a symbolic bridge between individualism and technology. The Paris UNESCO complex takes advantage of art and architecture in order to offer a compelling vision of the future. Via the juxtaposition of two distinct spheres, the subjective and the technological, free and peaceful human coexistence is emblematically shown by means of the confrontation between individual, abstract works of art and optimised technology.[30]

In July 1953, the General Conference authorised the setting up of an arts advisory committee; the architectural triumvirate was represented by Breuer, and the team of five advising architects by Markelius and Rogers.[31] Among other members were Jean Cassou,

28 UNESCO Archives, Paris, 2/CCA/5, p. 5.

29 UNESCO Archives, Paris, 2/XC/3 Add I, p. 2 and 24/HQ/2, p. 11. Among the best-known architects who participated in the design of the interior furnishings were Gerrit Rietveld, who was invited from the Netherlands to outfit the press hall in the basement level of the Conference Building, and Philip Johnson, under whose direction the International Council of the Museum of Modern Art of New York undertook the furnishings of the hall of the executive council.

30 Pearson 2001, p. 97.

31 The chairman of the headquarters committee also chaired the arts advisory committee, albeit without having a vote. The three architects worked as an independent group and were represented on the committee by just a single vote. Conversely, the five advising architects were allocated two seats, in recognition of their vital contribution.

354

Chief Conservator of the Paris Museum of Modern Art and a Picasso specialist; Francisco Javier Sanchez Canton, art historian, Acting Director of the Prado in Madrid, and a member of the National Commission of UNESCO; and Sir Herbert Read, Chairman of the Institute of Contemporary Art in London, and a member of various expert committees established by UNESCO. When Cassou was prevented from assuming the tasks assigned him, he was replaced by another candidate from the French National Commission, Georges Salles, head of the Musée de France.[32] All of the above were committed advocates of the diverse manifestations of modernist formalism that had emerged in the wake of Cubism. The first six artists chosen by the committee for the UNESCO complex were Picasso, Moore, Arp, Calder, Miró and Noguchi. Even if many of the art works are immobile – that is to say, physically bound to the architecture – they were none the less essentially applied to the building in an external fashion. They do not depart from the conventional genres of mural, relief and sculpture. Only the Japanese-American artist Isamu Noguchi, who designed the area between the Secretariat and the annexe as a garden inspired by the Japanese tradition, succeeded in fusing architecture, the plastic arts and garden design.

Henry Moore's monumental travertine sculpture "Reclining Figure" stands before the longest façade of the Secretariat. Alexander Calder designed a 10-metre high mobile entitled "Spiral", which is sited to the left of the entry to the Conference Building. The freestanding stone wall before the Salle des Pas Perdus was to provide a chromatic element. Since Fernand Léger died in August 1955 before he could fulfil his commission, it passed to Joan Miró. He designed two walls of equal size (15 x 2.2 metres), which meet at right angles: the "Wall of the Sun" and the "Wall of the Moon". These have been rebuilt, and are today found in an

As chairman of the advising architects, Gropius was entrusted with the nomination of two colleagues for this work. Altogether three architects, therefore, were represented on the arts advisory committee. Four additional votes were allocated to artists or art critics, who hence formed a majority on the committee. UNESCO began to collect nominations for the four representatives from the art world. To begin with, the National Commission was requested to supply candidate lists. These were sent to the Association internationale des Arts plastiques and the Association internationale des Critiques d'art, who compiled their own lists by selecting names from the existing ones and appending their own, so that by the end of February 1954, UNESCO had 106 names in all. The lists can be examined in the UNESCO Archives, Paris, 157HQ/4 Annexe I and Annexe II, 19 (March 1954); see also CPG/HQ/11, pp. 4–5; 2/XC/3, pp. 1–2; 11

◀ Sculpture exhibition in the UNESCO grounds.
▾ Miró's "Wall of the Moon".

interior space, sheltered from the elements. Hans Arp created four forms which he assembled on the exterior wall of the library as a relief. In the mid-1960s, these bronze elements were removed into the foyer of the patio complex, and installed on a travertine wall to the left of the entrance to the assembly hall. Pablo Picasso designed one wall, "The Bathers" (10.6 x 9.1 meters), in the Conference Building.[33]

The UNESCO building in Paris displays a wealth of architectonic details and unusual structures. In the context of Breuer's oeuvre, finally, the forms and materials of the complex should be mentioned. The ground plan of the Secretariat is based on the same Y-shaped figure Breuer had used almost twenty years earlier for his "Garden City of the Future". In his role as planner, the 1936 exhibition "The City Centre of the Future", mounted for the British Cement and Concrete Association, offered Breuer an opportunity to present an entire repertoire of fundamental design conceptions in model form. In that context, Breuer used the Y-shaped ground plan for the first time in an office building, albeit as a double-form. The inward-curving wings would have contained the offices along their outer perimeters, while elevators, transport and installation shafts were to have been sited towards the core. This design constituted the basic schema for both the UNESCO Secretariat Building and for the IBM research centre at La Gaude near Nizza, dating from 1960.[34]

HQ/SR.1, as well as Tillissen 1992, p. 148; and Emmanuel Devouge-Lamielle, "Ville et culture. Analyse du discours suscité par la création du Siège de l'UNESCO à Paris" (dissertation, Paris: Université de la Sorbonne, 1975), pp. 86, 101–4.

32 UNESCO Archives, Paris,13/HQ/5; 14/HQ/2; 15 HQ/4; 16 HQ/3-F; 1/CCA/8.

33 Afro Basaldella and Roberto Matta each designed one wall for the foyer in the seventh storey of the Secretariat Building: "The Garden of Hope" and "Three Constellation Beings Facing the Fire". For the restaurant and the bar area, also found in the seventh storey, Karel Appel produced the painting "Meeting in Springtime" and Gyula Brassai the photograph "Reds". In the large commission hall is a picture by the Mexican artist Rufino Tamayo, entitled "Prometheus Bringing Fire to Mankind". Jean Bazaine created a mosaic for the outer wall of the entrance

At the UNESCO complex, the range of variations employed in the patterns made by shuttering is especially conspicuous. With the registration of the joints and the grain of the wooden formwork, and via improvements introduced by subsequent treatment, the exposed concrete was structured and articulated. Breuer's elaboration of the problem of surface design is revealed not only in the surface textures, but equally in the volumetric structures, as exemplified by the pleated concrete walls of the Conference Building. At Breuer's suggestion, this constructive idea – which Nervi originally wanted to employ only for the ceiling of the plenary hall – was extended downwards across the entire façade.[35] The UNESCO complex is thus a representative example of Breuer's efforts to pattern and articulate large surfaces by means of the special technical and aesthetic properties of concrete.

Besides concrete, the exterior of the building is dominated by polished travertine and glass. Below the volume of the building itself, a platform spreads itself out that is dominated by undressed stone – an additional contrast between rough and smooth materials so typical of Breuer's architecture. And yet it is not this contrast alone that distinguishes the UNESCO complex. Just as the Y-form of the Secretariat Building, which Breuer referred to as "a generally applicable solution for an office building of the 'continental' type", offered him the possibility of completing the partially existing semi-circle of the historical plaza structure, so his utilisation of contemporary materials is an almost sensory response to the urban profile so typical of Paris.[36] One year after the completion of construction work on the UNESCO complex, he wrote that it had been a fortunate coincidence "that the glass industry developed grey solar glass just in time for it to be utilised in this project. (Previously, there had been only blue-green solar glass.) This made it possible for us to adapt the building to the grey

hall of the extension. See UNESCO, ed., Le Courrier de l'UNESCO [special volume], 11 (November 1958), pp. 10–36.

34 Jones 1962, pp. 14 f., 19.

35 Jones 1962, p. 18.

36 Jones 1962, p. 252.

panorama of Paris, the slate slabs of the mansard roofs, the grey window shutters, the 37 Jones 1962, p. 252 f. weathered stone of the bridges and the restless grey clouds of the Parisian skies, illuminated here and there by pale, slanted sunbeams. The grey tones of our exposed concrete, a pair of travertine façades in warmer tones, the sandstone from the vicinity of Paris and a lighter granite all correspond to the shifting greys and watery whites of the Parisian atmosphere."[37] Despite numerous architectural alterations and its lamentable state of preservation, the UNESCO headquarters essentially retains this harmony to the present day.

THE LATER MODERNISM OF MARCEL BREUER

THE LATER MODERNISM OF MARCEL BREUER

ISABELLE HYMAN

"With the rebirth of solids next to glass walls, with supports which are substantial in material but not negligent in structural logic and practical requirements, a three-dimensional modulation of architecture is again in view." Marcel Breuer, Matter and Intrinsic Form, 1963.[1]

1 Marcel Breuer, "Matter and Intrinsic Form", second annual Reed and Barton Design Lecture, presented at the University of Michigan, Ann Arbor, 6 March 1963 (Taunton, Mass.: Reed and Barton, 1963), n.p.

2 Robert McLaughlin to Breuer, 21 January 1954. Marcel Breuer Papers, Archives of American Art, Correspondence.

A brief synopsis of Breuer's status in the post-war period

When the war ended for the United States in 1945, Marcel Breuer was in Cambridge, Massachusetts, a member of the architecture faculty of the Graduate School of Design at Harvard where he had been teaching for the eight years since his emigration to America.

There he had trained dozens of young architects who went into practice grounded in the progressive instruction and inspiration received from Breuer and from Walter Gropius, who had encouraged and expedited Breuer's appointment at Harvard. Breuer's renown as a teacher was legitimated by later offers for teaching positions at prestigious institutions such as Massachusetts Institute of Technology and Princeton University – "We know how ably you pass on your understanding of architecture to the younger men," wrote the director of the School of Architecture at Princeton[2] – and by the frequently published testimonials of his students, many of whom went on to achieve their own professional celebrity. Both the built work and the unexecuted projects produced by the architectural partnership of Gropius and Breuer from 1937 to 1941 were also of critical importance in educating students about modern design, construction and materials.

◄ Marcel Breuer and Walter Gropius, Frank House, Pittsburgh, Pennsylvania, 1938–40, garden view.

During the war years restrictions and priorities were necessarily placed on building materials, and there was a virtual cessation of construction other than that needed for defence. But post-war America – with its automotive culture, accelerating economy and dynamic propulsion towards suburban family living – lay just around the corner. With his celebrated Geller House of 1945, Breuer had an early exposure to the potential of a new architectural market – single-family residences for middle-class and upper middle-class clients in business and the professions who were returning from military service and wanted architect-designed modern homes. It led him to give up teaching in Cambridge and to risk opening an independent architectural practice in New York City in 1946.

While the story of Breuer's career rightly spotlights his achievement as a residential architect as it evolved and expanded in this atmosphere, at the same time he also gained commissions and proposals for institutional, commercial and industrial buildings, and for programmes for urban development and housing. New buildings were needed to service the growth of post-war American industry and business, to accommodate the expansion of the US federal government and its agencies, and to provide for the increase of religious and educational institutions, many of them situated in the unfolding suburbs. Not least, there was the architectural restoration of Europe after the destruction of the war. Vigorously responding to all these opportunities, between 1945 and 1976 Marcel Breuer became one of the most productive and most respected of international architects. Many of his buildings are canonical examples of the genre now described as mid-century modernism. Already in 1956 he had been recognised as a leader in the modern architectural establishment when he was named one of the twentieth century's "form-givers", a group of thirteen architects who had

▼ Geller House I, Lawrence, Long Island, New York,
  1945, living room, view from east.
▼▼ Geller House I, view from north.

▼ Geller House I, view from north-west,
  entry situation.
▼▼ Geller House I, view from south.

made a major contribution to architecture including Wright, Mies, Le Corbusier, Saarinen, Gropius and Aalto.

3 Marcel Breuer, interview for Schokbeton [trade publication of Schokbeton Products, Corp.], October 1973, p. 4.

Breuer from mid-century to retirement

Breuer's preparation for these accomplishments can be said to have crystallised in London in the mid-1930s. There, during his two years as a partner of British architect F.R.S. Yorke, and before emigrating to America, he designed a large demonstration model to represent a segment of what was called the "Garden City of the Future", an urban plan based on utopian ideals for living well socially, physically and architecturally. The model was constructed on a scale of 1/20in:1ft on a base of about 10 x 6ft and was displayed at the London Building Exhibition of 1936. It represented the zone in a new seaside city where the business and residential sections converged. That it was commissioned by the British Cement and Concrete Association is highly signficant for any account of Breuer's architecture, for had this ideal modern city been built its principal material would have been reinforced concrete. "No material has more potential," Marcel Breuer later would say when speaking of concrete and of the kind of architecture it best produced and with which he felt most at home.[3] Equally significant were the office buildings Breuer designed at the eastern edge – the commercial quarter – of the "Garden City" model: they were formed as multi-storied Ys and double Ys, a configuration that would become one of the most fruitful formal inventions of his career. Before coming to America Breuer was, therefore, already in command of three elements that singly or together would most accurately define the monumental buildings he eventually

Marcel Breuer and F.R.S. Yorke, "Garden City of the Future", London, England, 1936, model.

produced for institutional, civic, private and governmental clients all over the world: the design of Y and Siamese-Y shapes; the material, reinforced concrete, considered by Breuer to be the building material of the twentieth century; and the construction technology made possible by poured concrete, prefabrication. That concrete parts could be prefabricated off-site appealed to Breuer immensely. Throughout his professional life he remained true to his belief in prefabrication and its promised benefits for the economics of a building project, a belief founded at the Weimar Bauhaus in the deprivations and economic depressions following World War I. By 1960 he had become a major prefabrication architect, probably the most creative designer of large standardised components fashioned of fins, cuboids and trapezial forms for the serial bays of his expansive buildings. Relevant for Breuer, too, as well as for many of his clients, was the fact that the costs for building in concrete were substantially less than for a structure of stone or steel.

Even apart from the cost factor, Breuer preferred concrete over all other materials for its versatility in architectural design rather than purely as a structural material. During his lifetime he gave interviews on many subjects but on few did he speak more eloquently or more passionately than on concrete and its potential to create a sculptural architecture. "'Garden City of the Future' was the turning point," he acknowledged. "In connection with concrete, it develops towards more plastic form."[4] The concept of "plastic form" and an appreciation for sculptural weight in architecture were at the core of Breuer's creative vision both early and late in his career. It is possible to recognise, for example, the compact cubiform masses of his 1966 Whitney Museum of American Art already present in his first piece of furniture – the cherrywood and leather Sommerfeld House armchair he designed and made

4 Quoted in Winthrop Sargeant, "Profile of Marcel Breuer (manuscript draft, prepared for the New Yorker, c. 1971-72).

◄ Walter Gropius and Adolf Meyer, Sommerfeld House, Berlin, 1921, entrance hall with armchair by Marcel Breuer.

at the Bauhaus in 1921, forty-five years earlier.[5] At the age of nineteen, Marcel Breuer had begun his designing career by manipulating heavy, dense and boxy forms, and it was in this distinctive mode that he continued to be most comfortable, and most himself, for the greater part of his life as an architect and designer.

Two decades after "Garden City of the Future", the essential architectonic and structural elements Breuer had developed there were given one of their most noble expressions in the Y-shaped Secretariat building for the UNESCO headquarters in Paris of 1955–58, elevated on 72 powerful tilted concrete *pilotis*. This was designed by an international team from Italy (Pier Luigi Nervi), France (Bernard Zehrfuss) and the United States (Breuer). Revealing through the glass skin of its façade the structural system of pier-supported slabs from ground to roof, the building was regarded as a monument of concrete construction and a powerful example of Breuer's sculptural idiom.

Monumental, too, were the laboratories and research facilities Breuer built for IBM in La Gaude, in the south of France, in 1960–62, a grand two-storey double-Y lifted by *pilotis* that were shaped as elegant abstract caryatids. The format was well suited to this project, as it had been for UNESCO, because among other virtues it made it possible for offices and laboratories to be peripheral and windowed – a highly desired feature in French office buildings at the time – and, in the case of IBM, for those windows to have views of the dramatic landscape characteristic of the region.

5 Also observed by Adam Eli Clem, "The City in Miniature: From Chair to Building in the Work of Marcel Breuer", art history thesis, Vassar College, 1993, n.p.

Because of the success of the La Gaude installation, IBM asked Breuer to design a complex near Boca Raton, Florida, for the offices, laboratories and manufacturing facilities of its south-east division. Built in 1968–72, this project called for a pair of administrative and laboratory wings, once again expressed in a curving double-Y contour – an arrangement that also allowed for physical growth and expansion in four directions. By using two floors of pre-cast concrete window panels with faceted sun-break systems above sculptured, poured-in-place tree-columns – a design and planning strategy with which he was to become identified – Breuer was again able to accommodate successfully the priorities of the client by providing a large number of windowed spaces for the work-force within a richly textured enclosure. That texture was also composed, predictably, of sculpturally formed pre-cast units repeated in series and defined by chiaroscuro patterns.

Between the time of his first and second IBM structures, Breuer built the first of his two Washington DC buildings. It was produced in collaboration with Nolen-Swinburne and Associates on a site considered difficult by the architects because it was bounded by streets on all sides. The client was the US Government's General Services Administration (GSA), and the building was to be headquarters for five to six thousand employees of the agency that eventually became the Department of Housing and Urban Development (HUD). Construction began in 1965 and was completed in 1968; it was the first federal building of pre-cast concrete. Its imposing scale and light colour made it a highly visible example of what was being promoted at the time as a new and forward-looking architectural policy wherein the government would make a genuine effort to improve the quality of federal architecture and set a high standard for public buildings. It was a policy also intended to call attention to

ISABELLE HYMAN

◄ Marcel Breuer and Robert F. Gatje,
IBM Research Center, La Gaude, France, 1960–62,
during construction.
▼ IBM Research Center, aerial view.

◀◀ Marcel Breuer and Robert F. Gatje, IBM Complex, Boca Raton, Florida, 1968–70, view of a support during construction.
◀ Marcel Breuer, Nolen-Swinburne and Associates, and Herbert Beckhard, Department of Housing and Urban Development (HUD) headquarters, Washington, D.C., 1965–68, view from north-east.

exceptional American architectural talent, expressed in a modernist idiom, by displaying it in a capital city that was traditionally understood to be culturally conservative. Again, Breuer found the Y-format to be the most efficient solution for a structure in which so many people worked; he could also utilise the areas where the formal elements intersected and terminated for the installation of the essential service cores (elevator shafts, stairwells, etc.).

The cost effectiveness and comparative speed of execution of Breuer's HUD building was appreciated by the GSA and in 1966 he received another significant government commission for a new headquarters building for HEW (Health, Education and Welfare, as the agency was then named; now the Hubert H. Humphrey Federal Building). After lengthy delays (it was not begun until 1972) HEW was finally completed in 1976. Another large federal office building requiring a huge floor area to house thousands of employees, in appearance HEW belongs to a type of brooding, assertive concrete structure designed by Breuer in the mid- to late 1960s, rich in the contrast of textures and scale and characterised by heavy volumes. Breuer's solutions to the formidable technical problems presented by the HEW site were regarded as innovative and were widely admired within the profession. A year after it was completed the Architectural Awards Committee of the Metropolitan Washington Board of Trade gave the HEW building its Certificate of Merit for "Excellence in Architecture in the Metropolitan Washington Area". The building height was limited to 90 feet; Breuer used the setback penthouse level for the main mechanical facilities, a large cafeteria and, most notably, a network of steel trusses from which vertical hangers were suspended and from which the six office floors of the building below were "hung". Those trusses provided the

distinctive 45-degree roofline, dramatised by massive triangular planes that humanised the working environment by creating terraced areas – outdoor extensions of the cafeteria that offered views over the city. HEW's rhythmic façade, almost mannerist in the complexity of its articulation, provided another characteristic Breuer contribution to the architectural language of Washington DC. The window walls of the structure had been pre-cast in an off-site plant: Breuer claimed that this process allowed him design possibilities beyond those of concrete poured at the site. For one thing, there could be a high degree of stone aggregate exposure to create surface texture and counteract weathering; for another, there was the comparative thinness of the concrete. This meant that the deep profiles of so three-dimensional a façade could be realised without excessive weight; and the depth of the profiles allowed the recessed windows to be shaded from the sun. It was an ingenious integral system, for within the shadowed bays there were also spaces to house and hide air conditioning and room heating units with their networks of ducts.

"The greatest aesthetic design potential in concrete," Breuer said, "is found through interrupting the plane in such a way that sunlight and shadow will enhance its form."[6] Sunlight and shadow are of course essential to the perception of three-dimensional sculpture, and Breuer perceived and conceived architecture as sculpture. Of the Whitney Museum he said unequivocally: "I formed the building as a sculpture."[7] Shadows caught in deep cavities to contrast with a raking light across surfaces gave Breuer the aggressive three-dimensionality that was essential to his notion of creative design for things both large and small. The sculptural nature of the shaped fireplaces he designed for the living rooms of many of his houses, for example, has always been recognised, as has that of the communion tables,

6 Schokbeton interview, p. 4.

7 Marcel Breuer, draft of comments at the presentation of the Whitney Museum project, November 1963, p. 2. Marcel Breuer Papers, Archives of American Art, Speeches and Writings.

◄ Marcel Breuer, Herbert Beckhard and Nolen-Swinburne and Associates, Department of Health, Education and Welfare (HEW) headquarters, Washington, D.C., 1972–76.

baptismal fonts, lecterns and other "furniture" for his numerous churches, chapels, monasteries and convents.

Interviewed in France in 1974, and speaking about the great sculptural possibilities for architecture inherent in reinforced concrete, Breuer used as an example his 1972 colossal forebay dam and power plant at the Columbia River basin in Grand Coulee in Washington State, with, as he described its interior, "dimensions truly Egyptian".[8] The engineer in Breuer, joined with his love of big massing shapes, produced this pylonic format with its sloping, thick-based and articulated walls, which expressed both his fascination with the possibilities of concrete technology and his innate "Egyptian" manner. By utilising the density and liquid plasticity of concrete, Breuer believed he could do with that material what the Egyptians did with stone.

Not only Grand Coulee Dam, but the church of St Francis de Sales in Muskegon, Michigan (1964–66) and the Campus Center for the University of Massachusetts in Amherst (1967–70) were shaped to express the kind of weight and density that gave Egyptian architecture its great power. In his preface to Jean Louis de Cenival's *The Architecture of Egypt* (1964), "The Contemporary Aspect of Pharaonic Architecture",[9] Breuer made it clear that he had a deep interest in the monumental architecture of Egypt and in its formal constructs: the ramps; the battered walls of the pylons; the flat-topped inclines of the low-lying *mastabas*; the trapezoidal masses of heavy stone, and the serial repetition of individual elements. Each of these found its way into his work. There are obvious equivalences between the bold geometries of the Egyptian *mastaba*, for example, and Breuer's Torin factory of the 1970s in Penrith, Australia, a forceful work with nearly windowless

8 Marcel Breuer, interview for Les Archives du XXième siècle, 30–31 March 1974. Marcel Breuer Papers, Archives of American Art, Speeches and Writings.

9 Jean Louis de Cenival, Living Architecture: Egyptian (New York: Grosset & Dunlap, 1964), p. 3–5.

 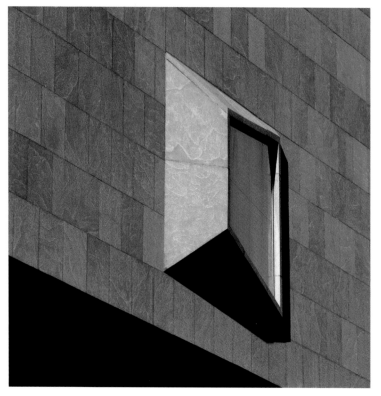

solids of rough-textured stone and concrete. Even IBM La Gaude was sited against the region's rocky peaks in a manner suggestive of the Middle Kingdom mortuary temples at Deir el Bahari.

Working in this Egyptian mode that he adopted particularly for smaller religious structures in the 1960s, Breuer designed the Kent School Girls' Chapel (an unexecuted project, known principally from a fine rendering) as a heavy, ground-based block with four large faceted projections for organ niches. It is a building of powerful expression, allied stylistically with the Whitney Museum completed a year earlier, and with other imposing geometric Breuer structures such as the Atlanta Public Library and Begrisch Lecture Hall at the former uptown campus of New York University. Profoundly committed to concrete for these effects, Breuer, when interviewed by Winthrop Sargeant, said: "I like to use concrete because it has a kind of rugged quality. It is not a sweet material. It is a relief in modern architecture from all that glass and steel."[10]

Breuer used glass and steel too, of course, often with stunning effect. "I don't dislike glass and steel buildings," he said. "There is a certain pleasing effect in the reflections that come from the glass."[11] His 1957 Van Leer Office Building in Amstelveen, The Netherlands, is a light-filled, weightless structure and one of his few curtain-wall designs. And about the glass curtain-walled annexe to Breuer's de Bikenkorf department store in Rotterdam of 1955–57, the eminent architectural critic Lewis Mumford wrote: "Here architect Marcel Breuer has produced one of the best office building façades I have seen anywhere."[12] Still, the building Mumford was referring to was the subsidiary office annexe located to the rear of one of Breuer's more characteristic (and more visible) "solids" of the 1950s – the massive box of the store itself, pierced only by narrow window slits.

10 In Sargeant, "Profile".

11 Ibid.

12 Lewis Mumford, "A Walk Through Rotterdam", in The Highway and the City (New York: Harcourt, Brace & World, 1963), p. 39.

◀ Marcel Breuer and Hamilton P. Smith, Grand
    Coulee Power Plant and Dam, Grand Coulee,
    Washington, 1972–75.
◀▼ Grand Coulee Power Plant and Dam, interior
    view of plant.
▼ Grand Coulee Power Plant and Dam, dam under
    construction.

▾ Marcel Breuer and Herbert Beckhard, Church of
St Francis de Sales, Muskegon, Michigan, 1964–66,
view from north-east.
▸ Marcel Breuer and Herbert Beckhard, University
of Massachusetts, Murray Lincoln Campus Center,
Amherst, Massachusetts,1967–70, view from
south-east.
▸▾ Marcel Breuer and Herbert Beckhard, Torin
Corporation, Penrith, Australia, 1976, view from east.

▾ Marcel Breuer and Robert F. Gatje, Kent School,
   Girls' Chapel, Kent, Connecticut, 1967, perspective
   view (unrealised).
▸ Marcel Breuer and Hamilton P. Smith, Atlanta
   Central Public Library, Atlanta, Georgia, 1977–80,
   view of southern façade.

In the 1920s, as a modern man and a young artist-designer, Marcel Breuer produced furniture and interiors that conformed to what Douglas Davis characterised as the "new dematerialised spatial quality that was in keeping with the ideals of freedom – political, economic, sexual – at the end of World War I: the promise of the modern world."[13] The world-famous tubular steel chairs and tables designed by Breuer from 1925 to 1928 exemplify this approach, in which transparency, lightness and pure space demonstrate an allegiance to the modernist revolution and its ideals of dematerialisation. But Breuer was never fully complacent – at least, not in his practice of architecture – about the diaphonous transparencies expressed in much of his early furniture, or an abundance of large glass panels, or glazed corners, or planar effects, or the predominantly glass and steel construction of "glass box modernism". Even though he shared the modernist's respect for industrial materials, he was never motivated to eliminate or to replace old bearing materials, such as stone. But he soon learned, from Le Corbusier at the 1932 Swiss Pavilion particularly, that he could cast those old materials in a modern format. He did so as early as 1936 in Bristol, England, with the sharp-edged geometric stone walls for his exhibition pavilion for Gane's, manufacturers of modern furniture, and he continued to do so in private and industrial buildings until his final residential structure, Stillman House III in Litchfield, Connecticut, of 1973–74. He was finicky about stonework; many of his houses had retaining walls and plinths of stone or stone veneer, and he instructed contractors to avoid stones of a rectangular shape with a cut appearance, small stones, stones with acute corners or triangular shapes, or smooth round stones. The top course in a freestanding wall was to be straight and flat.

13 Douglas Davis, essay in Modern Redux: Critical Alternatives for Architecture in the Next Decade, exhibition catalogue, Grey Art Gallery and Study Center, New York University, New York City, 4 March–19 April 1986, n.p.

Even at the height of the popularity of the transparent, vitreous cubes that were the residential buildings of Richard Neutra and Mies van der Rohe and their followers – in which material and substance evaporated in favour of light, space, sleek surfaces and weightlessness – Breuer was working with heavy massings of dense materials, and with depth. "Transparency through the use of glass is definitely one of our objectives," he said, "but transparency also needs solidity. Not for aesthetic reasons alone but because the total glass wall leaves out such considerations as privacy, reflections, transition from disorder to order, furnishings. Transparency becomes more crystalline next to solidity – and solidity makes it work."[14]

As early as the 1940s – in the Weizenblatt House of 1940–41, for example – Breuer had moved away from the goals of the new architecture as expressed by Walter Gropius, when he wrote that "the lightness of modern architecture has banished the crushing sense of ponderosity inseparable from the solid walls and massive foundations of masonry."[15] The structural system of the Weizenblatt House was based on an unexecuted project Breuer devised three years earlier for a ski resort hotel in the Austrian Tyrol, known from a few drawings and a crude model of cork, plywood and paper made later by Breuer's students at Harvard. About this project, Breuer said: "In 1937, I devised a taut framing system with truss-like forms made of cross-wise plywood boards that created for the Obergurgl ski resort project a structure that can be described as reinforced concrete in wood."[16] Even when working in wood, which Breuer did for the framing, balloon construction and the siding of houses that constituted much of his early practice in America, he was thinking of concrete and its effects. Writing about the 1940–41 Chamberlain Cottage, in which both the interior

14 In Sargeant, "Profile".

15 Walter Gropius, The New Architecture and the Bauhaus, trans. Morton Shand, 1935. Reprint (Cambridge, Mass.: MIT Press, 1965), p. 82.

16 Marcel Breuer, memorandum on Ober-Gurgl, 12 August 1938, prepared for the project's forthcoming publication in Architectural Record, September 1938, Syracuse University Library, Box 18.

◄◄ Atlanta Central Public Library, view of
north-eastern façade.
◄ Atlanta Central Public Library, entry area.
▶ Marcel Breuer and Hamilton P. Smith, New York
University, University Heights, New York City, 1959–61,
student residence and lecture hall in Begrisch Hall.
▶▼ New York University, Begrisch Hall, view from west.

▾ Van Leer office building, Amstelveen, The Netherlands, 1957–58, view from south.

▸ Marcel Breuer and A. Elzas, De Bijenkorf Department Store, Rotterdam, The Netherlands, 1955–57, partial view of northern façade.

◀ De Bijenkorf Department Store, view from north-west.
◀▾ De Bijenkorf Department Store, view from
   south-west showing sculpture by Naum Gabo.
▾ Thompson House, Ligonier, Pennsylvania, 1947–49,
   garden façade with pergola roof.

and the exterior finish are of Douglas Fir, Breuer said: "The traditional American frame construction is considered in this house, as in most of my others, as having truss-like walls which can be cantilevered or built over large openings without beams. It is very similar to reinforced concrete walls. On this principle the west end of this cottage is cantilevered eight feet over the foundation without heavy members – only by means of the slab-like stiffness of its walls."[17]

Private houses were one thing and public buildings another, but Breuer's intentions for producing images of solidity were consistent for both. The coursing of light and dark grey split-face granite on the exterior walls of his 1968–70 education wing for the Cleveland Museum of Art is one of his most striking effects.(He admired the striped dark and light stonework of the great thirteenth-century cathedral at Orvieto.) The textured granite panels bring vitality to the sharp-edged windowless planes, for Breuer's Cleveland Museum has no windows, and its immediate predecessor in New York, the elegant granite-clad Whitney Museum, has only seven. Both buildings in their uncompromising density serve as fully developed manifestations of the respect for material substance characteristic of Breuer's architecture.

More than a decade before the construction of the bold museum in Cleveland, Ohio, the Midwest saw religious buildings of great architectural daring that Breuer had begun to design there. His Benedictine churches and monastic community structures constituted the most significant advances in technology and design in mid-century modernist ecclesiastical architecture in America. Guided by the leaders and members of the religious communities by whom he was commissioned, Breuer designed buildings that reflected the liturgical reforms

17 Letter from Marcel Breuer to F. R. S. Yorke, 8 March 1943, Syracuse University Library, Box 45.

that the Catholic Church had been undergoing in this period, as well as a new spirit of community within the congregations. Heading the list is the now-famous church with its bell tower at St John's Abbey and University in Collegeville, Minnesota; in repeated campaigns from 1953 to 1968, residences, dormitories, a library and a science building were added, as part of the Abbey's "comprehensive hundred-year plan".

The planning of St John's began in 1953; within a year, the Benedictine Sisters at the Priory of the Annunciation in Bismarck, North Dakota, learned of Breuer's work at Collegeville and asked if he might be willing to undertake the planning of a small convent in Bismarck while he was engaged at Minnesota. The result of that commission – apart from the novelty of a New York City architect designing a convent complex in a remote location in the plains of North Dakota – is one of the most impressive illustrations of mid-century modernism in the United States. Since Breuer's buildings would need to contend with the vast emptiness of the surrounding prairie, a powerful architectural statement was called for. That power is dramatically signalled by a 100ft bell tower of reinforced concrete, with a bas-relief textured surface made from the carefully detailed imprints of the wooden formboards, which dominates the low-lying four-wing ensemble of the convent and its chapels.

The roof system of the principal chapel is that of half-hyperbolic paraboloid concrete shells. Breuer was fascinated by the formal and structural promise of the hyperbolic paraboloid, and he was one of the first architects outside South America to put it to significant use in his designs during the mid-1950s: at the Priory chapel; for the covering of the passenger ramp at the New London, Connecticut, station of the New Haven Railroad (unexecuted); and, most notably, for the roof of the library building at New York City's

Hunter College (1957–60), which was composed of six thin reinforced concrete shell sections bracing each other, each one formed as an inverted umbrella and supported by a slender concrete column. A roof structure configured in this way was light in weight, and since only six columns were needed for support the space below was open and relatively unobstructed so that an ideal library environment, spacious and luminous, was created.

In his religious buildings based on the hyperbolic paraboloid, Breuer carried out some of his most expressive and experimental constructs with the full approbation of the commissioning bodies. This is certainly the case at the church of St Francis de Sales, in Muskegon (1964–66): as the side walls rise to enclose the interior space, they revolve and twist into self-supporting hyperbolic paraboloids. Inside, the altar wall is composed of soaring concrete ribs that generate a mimetic association with the vertical linearities that energised the great Gothic churches of Europe.

But it was with St John's Abbey church – possibly the most frequently reproduced example of Marcel Breuer's architecture – and the library interior that Breuer first demonstrated his genius for bringing together sculpture and architecture, material and expression, technology and art. "I believe the architect can fully express himself as an artist by means of concrete," he said.[18] Writing in 1952 about American post-war architecture, Henry-Russell Hitchcock observed that compared to the Latin countries America still lagged in concrete construction.[19] Breuer himself noticed that until the time of the Korean War and its restrictions on the use and availability of steel, American engineers had been uncertain about structures of reinforced concrete compared with steel.[20] Not the least of the benefits of the change in attitude about concrete after the war was the effect on building costs. But if

18 In Sargeant, "Profile".

19 Henry-Russell Hitchcock, Introduction to Henry-Russell Hitchcock and Arthur Drexler, eds., Built in USA: Post-War Architecture. Exhibition catalogue (New York: Museum of Modern Art, 1952), p. 15.

20 Letter from Breuer to Abbot Baldwin Dworschak, 20 November 1956. Marcel Breuer papers, Syracuse University Library, Box 98.

Cleveland Museum of Art, view along
northern façade.

◄ Marcel Breuer and Hamilton Smith, St John's Abbey and University Complex, Collegeville, Minnesota, 1954–68, library (1964–66).

concrete was the appropriate material for cost-minded institutions with an expansive and expensive architectural enterprise at stake such as St John's Abbey, Breuer was able to elevate the material to something of grandeur, to exploit the possibilities it held for structural invention, spectacular cantilevers, folded walls enclosing a wide uninterrupted interior expanse (more than a million cubic feet in the church), and unexpected formal configurations in which the right angle was never obligatory. Surely the sculptural "trees" in the upper level of St John's library building are a supreme expression of the artistic freedom Breuer must have experienced when he was able to give concrete such form.

Breuer's response to the expressive possibilities inherent in raw concrete had been catalysed by a number of sources after the prime mover Le Corbusier (beginning in the 1930s) and included the daring design inventions of Pier Luigi Nervi (soaring thin shell structures and delicate vertical lines), from whom Breuer, by his own admission, learned a great deal when they collaborated on UNESCO and with whom he consulted about the folded walls used at St John's. The work of the great Swiss engineer-designer Robert Maillart was another inspiration; photographs of his lyrical and elegant reinforced concrete bridges that Breuer knew in Switzerland in the 1930s were kept in a separate file in the Breuer office.

The first building Breuer built, a landmark residence of 1932 in Wiesbaden for Paul and Marianne Harnischmacher, considered by Henry-Russell Hitchcock in 1938 to be "one of the finest modern houses in the world",[21] was destroyed in World War II. The commission in 1952 to design the Paris UNESCO complex brought Breuer back to Europe as an architect for the first time since he had gone to the United States and dissolved the 1935–37 London

21 Henry-Russell Hitchcock, "Marcel Breuer and the American Tradition in Architecture", essay and exhibition catalogue, Graduate School of Design, Harvard University, Cambridge, Mass., June–September 1938, mimeographed.

Marcel Breuer and Robert F. Gatje, Hunter College, Bronx, New York, 1957–60, classrooms and administration building, view from east.

◄ Hunter College, interior view of library roof.
▼ Hunter College, interior view, library.
▼▼ Hunter College, view of library from roof.
▶ Hunter College, side view with entrance ramp.

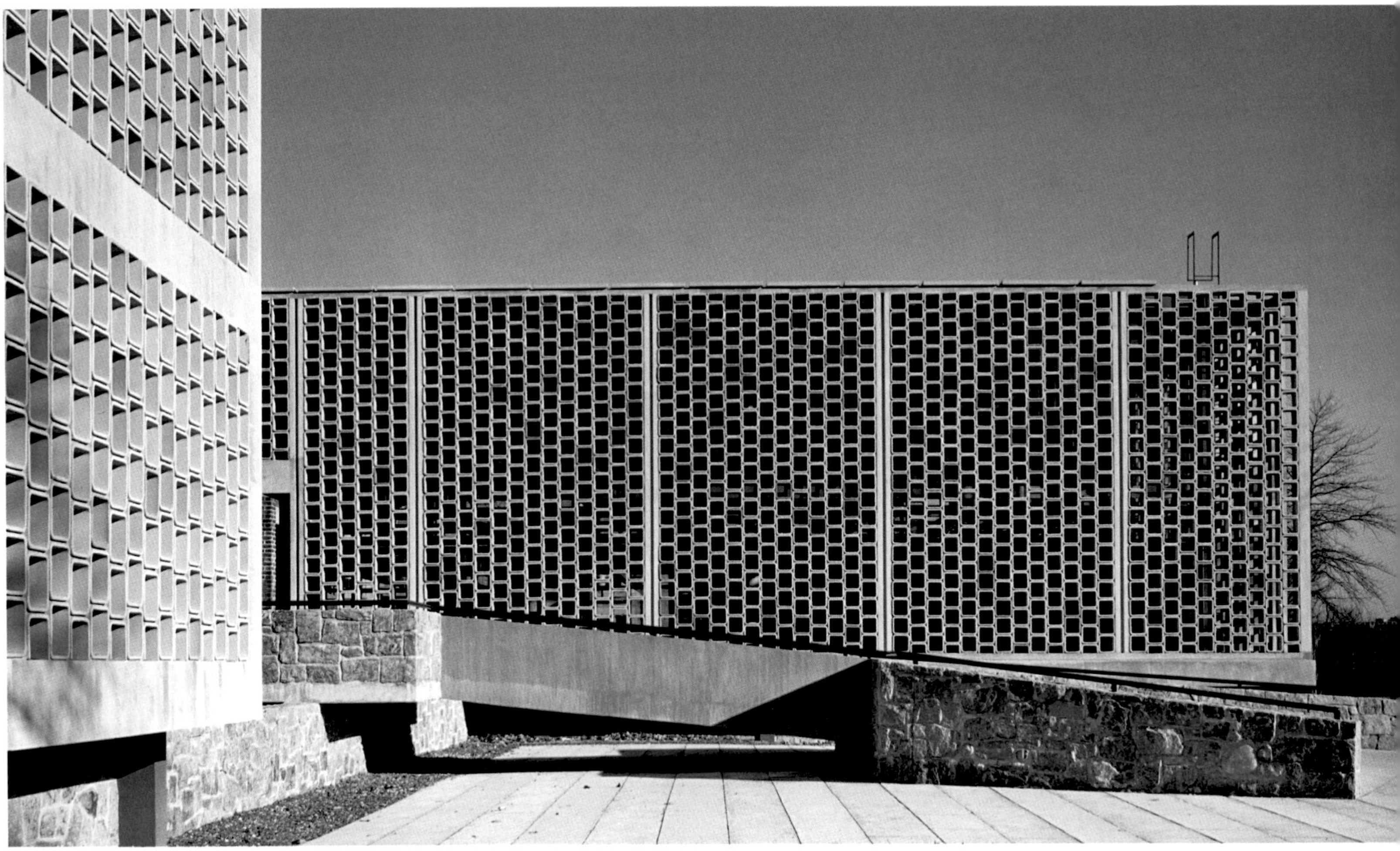

Marcel Breuer and Hamilton Smith, St John's Abbey
and University Complex, Collegeville, Minnesota, 1954–68,
reading room library.

practice of Breuer & Yorke. Despite a decidedly mixed critical reception, UNESCO gave Breuer immense prestige and visibility and, through the assignment (by members of the Art Committee) of works of art for the building, it "officially" allied him with exalted figures (most of them already his friends) of the mid-century international art world: Moore, Calder, Arp, Miro, Noguchi, Picasso. Commissions for buildings in The Netherlands, Switzerland, Belgium, France and Germany (including a second Wiesbaden house for the Harnischmachers) followed. This transatlantic and transcontinental momentum did not abate for a quarter of a century, not until Breuer's retirement in 1976 from what was a truly international practice. By that time both the modernist impulse that had been bred in the heroic period of the first generation (1910–30), and the limited appreciation for the effects of beton brut in the second, had given out. When he died five years later, Breuer was eulogised as "the last modernist".[22]

22 Newsweek, 17 August 1981, p. 70.

MARCEL BREUER – CHURCHES AND MONASTERIES

◄◄ Marcel Breuer and Hamilton Smith, St John's Abbey,
Collegeville, Minnesota, 1954–1968, Marcel Breuer in
front of the church building site (c. 1959).

◄ St John's Abbey, view of church with bell tower
from north.

▸ St John's Abbey, view from north-west with view to
church and bell tower

▾ St John's Abbey, view from south-west to bell tower.

St John's Abbey, baptismal font.

St John's Abbey, chancel.

▸ Marcel Breuer and Hamilton P. Smith, Annunciation Priory of the Sisters of St Benedict, Bismarck, North Dakota, 1956–1963, view from north.

▸▸ Annunciation Priory of the Sisters of St Benedict, view of bell tower from north.

▾ Annunciation Priory of the Sisters of St Benedict, aerial view, c. 1970, with cloister complex in foreground, university buildings to the rear.

◄ Annunciation Priory of the Sisters of St Benedict, view from south to bell tower and cloister living quarters.

◄▼ Annunciation Priory of the Sisters of St Benedict, chapel entrance.

▼ Annunciation Priory of the Sisters of St Benedict, interior courtyard in front of nuns' common room.

▼▼ Annunciation Priory of the Sisters of St Benedict, interior courtyard between chapel and seminar rooms.

◄ Annunciation Priory of the Sisters of St Benedict,
courtyard between chapel and cloister dormitories.
▼ Annunciation Priory of the Sisters of St Benedict,
view of chapel altar.

◄ Annunciation Priory of the Sisters of St Benedict,
interior of the chapel.

◄▼ Annunciation Priory of the Sisters of St Benedict,
view of left stained glass window.

▼ Annunciation Priory of the Sisters of St Benedict,
chancel, small chapel.

◂ Marcel Breuer and Herbert Beckhard, Church of
St Francis de Sales, Muskegon, Michigan,
1964–1966, view from south-east.
▾ Church of. St Francis de Sales, view from south-east.

▾ Church of St Francis de Sales, view from south.
▾◀ Next page: Church of St Francis de Sales, interior.
▾▶ Next page: Church of St Francis de Sales, chancel.

Marcel Breuer, Robert F. Gatje and Mario Jossa,
Convent of the Sisters of Divine Providence, Baldegg,
Switzerland, 1968–1972, view from south-east.

▾ Convent of the Sisters of Divine Providence, chapel.
▸ Convent of the Sisters of Divine Providence, cloister garden.

BIOGRAPHY

Marcel Breuer and siblings, c. 1907;
Marcel (Lajkó) is in the middle.

Members of the Bauhaus on the shores of the Elbe. From right, reclining: Marcel Breuer, Walter Gropius, El Muche, Georg Muche, László Moholy-Nagy, Lucia Moholy; gesturing: Xanti Schawinsky; right rear: Hinnerk Scheper, c. 1925.

Marcel Breuer and Martha Erps, c. 1926.

Marcel Breuer sitting in the B3, c. 1927.

Marcel Breuer at his typewriter, c. 1928.

In Ruth Hollos's studio. From left: Marcel Breuer,
Martha Erps, Katt Both, Ruth Hollos.

Marcel Breuer, c. 1949.

Marcel Breuer with Walter Gropius, mid -1950s.

Marcel Breuer with Achille Castiglioni, mid -1960s.

Marcel Breuer with Willy Brandt, early 1960s.

Marcel Breuer with Jacqueline Kennedy at the Whitney
Museum building site, 1965.

Marcel Breuer, summer 1975.

1902   Marcel Lajos Breuer born on 22 May in the Hungarian town of Pécs.

1920   After graduating from high school, Breuer receives a scholarship to attend the Academy of Fine Arts in Vienna, but leaves after only a few weeks. Following an apprenticeship at a Viennese architect's studio, he applies to the Bauhaus in Weimar.

1920-23   Breuer completes his training in the cabinet-making workshop of the Bauhaus in Weimar. He produces numerous designs in wood, including his African Chair (1921), furniture for the Sommerfeld House (1921) and the Slatted Chair (from 1922).

1923   Breuer is represented by several furniture designs in the Bauhaus "Haus am Horn" exhibition in Weimar, including his journeyman project, a dressing table. Together with Farkas Molnár and Georg Muche, Breuer organises an initiative to establish an architectural department at the Bauhaus; initial architectural designs follow.

1924   After his journeyman examination and a short period spent working in a Paris architectural studio, Breuer returns to the Bauhaus. He is appointed a "Young Master" and made head of the cabinet-making workshop.

1925-31   Breuer is commissioned to design the furnishings for the new Bauhaus building in Dessau. Initial development of his first tubular steel chair B3 (Wassily) and the stool B9. In the following years, he creates numerous furniture pieces in tubular steel.

1927   Establishment of his own company Standard-Möbel, which mass produces his early tubular steel designs. Breuer realises various interiors, including model dwellings at the Weissenhof estate in Stuttgart and the Berlin apartment for the theatre director Piscator. Breuer designs the BAMBOS Houses for the "Young Masters" at the Bauhaus, though the project is never executed for financial reasons.

1928   Along with Gropius, Bayer and Moholy-Nagy, Breuer leaves the Bauhaus to open an independent architectural practice in Berlin. Here he primarily produces apartment interiors, furniture and exhibition designs.

1930   Together with Gropius, Moholy-Nagy and Bayer, Breuer participates in the exhibition of the Deutscher Werkbund in Paris.

1931   At the Bauausstellung exhibition in Berlin, Breuer shows the 70m² Apartment and the House for a Sportsman.

1932   With the Harnischmacher House in Wiesbaden, Breuer is able for the first time to realise a design for a new building. Development of the first aluminium furniture, which is mass produced by the Swiss company Embru, starting in 1934.

1932-36   The Doldertal Apartments, designed in collaboration with Alfred and Emil Roth, are built in Zurich.

1934   At the Museum of Applied Arts in Zurich, Breuer delivers the programmatic lecture: 'Where do we stand?'

1935   Breuer follows his friend and mentor Gropius to England where he enters a partnership with the architect F. R. S. Yorke in London. For the British company Isokon, he designs diverse furniture pieces in plywood.

1936   Design of an exhibition pavilion for the furniture producer Gane. Plans for a "Garden City of the Future" together with Yorke.

1937   Breuer emigrates to America where his connections to Gropius get him a teaching position on the architecture faculty at Harvard University, Cambridge, Massachusetts. Gropius and Breuer found a joint architectural practice that remains in existence up to 1941 and primarily develops plans for single-family homes.

1938/39   Design and construction of Breuer's first house for himself in Lincoln, Massachusetts.

1941	Gropius and Breuer dissolve their partnership. Because of World War II, Breuer is able to realise only a small number of projects in the following years.	**1960-62**	IBM Research Center in La Gaude, France (subsequently expanded several times).
1946	Breuer gives up his teaching position and relocates his practice to New York City.	**1961-76**	Development of the Flaine ski resort in the French Alps.
1946-48	Robinson House in Williamstown, Massachusetts.	**1963-67**	Construction of the Koerfer House in Moscia, Ticino, Switzerland.
1947-48	Design and construction of Breuer's second house for himself and his family in New Canaan, Connecticut, which achieves renown through striking design features such as a widely projecting balcony.	**1964**	Breuer opens an office in Paris. His long-time employees Hamilton Smith, Robert F. Gatje and Herbert Beckhard become official partners in the firm, with Tician Papachristou joining later.

1941 Gropius and Breuer dissolve their partnership. Because of World War II, Breuer is able to realise only a small number of projects in the following years.

1946 Breuer gives up his teaching position and relocates his practice to New York City.

1946-48 Robinson House in Williamstown, Massachusetts.

1947-48 Design and construction of Breuer's second house for himself and his family in New Canaan, Connecticut, which achieves renown through striking design features such as a widely projecting balcony.

1948-49 The Museum of Modern Art in New York organises a travelling exhibition on Marcel Breuer, accompanied by a monograph by Peter Blake. Breuer constructs a model house in the Museum Garden, which attracts tens of thousands of visitors.

1952-58 Together with Pier Luigi Nervi and Bernard Zehrfuss, Breuer receives the commission to design the UNESCO Headquarters in Paris, resulting in an international breakthrough and further major public commissions.

1953-68 Breuer begins the plans for his first monastery project, St John's Abbey, and the affiliated university complex in Collegeville, Minnesota.

1955-57 De Bijenkorf Department Store in Rotterdam, The Netherlands.

1956 Founding of Marcel Breuer and Associates architectural practice in New York. Long-time employees Hamilton Smith, Herbert Beckhard, Murray Emslie and Robert Gatje become associates of the firm.

1956-59 Villa Staehelin in Feldmeilen near Zurich, Switzerland.

1956-63 Breuer designs a convent complex for the Benedictine Sisters of Annunciation Priory in Bismarck, North Dakota.

1959-61 Design of the Begrisch Hall lecture hall on the University Heights Campus, New York, the overall planning of which lasted from 1959-70.

1960-62 IBM Research Center in La Gaude, France (subsequently expanded several times).

1961-76 Development of the Flaine ski resort in the French Alps.

1963-67 Construction of the Koerfer House in Moscia, Ticino, Switzerland.

1964 Breuer opens an office in Paris. His long-time employees Hamilton Smith, Robert F. Gatje and Herbert Beckhard become official partners in the firm, with Tician Papachristou joining later.

1964-66 Whitney Museum of American Art in New York and the St Francis de Sales Church in Muskegon, Michigan.

1968-72 Baldegg Convent, Switzerland.

1972 The Metropolitan Museum of Art honours Breuer with a retrospective, the first ever devoted by the museum to a living architect; it travels to Paris and Berlin.

1976 Breuer retires from professional practice for health reasons.

1977-80 One of Breuer's last designs, the Central Public Library in Atlanta, is built; its initial plans go back to 1971.

1981 Marcel Breuer dies in New York on 1 July.

FURTHER READING

Argan, Giulio Carlo, *Marcel Breuer – disegno industriale e architettura*, Milan 1957

Bauhaus-Möbel. Eine Legende wird besichtigt, exhibition catalogue, Bauhaus-Archiv, Berlin 2002

Bayer, Herbert. *Das künstlerische Werk 1918–1938*, exhibition catalogue, Bauhaus-Archiv and Gewerbemuseum Basel, Berlin 1982

Blake, Peter, ed., *Marcel Breuer. Sun and Shadow. The Philosophy of an Architect*, New York 1956

Blake, Peter, *Marcel Breuer. Architect and Designer*, New York 1949

Marcel Breuer, Buildings and Projects 1921–1962, introduction and captions by Cranston Jones, New York 1962

Marcel Breuer, exhibition catalogue, The Metropolitan Museum of Art, New York 1972

Cohen, Arthur A., *Herbert Bayer. The Complete Work*, Cambridge, Mass., and London 1984

Driller, Joachim, *Breuer Houses*, London 2000

Droste, Magdalena and Manfred Ludewig, *Marcel Breuer. Design*, Cologne 1992

Ford, James and Katherine Morrow Ford, *Design of Modern Interiors*, New York 1945

Ewig, Isabelle, Thomas W. Gaehtgens and Mathias Noell, eds., *Das Bauhaus und Frankreich / Le Bauhaus et la France. 1919–1940*, Berlin 2002

Gatje, Robert F., *Marcel Breuer. A Memoir*, New York 2000

Geest, Jan van and Otakar Máčel, *Het museum van de continue lijn / The Museum of the Continuous Line*, Amsterdam 1986

Geest, Jan van and Otakar Máčel, *Stühle aus Stahl. Metallmöbel 1925–1940*, Cologne 1980

Giedion, Sigfried, "Befreites Wohnen", *Schaubücher* 14, Emil Schaeffer, Zürich and Leipzig 1929

Giedion, Sigfried, Space, *Time and Architecture. The growth of a new tradition.* Cambridge, Mass., 1956

Gräff, Werner, ed., *Innenräume. Räume und Inneneinrichtungsgegenstände aus der Werkbundausstellung "Die Wohnung", insbesondere aus den Bauten der städtischen Weissenhofsiedlung in Stuttgart*, Stuttgart 1928

Hassenpflug, Gustav, *Baukastenmöbel. Ein Beitrag zum Wohnproblem für Entwerfer, Hersteller und Käufer von Möbeln*, Pössneck 1949

Hassenpflug, Gustav, *Stahlmöbel. Beratungsstelle für Stahlverwendung*, Düsseldorf 1960

"The House in the Museum Garden. Marcel Breuer – Architect", *The Museum of Modern Art Bulletin* XVI, 1, New York 1949

Hyman, Isabelle, *Marcel Breuer, Architect. The Career and the Buildings*, New York 2001

Ichinowatari, Katsuhiko, ed., "Legacy of Marcel Breuer. Marcel Breuer Associates. Architects and Planners, Process", *Architecture* 32, Tokyo 1982

Izzo, Alberto and Camillo Gubitosi, *Marcel Breuer. Architettura 1921–1980*, Florence 1981

Máčel, Otakar, *Der Freischwinger. Vom Avantgardeentwurf zur Ware*, Delft 1992

Masello, David, *Architecture Without Rules. The Houses of Marcel Breuer and Herbert Beckhard*, New York 1996

Mehlau-Wiebking, Friederike, Arthur Rüegg and Ruggero Tropeano, *Schweizer Typenmöbel 1925–1935. Sigfried Giedion und die Wohnbedarf AG*, Zürich 1989

Möller, Werner and Otakar Máčel, *Ein Stuhl macht Geschichte*, Munich 1992

Ostergard, Derek E., ed., *Bent Wood and Metal Furniture 1850–1946. The American Federation of Arts*, New York 1987

Papachristou, Tician, *Marcel Breuer. Projets et réalisations récentes*, Paris 1970

Puente, Moisés and Lluís Ortega, ed., "Marcel Breuer. Casas Americanas / American Houses", *Revista Internacional de Arquitectura* 17, Barcelona 2001

Roth, Alfred, ed., *La Nouvelle Architecture. Présentée en 20 examples / Die Neue Architektur. Dargestellt an 20 Beispielen / The New Architecture. Presented in 20 Examples*, exhibition catalogue, Erlenbach-Zürich 1946

Rüegg, Arthur, *Ein Hauptwerk des Neuen Bauens in Zürich. Die Doldertalhäuser 1932–1936*, Zürich 1996

Scheidig, Walter, *Bauhaus Weimar 1919–1924. Werkstattarbeiten*, Leipzig 1966

Stoddard, Whitney S., *Adventure in Architecture. Building the New St John's. Plans by Marcel Breuer*, New York, London, Toronto 1958

Stoller, Ezra, *Whitney Museum of American Art*, photographs by Ezra Stoller, New York 2000

Vegesack, Alexander von, *Deutsche Stahlrohrmöbel*, Munich 1986

Vegesack, Alexander von, ed., *100 Masterpieces from the Vitra Design Museum Collection*, Weil am Rhein 1996

Vegesack, Alexander von, ed., *Dimensions of design. 100 classical seats*, Weil am Rhein 1997

Vegesack, Alexander von, ed., *Thonet Stahlrohrmöbel*, reprint of 1930 catalogue, Weil am Rhein 1989

Wilk, Christopher, *Marcel Breuer. Furniture and Interiors*, The Museum of Modern Art, New York 1981

Wilk, Christopher, *Thonet. 150 Years of Furnishing*, Woodbury, UK, 1980

Winkler, Klaus-Jürgen, *Die Architektur am Bauhaus in Weimar*, Berlin 1993

Wiseman, Carter, *I. M. Pei. A Profile in American Architecture*, revised edition, New York 2001

Yorke, Francis Reginald Stevens, *The Modern House*, 7th revised edition, London 1951 (1st edition, London 1934)

Esto is the definitive source for architecture and design with available stock images or new assignment photographs. From commercial buildings to domestic design, urban scenes to privat gardens, Esto describes the shape of the world.
Esto Photographics, 222 Valley Place, Mamaroneck NY 10543
www.esto.com, Tel 914 698 4060, Fax 914 698 1033, email esto@esto.com

AUTHORS

Barry Bergdoll teaches art history at Columbia University in New York. His current projects include a book on the architecture of Marcel Breuer.

Donatella Cacciola is an art historian who is currently working on a dissertation on the history of design classics and their reception in Germany and Italy.

Joachim Driller is an art historian who teaches in the Department of Architecture at the University of Wuppertal. He has published a highly regarded book on the single-family houses of Marcel Breuer.

Robert F. Gatje is an architect and former partner of Marcel Breuer. In 2000, he published the book "Marcel Breuer. A Memoir" in which he reports on his work with Breuer.

Gabriele Diana Grawe is an art historian working at the German Forum for Art History in Paris. She has published numerous texts on architectural and design history.

Isabelle Hyman teaches art and architectural history at New York University. In 2001, she published the first comprehensive monograph on Marcel Breuer's architectural oeuvre.

Otakar Máčel is an art historian who teaches as a member of the architecture faculty at the Technical University in Delft. His numerous publications have established him as an expert on the history of tubular steel furniture.

Mathias Remmele is a guest curator at the Vitra Design Museum and teaches architectural and design history at the School of Art and Design in Basel.

Lutz Schöbe is a research fellow at the Bauhaus Dessau Foundation. He has published numerous texts on the history of the Bauhaus.